T0311623

Ecolabels, Innovation, and Green Market Transformation

This book develops a path to decarbonization through a process of Green Market Transformation. Matisoff and Noonan assess the scope and impact of the green building movement, which is working towards decarbonizing a sector that accounts for more than a third of global carbon emissions. They describe the role of the movement in addressing sustainability challenges within the building and construction sector, and suggest new ways of marshalling markets through the voluntary efforts of industry to shift society towards a better future. Matisoff and Noonan tell the success story of green industry, seen through the lens of green buildings and ecolabels. By combining case studies with recent interdisciplinary scholarship, the authors provide a compelling narrative of the opportunities and limitations of reliance on voluntary approaches to regulation.

DANIEL C. MATISOFF is an associate professor of public policy at the Georgia Institute of Technology and the Director of the Sustainable Energy and Environmental Management master's program. He publishes in the areas of the economics and policy of renewable energy, information disclosure programs, and corporate social responsibility.

DOUGLAS S. NOONAN is the Paul H. O'Neill Professor of Public and Environmental Affairs at the O'Neill School at Indiana University–Purdue University Indianapolis. He is an economist who researches many topics, emphasizing the built environment and amenities affecting quality of life.

Organizations and the Natural Environment

Series Editors
Jorge Rivera, George Washington University
J. Alberto Aragón-Correa, University of Surrey

Editorial Board
Nicole Darnall, Arizona State University
Magali Delmas, University of California, Los Angeles
Ans Kolk, University of Amsterdam
Thomas P. Lyon, University of Michigan
Alfred Marcus, University of Minnesota
Michael Toffel, Harvard Business School
Christopher Weible, University of Colorado

The increasing attention given to environmental protection issues has resulted in a growing demand for high-quality, actionable research on sustainability and business environmental management. This new series, published in conjunction with the Group for Research on Organizations and the Natural Environment (GRONEN), presents students, academics, managers, and policy-makers with the latest thinking on key topics influencing business practice today.

Published Titles
Oetzel, Oh, and Rivera, *Business Adaptation to Climate Change*
Albright and Crow, *Community Disaster Recovery*
Grabs, *Selling Sustainability Short?*
Sharma and Sharma, *Patient Capital*
Marcus, *Strategies for Managing Uncertainty*
Marcus, *Innovations in Sustainability*
Bowen, *After Greenwashing*

Forthcoming Titles
Gouldson and Sullivan, *Governance and the Changing Climate for Business*
Matisoff and Noonan, *Learning to LEED*
Oetzel, Oh and Rivera, *Business Adaptation to Climate Change*

Ecolabels, Innovation, and Green Market Transformation

Learning to LEED

DANIEL C. MATISOFF
Georgia Institute of Technology

DOUGLAS S. NOONAN
Indiana University–Purdue University, Indianapolis

CAMBRIDGE
UNIVERSITY PRESS

CAMBRIDGE
UNIVERSITY PRESS

University Printing House, Cambridge CB2 8BS, United Kingdom

One Liberty Plaza, 20th Floor, New York, NY 10006, USA

477 Williamstown Road, Port Melbourne, VIC 3207, Australia

314–321, 3rd Floor, Plot 3, Splendor Forum, Jasola District Centre,
New Delhi – 110025, India

103 Penang Road, #05–06/07, Visioncrest Commercial, Singapore 238467

Cambridge University Press is part of the University of Cambridge.

It furthers the University's mission by disseminating knowledge in the pursuit of
education, learning, and research at the highest international levels of excellence.

www.cambridge.org
Information on this title: www.cambridge.org/9781108841085
DOI: 10.1017/9781108888769

© Daniel C. Matisoff and Douglas S. Noonan 2023

First published 2023

A catalogue record for this publication is available from the British Library.

ISBN 978-1-108-84108-5 Hardback
ISBN 978-1-108-74484-3 Paperback

Cambridge University Press has no responsibility for the persistence or accuracy
of URLs for external or third-party internet websites referred to in this publication
and does not guarantee that any content on such websites is, or will remain,
accurate or appropriate.

Dan would like to dedicate this book to wife, Sabrina, and to his kids Gabe and Evan.

Doug would like to dedicate this book to his wife, Kim, and to his kids, Jack and Cora.

We hope that our children will innovate greener futures for us all.

Contents

Figures

Tables

Preface

Toward Understanding Ecolabels, Innovation, and Market Transformation

This book marks the culmination of – or at least a pause in – our efforts to evaluate the Green Building Movement. It is a look back at our (and others') decade of scholarship on ecolabels and green building, and specifically at the accomplishments of the US Green Building Council's Leadership in Energy and Environmental Design (LEED) ecolabel program. It is an opportunity for retrospection and reflection on the progress that has been made in transitioning green buildings toward a more environmentally friendly footprint. It also enables deeper consideration of the opportunities that remain and allows us to take stock of what the academic literature has had to say about the design and application of ecolabels, and how those portend future opportunities in technological transitions.

Our Aims in This Book

First, we seek to develop a perspective of green market transformation built on the empirical evidence and our experience studying green buildings. The need to combat climate change through deep decarbonization requires a rapid and widespread deployment of innovative energy and environmental technologies. This puts the emphasis on the diffusion of innovation. While Bass (1969) posits a generalizable model that can be used to understand the deployment of innovative technologies, further work is needed to understand the derivation of the key input parameters to this model that determine the rate in which adoption ultimately occurs. One of our key insights in this book is that the initial deployment of technologies can be accelerated by attaching a marketing signal to those investments in the form of an ecolabel. We call attention to the core problem here – one that couples vital information problems (e.g., hard-to-market green upgrades, disincentives to innovate, and not enough peer learning) with the well-rehearsed pollution problem that typically features in policy discussions. The ecolabel pairs private and excludable marketing benefits with the provision of improved environmental performance. Once seeded by the ecolabels, the technologies can gain widespread adoption. Our book documents the inception of innovative technologies in the commercial context, the nascent uptake of these technologies in a series of pilot and demonstration projects, the leading edge of adoption through the spread of ecolabeled technologies, and finally the implications of widespread adoption in the marketplace.

Second, we seek to provide a rigorous analysis of the Green Building Movement and the impacts that LEED and other green building programs have provided. While there are a plethora of books on how and why to build a green building, and there are thousands of people who earn and maintain LEED Accredited Professional (AP) qualifications, there are no comprehensive independent evaluations of the LEED program that evaluate its accomplishments over the past decade. We see this book as an opportunity to take stock of the academic literature so that we can assess the role that the Green Building Movement has played over the past decade in pushing forward a new set of standards and technologies to improve the built environment.

Our Blueprint for the Book

We begin in Chapter 1 by introducing our perspective of greener market transformation in more detail. Chapter 2 summarizes and gives conceptual structure to the evidence about the Green Building Movement. Once we propose the framework that grounds how we see the transformation – and the Green Building Movement in which we observe this transformation taking place – the subsequent chapters detail different components of this story of market transformation through voluntary mechanisms. We intend these chapters to be largely self-contained. They each discuss an important facet related to ecolabels and market transformations for green buildings. Yet they also connect to one another and build out a story from the economic fundamentals of a market in need of transformation to how industries in the building sector can learn and change to a discussion of where we are and where we might go next. Our discussions cross many disciplinary lines, from economics to engineering to management to political science and more. The book's modular design facilitates readers' selecting just the components best suited to their interests. Yet we feel its strength lies in its whole, which connects several critical perspectives in shaping the story of the Green Building Movement.

Chapter 3 ("Choose Your Own Adventure! The Landscape of Ecolabel Design") introduces us to a vital element of ecolabels like LEED: They are noisy. Like so many other ecolabels, we can see the designation but that does not tell us much more than "it's greener." We argue for the importance of this ambiguity and unpack various other key elements that go into designing an ecolabel in Chapter 3. There is variation in what it takes to earn a particular green certification *and* variation across ecolabels in terms of what those labels prioritize. Within LEED and similar programs such as Green Globes, the broad flexibility in paths to certification means that comparing the "greenness" or some other outcome metrics of certified buildings is nearly impossible. Furthermore, there are many ecolabels that address not whole-building sustainability, but narrower smaller factors like energy footprints and other individual parameters that comprise green buildings. The Green Building Movement is explicitly more holistic than a focus on just energy or water efficiency. The flexibility inherent in many green building labels allows for a broader conception of whole-building sustainability in certification. The breadth and variety underscores the complexity of the Green Building Movement and the ecolabels and certifications so vital to its success. Earning certification in a program like LEED is a bit of a "choose your own adventure" exercise in that different certified buildings might take different paths to the end result. The diversity of ecolabels out there further complicates, and enriches, the landscape of ecolabels. Chapter 3 explores important aspects behind ecolabel design and the varied landscape that results. The rich landscapes of ecolabels arise across all sorts of products, not just buildings, as Chapter 3's special case study of agricultural ecolabels shows. Chapter 4 ("The Labeling Building Challenge: The World of Ecolabels for the Built Environment") describes in greater detail the ecolabel landscape for green buildings.

Chapter 5 ("The Public and Private Benefits of Green Building: Many Shades of Green") shifts the attention from the *design* of the ecolabels to the builders' and the adopters' perspectives. The complexity in the ecolabel landscape involves considerable flexibility in how and why builders "go green." Greener buildings can provide many different types of benefits. Design teams can customize their building solutions to the needs of the building's region, site, and function. This results in highly heterogeneous green buildings, even among those certified under the same label. We cover these "many shades of green" in greater detail in Chapter 5.

Yet the conceptual landscape complex ecolabels do not exist in a vacuum, but rather must interact with another layer of complexity – the peer effects that spur on a virtuous cycle of green building market penetration. Chapter 6 ("Tossing a Pebble in a Pond: The Anatomy of a Demonstration Project") provides a closer look at this phenomenon and shows how a demonstration project can effect greater change. Peer effects are positive spillovers in which the behavior of one green building adopter creates a snowball effect of observers being influenced to take similar actions. This concept is difficult to isolate and observe in the context of greening the built environment, but it certainly plays a vital role behind the scenes of demand for and supply of green buildings. This means that, outside of the measurable, positive environmental effects of one green building, its total effect could be considerably larger after considering these factors of imitation and "keeping up with the Joneses." The dynamics of peer effects are critical for greater and faster generation of not only additional certified buildings but also incorporation of green building techniques and processes. Chapter 7 ("Demonstrating Innovation in Green Buildings: Catalyzing Market Transformation") explains the vital role of these peer effects in catalyzing market transformation.

What does the rapid diffusion of green building mean? Does it mean that there is a small market for green consumers and that this market will get saturated quickly? Or does it signify a shift in norms and a broader movement to build green? In Chapter 8 ("Keep Raising the Bar: Green-lighting a Race to the Top!"), we investigate the roles of ecolabels and peer effects in driving the increased investment in green buildings. During the first generation of green buildings, we observed an increased penetration of green buildings into the market. What is more, we observed that, rather than learning to game the system and target the minimum requirements to become certified, firms have invested more over time, going beyond the minimum requirements. They, and the green building labels themselves, are raising the bar. We interpret this finding as evidence that firms have increasingly pursued technological investments as supply chains have lowered costs, and the benefits of these technologies have become better understood. As firms have sought to become greener and greener over time, this indicates a race to the top. Voluntary mechanisms like ecolabels have given the green light to start that race.

We show how green building practices and programs are noisy and rapidly diffusing and evolving. Yet has this flexibility and continued evolution really made a positive impact? Chapter 9 ("It's Not Easy Being Green: Environmental and Equity Impacts of Green Building") considers the issues and evidence regarding the environmental and social impacts of green building. These questions are critical, both in the sense of being important but also in the sense of the need to continue questioning the worthiness of the enterprise. Are footprints getting smaller? Are benefits, access, and costs equitably distributed? Have we reached the limits of this approach? Chapter 9 outlines these critical questions and reviews the evidence for the equity and justice implications of ecolabeling.

Chapter 10 synthesizes our theory for scholarly readers and formalizes our theory by describing key indicators and outcomes, as well as causal mechanisms that connect these constructs. We also discuss the generalizability and limits for the application of our theory and propose some conditions for and limits to the transformative power of these voluntary mechanisms.

We close with Chapter 11 ("Conclusions: What Are We Building To?") with a look to the future of the Green Building Movement and the more general prospects of catalyzing market transformation through voluntary mechanisms. This discussion frames the success story here in the context of broader policy and academic debates over responses to climate change and environmental problems more generally. We identify promising avenues for policy and practice to pursue going forward. As we make clear here, we cannot say "mission accomplished" yet. We very much need more effort and innovation. There is much to learn as we advance sustainability and wellbeing. We hope that this book contributes in its small way.

Acknowledgments

We extend our greatest appreciation to the many people who have contributed to this book. A few have contributed quite directly. We thank Mallory Flowers (Chapter 9) and Mohan Turaga (Chapter 3) for contributing to the case studies on green buildings and GreenCo, respectively. Mallory also contributed greatly to many of the research projects on green buildings that we conducted prior to this book and deserves special acknowledgement. We would also like to thank Fikret Atalay, Lin-Han Chiang Hsieh, Anna Mazzolini, Shuang Zhao, and Shan Zhou, who have all contributed to our prior work on green buildings. These are our finest students, collaborators, and co-authors. Fikret Atalay played a particularly large role in the research that developed into Chapter 6. We also acknowledge our previous research on demonstration projects – coauthored with Christopher Blackburn, Mallory Flowers, and Juan Moreno-Cruz, which provided the backbone for Chapter 7. We also thank Anna Benkeser, David Capati, Matthew Ellett, Rachel Mohr, and Valentina SanMiguel Herrera, who have contributed research assistance, case writeups, graphics creation and editing, and other valuable tasks to help make the book a success. Finally, we would like to acknowledge the academic communities of the Association for Public Policy Analysis and Management and the Alliance for Research on Corporate Sustainability. Much of this work has been presented multiple times at these and additional workshops, conferences, and seminars, and has been improved by valuable feedback from our colleagues.

Reference

Bass, Frank M. 1969. "A New Product Growth for Model Consumer Durables." *Management Science* 15, no. 5: 215–227.

1 | Advancing a Perspective of Green Market Transformation

Advancing a Perspective of Market Transformation through Ecolabels

To achieve carbon reductions necessary to stabilize the climate, it is essential to move emergent technologies to market and gain widespread adoption. When emergent energy and environmental technologies gain widespread adoption in the marketplace, we term this *Green Market Transformation*. This phenomenon has been studied through the lens of technology adoption for decades and has received much attention in the academic literature. More recently, a perspective of sustainable energy transitions has emerged in the academic literature. We view our perspective as complementary to an emergent body of research of sustainable energy transitions.

Three characteristics separate this book from previous research on technology adoption and green market transformation or sustainable energy transitions. First, and perhaps most importantly, we contribute to a theory of technology adoption and market transformation that explains the mechanisms by which technology adoption occurs. In past research, technology adoption is observed, but rarely are the mechanisms by which it happens understood. Rather, vague pronouncements of "peer effects" or "communication" are thought to drive market transformation. In this research we articulate a number of mechanisms by which technology adoption is accelerated. These mechanisms include supply-side effects, such as building supply chains, disseminating information and knowledge across the supply chain, and lowering the costs of new technologies through market development. On the demand side, we observe multiple types of learning associated with new technologies that might exhibit as peer effects, improved information about the appropriateness of new technologies, or improved knowledge about the operation of new technologies. Together we speculate that these factors lead to a reduction in information costs and other transaction costs, generating positive spillovers and leading to an uptake in new technologies. These positive spillovers create a virtuous cycle where the adoption of new technologies leads to even more market uptake. This self-reinforcing pattern defines market transformation.

Second, we explore specific mechanisms to seed this market transformation, answering a question that has long eluded academics. In the technology and innovation literature, the so-called Valley of Death explains the failure of promising technologies to achieve widespread adoption in the marketplace. While the reasons for this are complex, in general, it is thought that high upfront costs of promising technologies prevent broad market uptake. While broad market uptake is thought to lower costs, innovative technologies are caught in a chicken and the egg paradox. If they were cheaper, they would gain broad market uptake. But because they are not cheaper, they do not. Expensive but promising technologies lay scattered in the Valley of Death, never to gain traction commercially or to deliver widespread benefits.

The typical response of policy-makers is to deliver subsidies for the adoption of new technologies through the tax code. There are a number of reasons that the use of subsidies may be less effective or efficient than intended, though these tools certainly remain very popular. While market subsidies have been used in solar photovoltaic, electric vehicles, and other domains, there may be other tools available to help seed market transformation.

In this book, we build upon mechanisms that do not require federal government intervention that can be used to help bridge the Valley of Death. Primarily, we link market transformation in the built environment to ecolabels, a policy tool that relies on private sector action to spur market transformation. To date, ecolabels have not received much attention in the literature and this effort to identify their mechanisms and impact is unique. Ecolabels can come in many forms. They can be sponsored by NGOs, governments, or industry associations. These labels exist in response to hard-to-observe sustainability attributes of a product (and in this case, buildings). This is worth repeating for the many readers who believe that government action is the primary or only way to induce change. While some ecolabels are government-sponsored, many ecolabels are private-sector or NGO-led efforts to differentiate and certify higher-quality products. As a result, we demonstrate that they change investments in sustainable technologies that have cascading effects upon an entire industry. Ecolabels work by providing a market premium (Rivera 2002) that induces early adoption of new technologies, thus lowering their costs for future potential adopters. Further, the initial seeding of these new technologies can be induced by demonstration projects, which reduce information costs and provide initial experience with new technologies that can spur market transformation.

Third, this book draws upon our experience in the built environment with a particular emphasis on the United States Green Building Council's (USGBC) Leadership in Energy and Environmental Design (LEED) program, as well as other labels around the world such as the United Kingdom's (UK) Building Research Establishment Environmental Assessment Method (BREEAM) program, the International Living Future Institute's (ILFI) Living Building program, and others. Given that LEED is the world's most popular green building program with 100,000 registered projects[1] worldwide, and broad penetration of the standards into building codes, public policies, and standard building practices around the globe, we argue that the built environment serves as an example of successful market transformation, spurred by these ecolabels. Figure 1.1 shows the global distribution of green certified buildings.

The built environment is responsible for roughly 40 percent of total carbon emissions. Given the challenges that we face to rapidly decarbonize our economy, it is essential to understand how to do this in the built environment. Recently much attention has been paid to the electricity sector, where rapid advances in wind and solar have begun to transform the electricity market. In the concluding chapter, we compare the built environment with other sectors and technologies to draw out how these lessons may extend to other sectors.

While Chapters 2 and 4 of this book provide more information on ecolabeling and green building, it is helpful here to provide a brief overview of ecolabels and the built environment to explain a theory of market transformation.

---

[1] Registering a project with USGBC is a prerequisite to pursuing certification. As of 2020 there are approximately 75,000 projects that have achieved LEED certification.

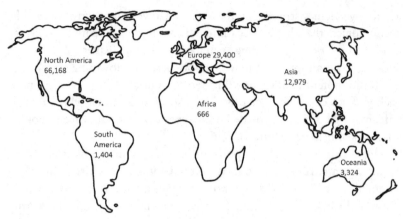

Figure 1.1 Green certified buildings around the world
Note: Data taken from project databases of the 14 most-popular ecolabels with public project data

Understanding the World of Ecolabels

Ecolabels are a type of third-party certification program that verify hard-to-observe characteristics of a good or service. Most ecolabels operate through a checklist approach. That is, labels offer a menu of product and process upgrades that relate to the sustainability of the production process or sustainability characteristics of a good.

There is significant variation across labels. Some are sponsored by governments. For example, at least 70 governing bodies around the world provide guidance on organic labels that can be placed on food products. Popular examples include the United States Department of Agriculture (USDA) label, the European Union (EU) Organic label, and the China Organic Food Certification.

Others are sponsored by nongovernmental organizations. For example, the Forest Stewardship Council (FSC) offers a timber and paper products ecolabel certifying forest management practices. The Sustainable Agriculture Network/Rainforest Alliance (SANRA) offers a Rainforest Alliance label that certifies economic, social, and environmental practices of farms producing a range of agricultural products such as coffee and sugar. The Marine Stewardship Council certifies sustainable fishing practices for seafood.

Still others are sponsored by for-profit entities, industry associations – or nonprofits that have close ties to industry. The Green

Good Housekeeping Seal is awarded for a range of product quality, safety, sustainability, and warranty characteristics by the Good Housekeeping Research Institute, a part of the Hearst Corporation. Greenguard, a label for low volatile organic compound emissions that impact indoor air quality, is offered by Underwriters Laboratories (UL). The Sustainable Forestry Initiative, which provides an alternative forestry certification to the FSC, while technically a nonprofit organization, has been accused by environmental groups of being fully funded by industry and a vehicle for greenwashing.

Not much is known about the broader impacts of ecolabels. One pressing and relevant question – perhaps unanswered by the research cited in this book – regards the design of and governance of ecolabels and how that translates to their effectiveness. Some research has assessed a broad range of ecolabels to conclude that third-party certification is an important feature of ecolabels that improves their rigor and ecolabels sponsored by nongovernmental organizations (NGOs) have the most stringent rules while labels sponsored by industry have the least stringent rules (Darnall et al. 2017, 2018; Rivera and de Leon 2004). But many questions remain about the wider landscape of ecolabels. Researchers have also pointed out a number of problems with ecolabels such as greenwashing, a lack of enforcement (Aragón-Correa et al. 2020), or even fraudulent ecolabels that lack any sort of legal meaning (e.g., antibiotic free chicken; GMO-free foods; and "all-natural ingredients") (Hamilton and Zilberman 2006). Others have been criticized for providing confusing or misleading claims, which can be compounded by having multiple competing labels in a particular product area (Roheim et al. 2018). Individual labels have received more attention on impacts. In particular, the LEED label from the USGBC has received significant attention. While we dig into these results in more detail in Chapter 2, these results highlight market premiums to green building, increased employee productivity, increased investment in energy and environmental technologies, and improved energy and environmental performance.

While the case of green building provides perspectives of success in green market transformation, we would be remiss to explore some of the risks associated with ecolabels and the promises of green market transformation. These include, but are not limited to: ecolabels that do not produce environmental benefits; greenwashing or providing misleading environmental information about a firm's behavior; or producing – instead of a virtuous cycle, produce a "race to the bottom" where organizations strive only for minimum levels of environmental performance or attempt to evade efforts aimed at producing improved environmental performance. In addition, it is important to recognize the conditions that enable the successes that we observe in the green building case and their applicability (or not) to other cases. We explore these risks in Chapter 3 (greenwashing), Chapter 8 (race to the bottom), and Chapters 10 and 11 (boundary conditions and limitations of our perspective).

The Green Building Movement and Ecolabels

Beginning in the early 1990s, there was a growing recognition of the need to think about energy efficiency and the environmental footprint of the built environment. The Building Research Establishment (BRE), which was a UK national lab (later privatized in 1997), launched its first certification in 1990, called the Building Research Establishment Environmental Assessment Method (BREEAM), aimed at benchmarking the performance of office buildings. In 1993, the USGBC formed and began to assemble a broad-based consensus-based process of stakeholders in the building and construction sector, seeking to launch a program aimed at improving the environmental performance of buildings. This consensus-based approach, which assembled diverse participants from environmental NGOs, government agencies, architects, engineers, developers, builders, product manufacturers, and other industry leaders, ultimately became the basis for a broad movement aimed at greening the built environment. The LEED program launched in 1998, though, as we discuss later, did not gain significant market traction until a couple of years later.

Originally, LEED worked as a checklist and what we like to call a "Choose Your Own Adventure" approach to ecolabeling (see Chapter 3). There were 69 different credits available divided across eight categories including energy and atmosphere, water efficiency, materials and resources, indoor environmental quality, sustainable sites, location and linkages, innovation and design, and awareness and education. Buildings could achieve certification levels based on points: 26–32 points achieved basic certification; 33–38 points achieved Silver certification; 39–51 points achieved Gold certification; and more than 52 points achieved Platinum certification. The technical committee aimed to make points roughly equivalent in terms of environmental impact, though certainly comparing water efficiency to innovation and design is like comparing apples and oranges. According to discussions with USGBC executives who were part of this early process, they just chose these cutoffs arbitrarily, intending for them to be like grades in school. Forty percent received a pass, 50 percent received Silver, and 60 percent received Gold. They wanted an extra step to get Platinum, so they required 80 percent of the total points to get Platinum.

At the time these systems were innovative for several reasons. First, while programs like Energy Star or product-labeling requirements in the EU labeled the energy-performance characteristics of a product (including buildings) or even labeled multiple performance characteristics, the BREEAM system and LEED system engaged in a more holistic rating of a building. LEED was not certifying just the energy performance of a building (and in fact, LEED attracted a fair bit of criticism for certification *not* being tightly tied to energy performance). Rather, LEED's multidimensional label and multiple-tier structure allowed it to provide an overall sustainability rating with a differentiated structure that encouraged competition to achieve greener buildings. This innovation has proven popular. Most building certification programs and many other ecolabels or rating systems have since adopted a similar structure.[2]

Over time, these systems have evolved. Both BRE and USGBC's systems have grown internationally and become popular around the world. Figures 1.2(a)–(c) demonstrate the number of buildings in the United States, Europe, and the rest of the world, with the total buildings listed as state and country labels, and the shading indicating the number of buildings per capita. These figures highlight a few unexpected leaders in the Green Building Movement. New Mexico, for example, with 1,942 certified buildings, leads all states in certified buildings per capita, just behind Washington DC, which has a mandate that requires all large buildings to be certified or equivalent and has a significant number of federal buildings that are also certified under the federal procurement policy.

---

[2] Costa Rica's Certification for Sustainable Tourism (CST) program also followed BREEAM and in 1997 established an ecolabel for hotels based on environmental excellence along four areas (Rivera 2002, 2004).

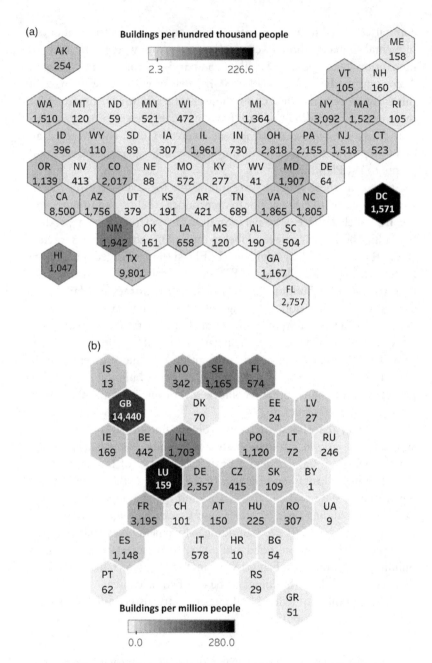

Figure 1.2 Total ecolabeled buildings and buildings per 100,000 people in (a) the United States, (b) Europe, and (c) the rest of the world

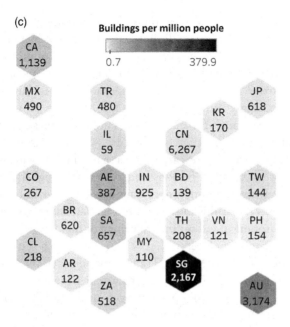

Figure 1.2 *(cont.)*

The United Kingdom leads the way in Europe, with 14,440 buildings, just behind Luxembourg in per-capita buildings despite its much larger size. This is likely due to the popularity of the BREEAM label, which is very popular in the UK. Not surprisingly, Sweden, Finland, and the Netherlands also have prominent ecolabeled buildings. These countries tend to certify under the LEED label. It is somewhat surprising that Germany, with its DGNB Sustainable Building Council certification and just over 1,500 certifications, does not have more popularity, although conversations with experts suggest that LEED has recently begun to gain uptake momentum in Germany. Other labels have also not gained significant traction in Germany.

Australia and Singapore are significant green building leaders in the rest of the world. Australia's Green Star ecolabel and Singapore's Green Mark ecolabel have become quite popular, with Singapore's Green Mark covering 20 percent of gross floor area in the country.[3]

---

[3] www.constructionglobal.com/company/singapore-green-building-council-sgbc

These systems have developed multiple labels and certify a growing array of products. In LEED v2009, the point totals were expanded to move to a 100-point scale and incorporate additional opportunities for credits. Version 4 expanded the point total to 110 and incorporated a large shift from a checklist-based approach toward an approach focused increasingly on performance. Over the past 10 years or so, the concept of ecolabels for buildings has grown increasingly popular, demonstrating the growing importance of the Green Building Movement. Our previous research shows that firms participate in these programs for a variety of reasons and achieving a higher tier corresponds to receiving additional marketing benefits. As will be discussed throughout this book, this movement has had an enormous impact on the built environment and on the trajectory of building improvements that are now commonplace.

Our theory of Green Market Transformation lays out a model in which these ecolabels and associated marketing benefits of certification drive early movers to adopt advanced technologies. This early adoption is strategic. Firms may be experimenting internally to earn a competitive advantage, to gain experience with cutting edge technological systems, to showcase their firm's identity, or to hire and retain employees. Other cases are oriented toward a broader public mission. The Kendeda Building for Innovative Sustainable Design at the Georgia Institute of Technology was initiated by the gift of a philanthropist as a mechanism to facilitate the transformation of the building and construction industries in the Southeastern United States. This building – and others built by foundations and universities, like the Bullitt Center in Portland and the Brock Commons tower at the University of British Columbia in Vancouver – highlights the role that foundations and universities can play in demonstrate innovative technologies to the private sector. Government-owned buildings such as the Vancouver Convention Center, Chicago's City Hall, and the ACROS Fukuoka Prefectural International Hall in Japan might be built to appeal to a wide range of stakeholder interests. And private sector investments like the Pixel Building in Melbourne, Australia, Bosco Verticale in Milan, One Bryant Park in New York City, the Edge in Amsterdam, Netherlands, DPR Construction's offices in Phoenix, Arizona, and Shanghai Tower in China highlight the role of the private sector strategically catering to niche markets or leveraging branding. The adoption of advanced technologies by early movers facilitates the broader uptake of these technologies. Here, we highlight several cases where firms or organizations that were early adopters of emergent technologies have paved the way for their widespread adoption.

Examples of Prominent Ecolabeled Buildings

Johnson Controls

Johnson Controls highlight a case where gaining experience with new technologies is key to the strategic practice of the firm. Johnson Controls, which builds and operates building automation technologies, is an obvious candidate to be an early adopter of leading energy technologies. Johnson Controls certified one of the very first LEED New Construction buildings in the world, the Brengel Technology Center in Milwaukee, in 2000. In 2010, the firm built a Corporate Campus in Glendale, WI, with four LEED Platinum buildings. These investments were seen through the lens of gaining experience with innovative technologies so that Johnson Controls could highlight to potential clients "what technologies provide the best financial investment while having the least impact on the environment, and at the same time create a productive workplace for employees," notes facilities and building services director Ward Komorowski.[4] The Johnson Controls case shows how corporations adopt these new technologies to communicate with employees, customers, and the public. Komorowski insists "It's important that our employees, customers and the public understand every aspect of our commitment to the triple bottom line, and the new corporate campus helps that happen."[5] Not only does this case highlight some of the strategic reasons that firms are likely to pursue ecolabeling and adopt new technologies, but also the dissemination of these new technologies across borders. In 2018, Johnson Controls completed a second headquarters in Shanghai, China, certified LEED Platinum. They also certified with the Chinese label Three Star and the International Finance Corporation (IFC) - World Bank label Excellence in Design for Greater Efficiencies

[4] www.johnsoncontrols.com/insights/2015/building-efficiency/case-study/johnson-controls-corporate-headquarters
[5] www.johnsoncontrols.com/insights/2015/building-efficiency/case-study/johnson-controls-corporate-headquarters

(EDGE). As we will discuss in more depth throughout the book, this repetitive and iterative certification represents evidence of learning and the transfer of knowledge across borders that is important to the market transformation process.

Genzyme

Other firms have less obvious strategic relationships with energy and environmental technologies. In 2001, biotechnology company Genzyme pursued one of the first LEED Platinum buildings in the United States at a time when Green Building certification was a new idea (Toffel and Sesia 2010). While Genzyme did not have a strategic relationship with energy and the environment, they saw the pursuit of a sustainably certified building as part of their global citizenship efforts and corporate social responsibility initiatives (Toffel and Sesia 2010). Henri Termeer, Genzyme's Chief Executive Officer (CEO), discussed that Genzyme wanted to do something different and to make a statement with their new headquarters. "I wanted the building to explain what we stood for – innovation, doing the right thing, sustainability, transparency, life sciences" (Toffel and Sesia 2010).

This case highlights many of the challenges, barriers, and costs associated with being an early adopter, as well as some of the motivations to pursue something truly innovative. When high costs associated with initial designs deterred the design team from pursuing a LEED Platinum certification, Termeer asked the Green Building Team to explore alternative green features to achieve Platinum certification. Back in 2001, senior Project Manager Gordon Brailsford explained the risks, costs, and uncertainties associated with being an early adopter of green building technologies: "This is a big challenge because it is not so easy to map a green feature to a LEED credit ... there are so few 'green' products and materials in the marketplace that costs are ballpark estimates ... making [design] changes could jeopardize LEED credits that we have in the bank." Still, Termeer argued that "The difference between meeting the highest standard and a good standard such as Silver or Gold is very large for a company of this kind. Setting a good standard simply falls short and sends the wrong signal to potential partners, regulators, our employees, and our patients." Early adopters of environmental technologies are subject to increased risk, uncertainty, and costs but are able to use these investments to

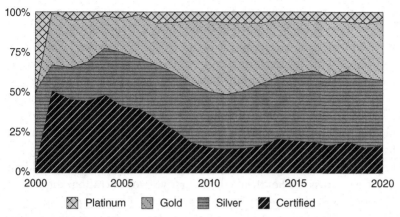

Figure 1.3 Tier breakdown of new construction LEED US buildings

signal to stakeholders that they are high quality, innovative, and sustainable.

As we will highlight throughout the book, individual choices like Genzyme's decision to invest additional resources to pursue a higher level of ecolabel can produce positive spillover effects that ultimately lead to the widespread uptake of these new technologies. Indeed, by 2020, roughly 1,200 projects worldwide had been certified Platinum under the LEED standard.[6] Figure 1.3 shows the growth of Gold and Silver new construction certifications in the United States relative to the lowest certification level throughout LEED's 20-year history. The stringency of standards for achieving LEED Platinum ecolabel have only increased over time, demonstrating that firms consider the benefits of high certification to be worthwhile even under conditions of increasing costs. In spite of cost, high levels of ecolabeling have become achievable for many, and market transformation has occurred.

The Kendeda Building for Innovative Sustainable Design

This Living Building was built as a collaboration between the Kendeda Fund foundation and the Georgia Institute of Technology (Georgia Tech or GT). The developers aimed to build one of the largest Living Building projects constructed as a demonstration of sustainable

---

[6] Our calculations, based on Green Building Information Gateway (GBIG) data.

engineering and design, with an overarching goal to transform the built environment in the Southeastern United States. Demonstration projects serve to disseminate state-of-the-art practices by reducing uncertainty associated with the performance of untested technologies. As one of the first Living Buildings in the Southeast, it faced incumbent climatic difficulties as well as a challenging lab and classroom environment. In addition to the adoption of a number of the advanced technologies highlighted in Chapter 5, the sponsoring partners and building team have actively undertaken a number of steps aimed at increasing the broader impact of the building and disseminating the new building practices across the Southeast. In its first year of operation, thousands of people were expected to tour the building.[7] They represent colleges and universities around the world considering similar building projects. Other folks come from corporations in the building and construction industry, sustainability professionals, and a diverse array of businesses and organizations hoping to learn about the leading edge of building technologies.

The building itself represents a transfer of technology and learning within the construction industry. When Georgia Tech initiated the design competition, all competing entries were made public. To the participants in the program, this represented a departure from the typical close-to-the-chest approach that design teams had observed in this cutting-edge technology space. Alissa Kingsley from the winning team at Lord Aeck Sargent explained that showcasing all of the designs, including those that did not win, allowed the design teams to build an understanding of varying approaches to meet ambitious performance targets. The winning team was a collaboration between Lord Aeck Sargent, Skanska, and Newcomb & Boyd. They partnered with Miller Hull and PAE Engineering, a design and engineering team from Seattle and Portland that had worked together on the Bullitt Center in Seattle, a Living Building that had been completed six years earlier. Together, these firms adapted many of the technologies that were employed in the Bullitt Center to use in the Kendeda Building for Innovative Sustainable Design (KBISD). This transfer of technologies and expertise from the Northwest-based design team to the Southeast-

---

[7] Due the COVID-19 pandemic, in person tours were suspended in March 2020. Roughly 6,000 people toured or attended events in the building between August 2019 and March 2020.

based design team allowed these technologies to be calibrated and adapted for a different climate zone and operating conditions. This transfer of knowledge as a result of collaboration on an innovative project is a unique example of learning by doing that we will explore further throughout the book.

Although the building has only been open since August 2019, a number of lessons have already emerged that have allowed this building to spur the diffusion of improved managerial practices. First, this building uses only off-the-shelf technologies that make broader uptake more likely. It highlights that innovation can look like the combination of various technologies together to build a cohesive sustainable system. Second, it engages a wide range of stakeholders through frequent tours, meetings, and large events that increase the number of people who interact with the building. Third, by placing the project within a large organization and frequent builder like a major state university, the visibility of the project is increased. This allows for the external transfer of technologies. Finally, engaging in a demonstration project like this requires enhanced coordination by the design and construction team as well as the development of new forms of communication and engagement. By engaging committed contractors and subcontractors in the project to build their own expertise, the project has an increased chance of success.

Soldier Field

Soldier Field, home of the National Football League's (NFL) Chicago Bears and one of Chicago's largest and most recognizable event facilities, was renovated and reopened in 2003. The project incorporated a number of energy conservation and recycling programs, use of green cleaning materials, and reuse of waste material such as old soil from sod. Like many stadiums, Soldier Field is publicly owned (in this case by the Chicago Park District) and managed by SMG, a large private venue management and consulting firm that operates stadiums, convention centers, and other large facilities across the United States. The building, first constructed in 1924, became the first stadium to receive LEED for Existing Buildings certification in 2012. To achieve this certification, the Chicago Park District made a conscious effort to lessen its environmental impact by reducing water usage, increasing energy efficiency, and creating waste management programs.

Compared with other advanced buildings, Soldier Field does not incorporate high end technologies or systems. Its scorecard, available on the USGBC website, shows that it barely achieved certification (with 37 out of 85 possible points for Existing Buildings) and earned few points in water efficiency and energy and atmosphere. The project was unique, however, in its leverage of a government-owned building to help spur a worldwide competition for green construction and operation of large event spaces and stadia around the United States. This highlighted a connection between cities' sustainable development strategies and opportunities to involve private-sector construction.

Chicago has had a sustainable development policy to improve sustainable performance of projects receiving City assistance in place since 2004. As a result of this policy, Chicago has become an international leader in green building technologies such as green roofs. In 2018, it was one of seven entire cities worldwide to be certified LEED Platinum.[8] Chicago also operates its own building certification program. New construction projects and renovations for existing buildings are required to either certify through LEED or another existing certification program, or they need to select amongst a series of strategies to earn points through the city's certification program.

Research suggests that public procurement programs like Chicago's can help drive the market for green buildings (Simcoe and Toffel 2014). This research suggests that government agencies that adopt green buildings play a role in highlighting the performance of these buildings, making them less risky and more attractive to the private sector. In addition, they build supply chains and expertise in the private sector, which lowers their costs and makes them more widely available in the market. These market driving forces, which are similar to those for pilot and demonstration projects, help facilitate market transformation and highlight a mechanism that cities and governments can utilize to transform the private-sector market.

Diffusing Technologies through Competition

While National Basketball Association (NBA), National Hockey League (NHL), Major League Baseball (MLB), and NFL teams

---

[8] www.usgbc.org/articles/mayor-emanuel-announces-chicago-achieved-leed-cities-platinum-certification

compete on the court, ice, or field, their ownership and management groups have been competing in sustainability management. There are over 30 LEED ecolabeled sports venues in the United States.[9] The Miami Heat's American Airlines Arena was the first NBA facility to earn the LEED for Existing Buildings certification in 2009, as well as the first sports and entertainment facility in the world to earn a LEED Gold recertification. This spurred a long list of stadiums and arenas around the world employing green building techniques and certifications. Here, we describe some of the most recognized green sporting facilities that demonstrate a competitive dynamic relationship and have pushed the bar for green building and inspired additional uptake of green building practices – both in the sporting world and in the communities they reside in.

In 2010, Target Field in downtown Minneapolis became the first MLB stadium to earn the LEED Silver ecolabel, and then earned LEED Silver for Existing Buildings – Operations and Maintenance the following year. By switching to compostable packaging and making improvements in recycling and composting management, the facility diverted 5,419 tons of waste in its first several years of operation. The facility was one of the first to adopt light-emitting diode (LED) systems for stadium lighting and to collect rainwater for purification and re-use. It inspired a number of additional adoptions both nearby and around the world. Demonstrating some of the local effects of greening stadiums, the Xcel Energy Center in Minnesota was the first NHL facility to earn LEED for Existing Buildings in 2014,[10] drawing upon the management firm's experience managing the Saint Paul RiverCentre, a convention center next door. The building boasts a solar photovoltaic (PV) and a solar thermal array and supports wind-power offsets. In addition, the facility is achieving recycling rates of 60 percent and has successfully encouraged 40 percent of employees to use public transportation. The success of this initiative has also inspired the nearby Edmonton Oilers to build Rogers Place, a LEED-Silver certified facility, in 2017.[11] In 2019, this building upped its certification level to Platinum during a recertification process.

[9] www.greenmatters.com/travel/2018/07/31/2f5fvD/sports-stadiums-sustainable-design

[10] www.usgbc.org/projects/rivercentrexcel-energy-center

[11] http://plus.usgbc.org/sustainable-stadiums

A number of other stadiums around the world have demonstrated leadership in energy and environmental design. The Levi's Stadium, home of the San Francisco 49ers, earned the first LEED Gold certification for a stadium hosting a professional team, and in 2016 received a second Gold certification for Existing Buildings – Operations and Maintenance. The building includes state-of-the-art solar arrays and solar-covered pedestrian bridges, as well as a green roof. The building employs a sustainable purchasing program for cleaning materials and local food sourcing. The Golden 1 Center in Sacramento became the first LEED Platinum building hosting a professional sports team in 2016 and is in the top 3 percent of high performance buildings in the world.[12] It achieves 100 percent solar energy and uses 45 percent less water than required by California's (already strict) code. Lincoln Financial Field in Philadelphia, certified LEED Gold in 2018, has 11,000 solar panels and 14 wind turbines, producing 3 megawatts (MW) of peak power.

The Atlanta Falcons and Atlanta United FC's Mercedes-Benz Stadium, completed in 2018, is the first LEED Platinum professional sports stadium in the United States. Arthur Blank, the founder of Home Depot and the owner of the Falcons and Atlanta United, built the first LEED building in Georgia in 2004. He notes,

We set out to build a venue that would not only exceed expectations, but also push the limits of what was possible in terms of stadium design, fan experience, and sustainability … We set a goal of achieving the highest LEED rating because it was the right thing to do for our city and the environment and with this achievement. We have a powerful new platform to showcase to the industry and to our fans that building sustainably and responsibly is possible for a venue of any type, size and scale.[13]

"In many ways, this project is influencing the future of LEED for sports facilities," says Carlie Bullock-Jones, founder and principal of Ecoworks Studio.[14] The stadium hosted the Super Bowl, the College Football championship games, and the Major League Soccer championship and all-star games, exposing hundreds of thousands of

[12] www.climateaction.org/news/the-5-most-sustainable-sports-venues-in-the-world

[13] https://footballstadiumdigest.com/2017/11/mercedes-benz-stadium-earns-leed-platinum-certification/

[14] http://plus.usgbc.org/sustainable-stadiums/

attendees, personnel, and fans watching the broadcasts to this innovative approach to construction. It is also slated to host a number of additional high-profile sporting events and conventions. This international exposure is expected to help boost awareness of the opportunities associated with a LEED Platinum certification.

Many of the advanced technologies employed in the Mercedes-Benz Stadium are unlikely to be cost-effective solutions on their own. In the context of a large public project that requires public assistance and has complex politics, however, many of these technologies may have major public benefits that help smooth the contentious politics of a major development project such as a stadium. Scott Jenkins, the general manager for Mercedes-Benz Stadium, notes that a 680,000-gallon cistern used to collect rainwater and irrigate vegetation around the building also serves as flood control for the flood-susceptible West End neighborhood nearby the stadium that has a median family income of just a fraction of Atlanta's wealthier neighborhoods.[15] Jenkins states, "It's a community play as much as an environmental play, to do our part around issues in the neighborhood ... If you looked at the return on investment for the water, it will take a long time to pay off. But some of this is good for business and some is good for community."

It has arguably become commonplace for large stadiums to pursue an ecolabel as a matter of standard operating procedure. The Banc of California Stadium for the Los Angeles Football Club certified LEED Gold in 2019. The new SoFi Stadium for the LA Rams and LA Chargers, which opened in 2020, certified Gold as well. Indeed, all six stadiums used for the 2014 World Cup in Brazil had some form of LEED certification. Mane Garrincha Stadium in Brasilia, Brazil can generate up to 2.5 MW of energy. BREEAM has been involved with stadium certification as well – with Moscow's Luzhniki Stadium, Kaliningrad Stadium, and Rostov Arena featured in the 2018 FIFA World Cup achieving the BREEAM label. The Austrian and German sustainable building councils, ÖGNI and DGNB, respectively, have created their own label specifically for sports stadiums in central Europe.

It is worth noting, however, that stadiums have been used to demonstrate innovative energy technologies even before ecolabeling was popular. For example, the Amsterdam ArenA – built in 1996 as a

---

[15] www.wabe.org/map-atlantas-highest-and-lowest-income-neighborhoods/

climate neutral facility – hosts solar panels, a wind turbine, and an energy storage system with used car batteries. This storage system for the local grid also works as backup generation for the stadium. It also boasts the use of renewable sugarcane materials for seating, various natural heating and cooling mechanisms, and the re-use of rainwater. In the United States, the MetLife Stadium, built in 2010, was an early adopter of solar panels and LED lighting, and consumed 30 percent less energy than its predecessor.

With green building becoming standard within the stadium market and in other high-profile buildings, it is apparent that market transformation has occurred. No longer is it acceptable to build a large building without paying attention to the sustainability features. The focus on sustainability features and the certification of those features has created an enormous industry around ecolabeling and sustainable building. This development has truly transformed the building and construction market. In the following section we explore the drivers of this market transformation.

How Market Transformation Works

Early adopters pave the way for broader market uptake by reducing a number of uncertainties and search and transaction costs that typically inhibit the adoption of new technologies. Viewed from a traditional economic lens, these might affect the supply curve or the demand curve for these technologies. In the green building market, uptake of technologies has followed a traditional S curve for technological adoption, which is well known in the technological adoption literature. This S curve suggests that at first adoptions are slow but, eventually, the pace of adoption speeds up, facilitating market penetration and ultimately market transformation.

Figure 1.4 demonstrates this S-curve trend in the international market, highlighting a very gradual uptake of new technology followed by a period of more rapid uptake. The leveling off of the version 2 vintage is also typical of an S adoption curve, as the new technology becomes the market standard. In this particular graph, we see total adoptions continuing upward as new varieties of LEED are offered.

We next explore the supply-side and demand-side drivers of market transformation that brought the LEED program into the mainstream and may (or may not) provide a similar trajectory for Living Building

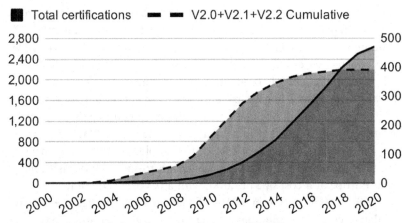

Figure 1.4 S-curve derived from cumulative total LEED-new-construction certifications (international market)

technologies. Other trends where nascent technologies eventually achieve rapid uptake include solar and wind electricity and hybrid vehicles. Other technologies such as fully electric vehicles are currently in the nascent stage but show widespread market potential. Still others, such as various nuclear energy technologies, hydrogen fuel cell technologies, and others, appear to have failed to gain widespread market uptake. We turn next to exploring some of the drivers that may have facilitated successful market transformation in the built environment, as well as some parallels and contrasts with other technologies.

Supply-Side Drivers of Market Transformation

On the supply side, one major barrier to the adoption of new technologies is the lack of knowledge or expertise across the supply chain, which increases costs. If there are few or no suppliers of a product, it can be difficult to find potential product suppliers to bid into a project. Public buildings such as Georgia Tech's KBISD are subject to public procurement and bidding requirements that might require three competing bidders. Even if these suppliers are found, they may demand a market premium because they do not have much experience with the product and perceive high risk in engaging with a new product space. Consider Genzyme's comment that green features added uncertain costs to the project because there was little market experience available. Or consider comments from other contractors on innovative projects that note "nobody wants to be the first to try something." Building systems are large, costly investments, and few want to gamble with new technologies.

In addition, a lack of competition in this space drives up prices. The initial products in a market pave the way for additional adoption, in part by building supply chains. Once suppliers gain experience with a product, it will be more readily available in the marketplace and prices will decrease. In the extreme case, for example, in 2001 the Genzyme LEED Platinum headquarters building had to import no-flush toilets from Europe at a cost of $117,000, with a payback rate of just $6,600 per year (Toffel and Sesia 2010). Today, no-flush toilets are widely available with only a minimal market premium that has quick payback times. This principle also explains the importance of successive pilot and demonstration projects, and why it appears from the data that there is a critical mass of projects required before widespread adoption of new technologies can take place.

One factor that seems to have driven the success of market transformation in LEED and in solar manufacturing is the presence of a critical mass of projects in a particular geographic location. Building markets are extremely local, with prime and sub-contractors working regionally or locally due to regional expertise and conditions and high transportation costs. The co-location of projects establishes supply chains and brings down costs.

Several pieces of evidence from the LEED building dataset support these claims. When LEED starts a new label or vintage (e.g., New Construction 4.0, Retail Interiors, Core and Shell, Existing Buildings) they run a set of pilot projects to develop the label. These pilot projects are the earliest adopters of a new standard, and USGBC works with potential adopters to seed these projects into geographically dispersed building markets. In exchange for participating in the pilot project and agreeing to disseminate results, early adopters get technical assistance from the USGBC, a head start on experience with new technologies, and the right to advertise their status as innovative early adopters.

Examining these pilot projects can inform us about how the experiences of the earliest adopters impacts the eventual uptake of new technologies. Research described in this book (Chapter 7) highlights the role of pilot and demonstration projects in driving the adoption of new LEED projects. Further, once a market is established, building additional LEED ecolabeled projects leads to ever-lower costs as eco-practices are routinized, are incorporated into building codes, and ultimately become standard practice.

Demand-Side Drivers of Market Transformation

The earliest adopters of LEED Pilot projects take on the riskiest projects that have the most additional costs. By iterating projects and lowering costs, uncertainty associated with new technologies decreases, the recognition of the ecolabel and opportunities to build green increase, and demand for these new buildings increases. As this demand increases and green buildings become more commonplace, the dissemination of projects across the building industry represents market transformation. A similar story follows in the solar industry and demand for a range of green products, where people adopt green technologies to reduce their environmental impact or communicate their green values to others. These early adopters help drive down prices allowing the industry to expand. Further in solar and manufacturing, we see economies of agglomeration where the co-location of many suppliers has driven down costs. Policies and incentives that have been plentiful in the solar industry have furthered the demand for solar panels. Additionally, significant research points to the role of peer effects in boosting demand for hybrid and electric automobiles, solar panels, and even energy-efficient heating, ventilation, and air conditioning (HVAC) systems. This "keeping up with the Joneses" effect suggests competition and – even at the individual level – pressures people into green investments.

This phenomenon might also underpin the failure of promising technologies to gain widespread traction in the market. The federal government has invested massive amounts of resources in new designs of nuclear power plants since 1950. One estimate suggests that from 1950–2016, the government spent over $85 billion on civilian nuclear energy R&D (Management Information Services 2017). Yet few nuclear plants have come online since the 1970s, and none have used advanced reactor designs. While part of the failure of nuclear can be attributed to cost, political opposition, and other factors, it is also plausible that high costs have been driven by the low volume of plants constructed. An alternative strategy of iterating a small number of designs and increasing focus on the commercialization of these technologies could have produced a different outcome.

Early adopters of technologies also provide positive spillovers to other market participants on the demand side. First, new technologies have uncertain costs and benefits, as well as performance and reliability characteristics, meaning uncertain costs and benefits. Kotchen and Costello (2018) argue that both pilot projects and full-scale demonstration projects may warrant significant government subsidies because of the value generated by the learning that results from their construction. Adopters of new technologies supply other potential adopters with information about these factors of new technologies. Demand might also be influenced by peer effects, marketing benefits, and suppliers pushing a new product that they believe is a cost-effective solution.

As individual firms gain experience with new technologies, they may seek more widespread adoption. For example, large firms may choose to apply specific technological standards or adopt new technologies across an entire product line or in multiple locations. Visual cues like seeing a new technology being used by a rival firm might signal a firm that a new technology is market-ready, or spur the demand by those who are exposed to this new technology. Research on electric vehicles, rooftop solar, and even zoned HVAC suggests that these peer effects can be powerful tools for disseminating new technologies.

As new practices become standard practices, costs continue to come down and the marketing advantages of adopting these practices eventually diminish. When new technologies become standard practices, market transformation is complete. In the built environment, we have seen energy efficiency, LED lighting, and a number of other technologies that were once costly and premium products become standard practice in new constructions and in retrofits.

Conclusion

In conclusion, ecolabels help enable early adopters to invest in innovative technologies and practices. These early adopters see strategic benefits to adopting ecolabels and signaling leadership. These benefits might be market premiums, growing market share, preempting or steering regulation, etc. Even more simply, this may be about bragging rights, similar to early adopters of Tesla vehicles or solar panels on a house.

But early adoption is about more than bragging rights. These early adopters play an important role in the innovation cycle and bringing new technologies to market. By ponying up the extra costs of new technologies, they play an important role in bringing about market transformation. Early adopters provide valuable information to the market. This information can come in the form of performance data for new technologies, or it may come in the form of training up a supply chain. The reduction in costs of new technologies, combined with improved understanding of benefits, leads to widespread adoption of these technologies. As the (previously new) technologies become standard in the market, ecolabels can change the standards to push the bar further and introduce more advanced, greener technologies to the market. This sets the stage for the next wave of innovation. Ecolabels can ratchet up requirements and require a new round of innovation and technological adoption, again rewarded by a marketing benefit and premium associated with being an early adopter. We explore this virtuous cycle in more depth throughout the book.

References

Aragón-Correa, J. A., A. A. Marcus, and D. Vogel. 2020. "The Effects of Mandatory and Voluntary Regulatory Pressures on Firms' Environmental Strategies: A Review and Recommendations for Future Research." *Academy of Management Annals* 14, no. 1: 339–365.

Darnall, Nicole, Hyunjung Ji, and Matthew Potoski. 2017. "Institutional Design of Ecolabels: Sponsorship Signals Rule Strength." *Regulation & Governance* 11, no. 4: 438–450.

Darnall, Nicole, Hyunjung Ji, and Diego A. Vázquez-Brust. 2018. "Third-Party Certification, Sponsorship, and Consumers' Ecolabel Use." *Journal of Business Ethics* 150, no. 4: 953–969.

Hamilton, S. F. and D. Zilberman. 2006. "Green Markets, Eco-Certification, and Equilibrium Fraud." *Journal of Environmental Economics and Management* 52, no. 3: 627–644.

Kotchen, Matthew and Christopher Costello. 2018. "Maximizing the Impact of Climate Finance: Funding Projects or Pilot Projects?" *Journal of Environmental Economics and Management* 92: 270–281.

Management Information Services, Inc. 2017. "Two Thirds of a Century and $1 Trillion+ U.S. Energy Incentives: Analysis of Federal Expenditures for Energy Development 1950–2016."

Rivera, J. 2002. "Assessing a Voluntary Environmental Initiative in the Developing World: The Costa Rican Certification for Sustainable Tourism." *Policy Sciences* 35: 333–360.

2004. Institutional Pressures and Voluntary Environmental Behavior in Developing Countries: Evidence from Costa Rica. *Society and Natural Resources* 17: 779–797.

Rivera, J. and P. de Leon. 2004. "Is Greener Whiter? The Sustainable Slopes Program and the Voluntary Environmental Performance of Western Ski Areas." *Policy Studies Journal* 32, no. 3: 417–437.

Roheim, C. A., S. R. Bush, F. Asche, J. N. Sanchirico, and H. Uchida. 2018. "Evolution and Future of the Sustainable Seafood Market." *Nature Sustainability* 1, no. 8: 392–398.

Simcoe, Timothy and Michael W. Toffel. 2014. "Government Green Procurement Spillovers: Evidence from Municipal Building Policies in California." *Journal of Environmental Economics and Management* 68, no. 3: 411–434.

Toffel, Michael W. and Aldo Sesia. 2010. "Genzyme Center (A)." *Harvard Business School Case* no. 610-008 (September).

2 | *The Architecture of Green Building Policies and Practice*

Defining Green Building and Related Policies

Green building has risen in prominence in recent years for architects, engineers, planners, environmental economists, and policy-makers alike. Yet green building policy is a fuzzy concept. In our definition, we distinguish it from policies that promote only energy efficiency, such as appliance standards, building codes, and other technology-specific regulations. Though there is not one definition for "green buildings" or their policies, they usually prioritize resource efficiency and reduce negative impacts on human health and the environment. This includes every stage of the building process, from siting to design, construction, operation, maintenance, renovation, and demolition.[1] To bound our definition, we focus on whole-building investments and policies rather than on component-level policies (e.g., weatherization subsidies, Energy Star appliances) or more general policies (e.g., wetlands offset policies, anti-sprawl policies). We distinguish between green buildings and energy-efficient buildings in order to highlight the Green Building Movement's attention to the entire building lifecycle and to nonenergy impacts. To the outside observer, identifying green buildings presents challenges, regardless of the criteria used. Most rely on formal designations or certifications to identify which buildings are green, but that list represents a lower bound on the total number of green buildings – some buildings would qualify as green but do not get certified.

Flexibility of certification paths is one of the key features (and criticisms) of green building. Green building labels rarely require or disclose individual building improvements or technological upgrades. For most non-confidential building projects, the United States Green Building Council's (USGBC) Leadership in Energy and Environmental

---

[1] www.epa.gov/greenbuilding/pubs/about.htm

Design (LEED) certification program totals points across many categories to calculate a tiered certification, though more recent initiatives
by the Green Building Information Gateway (www.gbig.org) have
increased the transparency of the individual building scorecards by
demonstrating category scores for each building and point category.
A variety of other programs around the world, discussed in more detail
in Chapter 4, function similarly. There are numerous steps and
improvements a design team can take to certify the lifecycle impacts
of a building and achieve LEED-certified, Silver, Gold, or Platinum
status. Firms can select from a menu of options rather than have
certain technology standards prescribed, thereby permitting solutions
that are customized for each building.

Two key motivations for the Green Building Movement have been to
incentivize firms to internalize externalities or to privately provide a
public good (Kingsley 2008; Kotchen 2006). *Externalities* are negative
or positive effects created by a firm that impact others, such as pollution. *Public goods* are resources that cannot be exhausted by any one
user and cannot be denied to any user, such as clean air or less carbon
in the upper atmosphere. Buildings that are good for the environment
provide benefits to the public, also known as positive externalities. One
strategy behind LEED, like other voluntary programs, is to link a set of
private benefits to public-good production via program participation
(a club good approach) (Prakash and Potoski 2006). This means that
LEED-certified buildings earn profits for their owners while creating
these beneficial public goods. By being part of the "club" of certified
buildings, organizations may enjoy financial value for reducing negative externalities. By *building* green, a developer avoids inflicting environmental damage. By *certifying* green, a building owner signals this
value to stakeholders (such as regulators, employees, investors, and
customers), who will often pay more (a premium) for their product
because the firm is benefiting society. Additionally, organizations may
bolster their profits by certifying operational improvements that are
hard to observe. The ability to prove to stakeholders that your building
is of high quality is a similarly valuable signal in the market.

While private-sector certification systems like LEED utilize voluntary participation, a wide range of federal, state, and local government
entities have also promulgated policies to promote green building.
Some policies take the form of mandates – sometimes even requiring
participation in private programs like LEED. Others alter government

procurement policies or otherwise encourage voluntary greener building. The justifications for these policies include several perspectives. Encouraging more private firms to produce public goods that benefit communities is one motivation. Another is that, without good information about which building choices are best, builders and owners may make suboptimal choices when building. Energy-efficiency policies can help nudge decision-makers into making more efficient choices, raising the quality of the built environment (Allcott and Greenstone 2012). Special interest politics and administrative costs also figure into a positive political economy of green building policy instrument choice.

In this chapter, we first review the theory and empirical evidence of market failures and various barriers that have shaped the Green Building Movement, which aims to improve environmental footprints in a way that is profitable to participants. To the scholar, this mission seeks to align public and private benefits through reduction of information asymmetries and externalities of building practices. We then characterize the scope of green building policy initiatives across the United States and across the globe. We also show the prevalence of the Green Building Movement around the globe.

Why a Builder Goes Green

The challenges and opportunities of the Green Building Movement can be understood through the economic lens of market failures, credence goods, and signaling theory. The market for buildings suffers from market failures, many of which relate to the external or hidden environmental costs of construction and building maintenance. Addressing these market failures can benefit the public and those who are directly involved in the market. Another, overlapping set of market failures regards information and green signals. Builders' choice to "go green" often includes the choice to "*certify* green." Traditionally, markets may not make it easy for builders to recoup higher costs of greener construction. Green building certifiers seek to overcome these market barriers by incentivizing greener practices by linking certification to profitability. Most additional costs associated with green buildings are related to innovative design costs and certification costs, including uncertainty in the certification process. Plus, green building entails additional materials costs (Chegut et al. 2019). There may still be concerns in the market about whether green buildings are "better." Like the worry that recycled paper might be inferior, greener products could be seen to entail inconvenience, discomfort, or greater operating costs. Misgivings about quality aside, builders still face challenges in making the business case that reducing environmental footprints is profitable, connecting the triple bottom line.

Thus, the first challenge to overcome in builders opting to "go green" involves realizing sufficient gains from greener design to justify the additional costs. Undoubtedly, much of the advantage of greener buildings arises from their smaller ecological footprints and the broader benefits to society and their environs. These advantages represent spillovers to others. Those benefits may do little to justify the building bearing the full costs of designs that are more expensive, complicated, or risky. In light of these externalities, discussed later in this chapter, the Green Building Movement often shifts attention to the improved building performance that comes with greener designs. Positive environmental spillovers may just be a bonus if builders choose to "go green" in order to capture the gains from better performing buildings. Green buildings are not just a boon to their neighbors; they can be superior buildings in their own right.

A key question then might be why firms certify at all if most additional costs are due to certification and firms could build to similar specifications without certifying. One motivation for firms to certify green is to overcome market barriers such as information problems, uncertainties, and misaligned incentives between the builder and the building owner, between the building owner and the tenant, or between the seller and the buyer. Certifying can allow the development of a market for high-quality buildings, reducing the dominance of shoddy quality buildings in the market. By linking profitability with quality, certifiers provide a strategic opportunity for builders to overcome market barriers in the built environment.

Without certification, even the modest costs of green building may become unattractive. Building owners may lack quality information about a building's future operating costs or the ability to monitor construction characteristics such as the disposal of the construction waste, the indoor air quality, or the qualities of the physical barrier between the interior and exterior environment (i.e., the building envelope). Green building certification can reduce the cost of obtaining this information and credibly verify information about the building's qualities through a third-party certifier. Similarly, certification can reduce imperfect information that can complicate arrangements between a potential tenant of a building and an owner, or between a buyer and a seller at resale. Certification provides an inexpensive option for consumers to judge the overall quality of a green building and reward building owners for the better building performance. Though this works in theory, however, the flexibility of many certification programs may also be considered a weakness. Because these programs do not prescribe specific technological requirements, the "noisy" signal of building quality (Fuerst and McAllister 2011b) in green certification can make it unclear what improvements buyers are really paying for. We discuss noisiness in ecolabels, where the certification refers to a holistic or general "greenness," and the tensions between flexibility and ambiguity in Chapter 3.

Improved Building Performance

Builders may opt to "go green" because green buildings often promise improved performance – lower construction or operating costs, more reliable or stable energy use, better indoor environments, etc. (Kats 2003). While green certification may not be directly tied to building performance, a number of the tactics available for certification reduce the costs of building operation (e.g., improved building envelope, increased water efficiency, high efficiency HVAC system). Certified buildings, on average, are more energy efficient than uncertified buildings (Asensio and Delmas 2017). Energy efficiency is a key factor in operational-cost reductions and a lever to be pressed to obtain cost-effective green building upgrades. Some green building policies require or incentivize particular tactics that have positive returns to the occupant or owner, as discussed later in this chapter. Often, the institutional investors financing building projects have a stronger belief in the cost-effectiveness of energy-efficiency upgrades (Chegut et al. 2014). This leads developers to invest more heavily in energy efficiency investments. The productive benefits of green buildings may go beyond water and energy efficiency as well. Green buildings may command a market premium (e.g., Rivera 2002) because of enhanced quality for residents, tenants, and employees. Some green building points are awarded for features that improve the experience of the building inhabitants, such as daylight and window access. Studies show that employees take fewer sick days and are more productive in green buildings (Singh et al. 2010). This indicates that green building certification can improve employee productivity and retention for tenants.

The operational benefits of green buildings suggest that there is value in the marketplace for reducing building operating costs. A number of studies have found that this operational value translates into increased profitability for these building owners. For instance, Real Estate Investment Trusts with more LEED-certified projects in their portfolio have a higher capitalizable value and lower volatility than those that do not (Eichholtz et al. 2012). Research also shows that BREEAM-labeled buildings attract longer rental contracts, with a 28 percent rental premium, even after controlling for basic building characteristics (Chegut et al. 2014). The international experience has been similar. Green Mark Singapore-labeled buildings achieve a 9.9 percent resale market premium. Interestingly, initial purchases bring a smaller premium (4.4 percent), demonstrating the role that ecolabeling plays in minimizing information asymmetries which may be higher in the resale market (Deng and Wu 2013). Rental properties enjoy greater premiums from being green labeled relative to those that are for sale (Chegut et al. 2014). This differential again highlights the reduction of information asymmetries and the signals that allow prospective tenants to discern the overall quality of a property (Verma et al. 2020). Moreover, these premiums are a fundamental indicator of a successful strategy in the Green Building Movement. Ecolabeling provides a marked link between green practices and profitability, incentivizing future ecolabeling.

A market premium may also be associated with a hedge against weather, climate, or regulatory risk (Kahn et al. 2014). For example, investments in Green Mark buildings were more profitable under stricter environmental regulations (Deng et al. 2012). Further, ecolabeled homes in California experienced increases in their price premiums after climate shocks (Kahn and Kok 2014). Less reliance on inputs with potentially volatile prices, such as water and energy, can reduce a firm's risk exposure (Jackson 2010; Juttner et al. 2003).

Marketing Value

The capitalizable value of green buildings is not solely realized in reduced operational costs. While operating expenses are lower in

LEED buildings, this only explains a portion of the price premium of LEED buildings. This suggests that a portion of a building's price premium comes from other sustainability aspects of the certification, rather than just reduced operating expenses. A premium exists for not just the energy efficiency of a building, but also its overall sustainability (Eichholtz et al. 2013; Li et al. 2021; Reichardt 2014). This premium can be an attractive lure to builders considering greener designs.

Green building ecolabels also aim to minimize negative externalities in the lifecycle of buildings. Evidence that certified buildings command a price premium beyond reduced operating costs suggests that firms may be able to capitalize on this reduction in lifecycle costs by certifying. This is possible because certification, as a token of corporate social responsibility, signals to potential tenants that the building management and its output is of higher quality. These social values are difficult to observe in the absence of some form of product label or certification but, once visible, may confer higher value to investors, consumers, employees, or other stakeholders (Saha and Darnton 2005; Sen and Bhattacharyra 2001; Turban and Greening 1997; Wood 1991). The design of green building programs directs builders and building owners to address the numerous potential externalities of a building's lifecycle through the point categories. When design teams select how they certify, they have flexibility in which of these externalities they address. Because these externalities may impact the environment on a highly local (indoor air quality), regional (construction run-off management), or global (atmospheric emissions) scale, the choice of strategy impacts who benefits from environmental improvements. However, as discussed in the next section, some green building policies specify tactics that must be used in order to comply with mandates or receive incentives, shaping or limiting this flexibility.

In summary, green buildings provide a set of advantages to their occupants and owners. The additional costs and benefits of building green are both varied and uncertain. But green buildings tout numerous performance advantages from more efficient and more sustainable operations. Operating a green building is typically more efficient in the areas of energy, water, and employee productivity, and thus produces higher quality outputs and improves tenant and worker recruiting and retention. Green buildings can also reduce reliance on inputs with volatile prices and reduce exposure to climatic risks. The structural asset value in resale and rental markets can be enhanced by these savings accrued from operational efficiency and improved productivity. Green marketing opportunities and appeals to other environmentally minded stakeholders may enhance this economic value. If the green building improves a firm's reputation and yields greater demand for their products, then that firm may cash in on its building's green cachet. Not always, but sometimes there are compelling reasons that builders will "go green."

Market Failures

With many possible motivations for owners to build green, the presence of key market failures leads us to suspect that the market will systematically underproduce green buildings. The Green Building Movement can thus be understood through economic lenses as a way to better align the built environment's social costs with its private costs (Allcott and Sunstein 2015; Kotchen 2006) by providing private benefits to participants (Fuerst and McAllister 2011a; Prakash and Potoski 2006). The two primary market failures addressed through this alignment and signaling mechanism are information asymmetries and externalities. These dual problems combine in the green building context to produce a built environment that is generally worse than it could be in terms of both economic and environmental performance. Competitive markets simply will not produce enough green buildings without addressing these problems. Remedying just one of the problems will not be enough if the other problem persists. Even in a world where greener, low-impact buildings could be easily identified and understood by stakeholders and buyers, builders would still not internalize all the environmental impacts of the built environment. And vice versa. Internalizing the environmental impacts without enabling high-performance buildings to recoup the costs of their investments would leave us with market outcomes that under-delivered on green buildings. Thus, we need to appreciate these dual market failures in order to see how the Green Building Movement redirects market forces for greener ends.

Information Problems

Innovative green buildings commonly pose hidden-information problems, where the builder has more information about the construction

A Closer Look: Signals and a Market for Lemons

Before we wade into some details on market failures for green buildings, let us walk through the classic "origin story" behind how certifications and signals arise.

The difficulty in observing the efficiency of a building – or many of its other attributes – points to some key defining characteristics of goods like buildings. First, much of a building and its services can be described as *experience goods*. These sorts of goods are those that buyers can only really appreciate their quality by actually experiencing the good itself. Movies and books can fall into the category of experience goods, just as meals at a restaurant or even new cars. There is a reason why we tend to shop for homes via in-person visitations, and even those visits only imperfectly remove the shroud of mystery around a home's qualities. Of course, there are other aspects of buildings that go even beyond the realm of experience and become a matter of faith. These *credence goods* have attributes that cannot be known merely by experiencing them, but rather require owners or users to simply take it as a matter of faith that the attribute is as claimed. No amount of experience can validate the claim of a credence good. Examples of these kinds of goods might include fair-trade coffee, sustainably harvested timber, or even made-in-the-USA labels. Simply buying and using a credence good or service offers little confirmation of those attributes' veracity.

Experience goods and credence goods can be difficult goods to sell in a market at a price that reflects their full value, because buyers may be particularly wary of the sellers' claims. When the claim cannot be verified until after purchase, the seller may be tempted to exaggerate claims of quality, especially if they do not go so far as to make a technically fraudulent claim. Even in the best case, the cost and risk of contesting these claims after purchase typically falls on the buyer. Thus, they would need to discount the amount they would be willing to pay to compensate for the expected risk of disappointment or contesting the sale. For experience and credence goods then, third-party verification or other certification of these attributes holds great appeal and potential to facilitate these transactions. When a trusted entity is able to verify the claims of the seller, buyers obviously will have more confidence and trust in the signal in the first place. This facilitates the market as buyers more eagerly take the chance and buy the product. Sellers are then more willing to make costly investments in improving quality or producing that hard-to-observe attribute, knowing that they will be able to recoup that expense through higher market prices.

(cont.)

This dynamic is famously explained in the "market for lemons" story. The lemons in the classic textbook example refer to used cars that might have difficult-to-observe flaws, especially for a typical car buyer. In a marketplace where everything about a product's qualities is difficult to observe for buyers, *and* the sellers know about these qualities, we have a situation known as *hidden information*. Hidden information markets operate inefficiently in the sense that the low-quality products crowd out the high-quality ones, leaving an incomplete market where, paradoxically, despite the willingness of potential suppliers, demand is not fulfilled. This inefficiency arises because the buyer, knowing that at least some flawed or lower-quality products are on the market, would be foolish to assume all goods are just as high-quality as advertised. Thus, rational buyers who confront the hidden information will discount these mystery goods. We would be reluctant to pay the full value of a perfect used car when there is a strong likelihood that the car in front of us is less than perfect, or "a lemon."

But the lemons story does not stop there. Once a buyer starts to discount the price that they are willing to pay for the potential lemon, the sellers adjust their behavior as well. Sellers, in turn, would be reluctant to bring their "plum" (i.e., high quality) cars to market, if they know they will command only a discounted price. Once the plums stop coming to the marketplace, the likelihood that a remaining used car is a lemon goes up. This leads buyers to revise their estimates and thus further reduce their willingness to pay. This, in turn, drives away more sellers of higher quality cars. We can iterate this example back-and-forth until we are left with an equilibrium where only the lemons ever make it to the market. The buyers expect lemons, pay what a lemon is worth, and get lemons. In that regard, the buyers and sellers are content. This looks like a story of a well-functioning market for beat-up, used cars or "lemons." *To be clear: this market in our context is characterized by only low-quality, "brown" buildings – sold for cheap but with low sustainability and higher long-term operational costs.*

The inefficiency in this market lies in what is missing. If the plums represent environmentally friendly products – like an energy-efficient building – the absence of plums or high-quality products represents a major loss. The market equilibrium where people (rightly) assume all goods are low quality and are only willing to pay a low price is a real barrier to greening industries. The presence or possibility of buying a lemon masquerading as a plum has effectively crowded out the genuine

(cont.)

plums from the marketplace. Because the premium-quality vendors cannot receive a premium for their product, they have little incentive to supply to the market. And, in our context of green buildings, this would be a case of building designers or owners either choosing not to make the initial investment in quality or being stuck unable to recoup their costs for a premium green building.

The absence of (plum) green buildings poses a major threat to the development of a green building industry and the general greening of the built environment. In some ways, it is a harder environmental problem than a traditional "pollution" problem because the problem is the absence of something (greener products) rather than visible pollution or hazards. As in the classic treatment of this hidden-information problem and a market for lemons, there is a significant value to both buyers and sellers of plums if something could provide a credible signal of the plums' quality. The trick is providing a credible signal that enables a market for plums to function even in the presence of lemons.

Consider a simple situation with two kinds of good: green and brown. Imagine the green good is an energy-efficient building with, say, superior insulation – a feature difficult or impossible for buyers to observe prior to purchase. Green goods cost $10 to produce and are worth $15 to buyers, while brown goods cost $5 to produce and are worth $6 to buyers. Sellers know the kind of goods they have made, but the buyers cannot tell them apart. The "lemons" equilibrium has only brown goods being sold for some price between $5 and $6 each; no green goods get made or sold. If a seller could get their green good certified for an additional cost of $0 to $4.99, and the buyer trusted the certification, then green sales could also occur. That $5 gap between production cost and value to buyers represents both the lost gains to society *and* the upper limit for the cost of the certification system. If the certification costs too much, then it is not worth the investment and the inefficiency remains. Generally, lowering the cost of certification will make more green markets possible. Thus, while a cheaper certification seems desirable from one vantage, cost is a necessary element to a credible signal. If brown sellers can also buy the same certification (and sell '"fake" green goods), the certification solution might break down. Certifying green must always cost more for brown sellers than green sellers (Mason 2012). As long as it is so onerous to certify a brown good that it costs the brown seller a lot, say $10 or more in this example, then buyers can credibly believe the certificate's signal of quality and pay up to $15 for the green good.

(cont.)

In this context, what we are looking for is a signal of quality that is more costly for the low quality (lemon) to obtain than it is for the plum to obtain. In our context of green buildings, that would mean the energy-*in*efficient building would find it extremely difficult or costly to obtain an energy-efficiency premium signal, while the energy-efficient building would find it much easier. In other words, the signal needs to work in (a) accurately reflecting the quality but also (b) implying that the low-quality products cannot simply fake or steal such a signal for themselves. These signals can be provided in a number of fashions, ranging from certification or licensing by third parties to sellers providing warranties to strong reputational mechanisms. Once the signal of high-quality is provided, then the buyer can reliably pay the premium price for the premium quality, and those desiring lemons can still find those in the uncertified market.

Thus, signals of a difficult-to-observe green quality in a building can be of enormous value. This value need not be just that those who can afford the high-end of the marketplace are made happier. Sure, that happens if you can solve the information problem here. But the other nice value is that the quality of buildings increases in a way that improves environmental impacts so others can benefit as well. It is not just a matter of having high-end buildings going to high-end consumers, like people buying diamonds of a certified quality. Instead, it is the case where these greener buildings are replacing browner buildings and bringing greater profits, lower operational costs, improved wellbeing, and reduced environmental footprints along with them.

process than the building owner, and the building owner or occupant has more information about its design and performance features than a potential buyer or tenant. It is difficult to assess building qualities prior to purchase or lease, which makes buildings "experience goods" (Nelson 1970). These qualities include efficiency and indoor environmental health. In some respects, however, a building's "greenness" is a "credence good" – that is, the building has qualities difficult to observe even after experiencing it, so that a third party is needed to verify the quality (Vining and Weimer 1988). Green building certification verifies difficult-to-observe building performance improvements, such as the building envelope, indoor air quality, or the environmental impact of the construction process. Because the building user cannot experience many of these traits such as construction waste diversion and sustainable material sourcing, green buildings can be thought of as credence goods (Fuerst et al. 2014; Giraudet 2020).

This difficulty in reliably detecting building quality applies to numerous stakeholders, including building buyers, tenants, employees, customers, and investors (Chegut et al. 2014; Eichholtz et al. 2012; Kahn and Kok 2014; Singh et al. 2010). All these groups may value the green building signal. Buyers and tenants of buildings seem like the most obvious shoppers who care about otherwise difficult-to-observe building quality. But employees may care as well, as green building criteria favor working conditions (e.g., daylighting, low emissions materials, better ventilation) that tend to enhance the worker experience as well as productivity. Similarly, a green building certificate may signal to prospective employees something about the management/corporate values and responsibility of their potential employer. Customers may also pay a premium for products and services that come from the green building, perhaps because they perceive the output itself to be more valuable or because they have preferences for greener firms. Investors may act likewise, using the signal of green building to guide investments in otherwise difficult-to-detect building quality. In some cases, green building certification may simply provide a convenient way to reduce search costs for those shopping for greener buildings, thus bringing value from the certification even to owners who would have built green anyway.

In the absence of green building certification, conditions of insufficient information go unsolved, and a sort of market for lemons is created where low-quality (traditional) buildings crowding out the high-quality (green) buildings prevents new investments targeting green buildings (Akerlof 1970). This argument is a key motivator for policy-makers who want to encourage green certification. Green building labels send signals that generate a market where investors in green buildings can earn a premium. This may come in the form of higher rental or sale prices for the property, lower wages for employees, more available financial capital, higher prices for outputs, or others.

To induce this efficient market, the basic green building certification scheme must reliably mark green buildings as distinct from and more valuable than other buildings. Higher quality buildings are presumably more expensive. Certification schemes verify concrete building qualities (e.g., installation of certain types of technologies, use of renewable fuels, use of certain building materials), distinguishing high-quality buildings from low-quality buildings. To signal more intangible qualities (e.g., quality of management), the presumption is that it would be more costly for less able or lower-quality management to successfully certify a green building.

A closely related reason for certification involves "principal-agent" problems. Principal-agent problems are well-known in economics and political science, where one party (the principal) wants another (the agent) to do something but an inability to monitor behavior makes it hard to align incentives and can lead to one party acting contrary to the interests of the other. Agents might not build green enough if the principals cannot observe and reward greener investments. Would a developer or a landlord go through extra trouble to make greener investment decisions if the downstream buyer or tenant who they ultimately sell to, perhaps years later, cannot see and reward that behavior? And if future tenants will not go to the trouble of optimally operating greener buildings, then why would the principals or landlords invest in costly innovations in the first place? Because developers or building owners are not necessarily knowledgeable about green building, or because building owners may not be knowledgeable about the cost-effectiveness of specific building improvements, the green certification allows builders to build to a target with flexibility within each tier. This provides a signal of building quality to building owners or developers (Patel and Chugan 2013), mitigating some of the information problems of hard-to-observe quality investments. By requiring third-party certification, building developers and owners can improve the alignment of incentives between the developer and builder and reduce the barriers associated with monitoring the building construction process and building features (Steelman and Rivera 2006).

These principal-agent problems can undermine the production of green buildings through the nature of contracting and the problem of "split incentives" in greener buildings. When a building's owner is not the occupant, the owner may not have sufficient incentives to invest in greener, high-efficiency upgrades to the property. Landlords underinvest because making the most of the upgrades can require use and maintenance by the tenants, which the landlord cannot enforce. And of course tenants lack incentives (and often authority) to make permanent upgrades that they might not be around to enjoy the return on investment (ROI). For instance, a friend in New York City installed expensive, insulated curtains in his apartment and left the customized curtains behind when he moved out. His landlord then charged him $400 for their removal because the tenant was not allowed to leave curtains behind. This split-incentives problem compounds the usual hidden-information problem. We can see this reflected in market prices. It is not just that green-certified buildings command a premium in the sales prices, they command an even greater premium in rental markets.

Beyond green buildings' additional construction costs, there still may be several reasons that may explain variations in adoption behavior. First, organizations may fail to discover cost-effective investments in green technologies due to the transaction costs or search costs involved with seeking a new design or green technologies. These costs may be substantial for some organizations. Alternatively, due to limited attention, misaligned incentives, or other internal organizational factors, organizations may fail to invest in cost-effective design improvements. Searching for greener technology and learning new approaches have real costs. Volumes of research have been written on the "energy efficiency gap" – efficiency upgrades with a positive ROI that are nonetheless not adopted (Gerarden et al. 2017). This view suggests major barriers exist to prevent us from grabbing those benefits. Some of this results from strategic priorities in practice that diverge from financial investment logic (Cooremans 2011). Green building standards represent one way to push decision-makers to claim those benefits that they might otherwise overlook. Without a good signal of greener qualities to mitigate some of these information problems, then surely many builders would not make the costly investments that they cannot recoup. This addresses the question of "why certify green?" without addressing the question of "why go green?" in the first place. Addressing information problems has its limits for addressing the deeper challenges of sustainable building. Even in a world of perfect information, we still face the problem where reducing pollution might not be profitable when it is free to pollute and costly to go green.

Externalities

The built environment produces considerable pollution. The building lifecycle has a large number of often unpriced social costs related to building construction, operation, and deconstruction. Water and air quality can be affected by the construction process or construction waste (Ding 2008). Operating the building also generates unpriced externalities due to energy use and affects air and water quality as well. Site selection and site remediation have effects on patterns of urban development, which in turn impact congestion, air quality, and more.[2] There is even evidence that the presence of green-certified buildings enhances the value of surrounding properties, creating a gentrification effect (Chegut et al. 2014; Yeganeh et al. 2019). On the whole, greener buildings promise to reduce the negative spillovers from traditional construction.

These negative externalities imply an equilibrium where green buildings are under-supplied by the market – which would happen even in the absence of information asymmetries. While business may react strongly to a certification system that addresses their information issues, they are still unlikely to internalize their externalities. Other organizations like nonprofits and governments also construct and occupy buildings, and may have goals that include social benefits, unlike for-profit firms. Not surprisingly, nonprofits and governments account for a large share of the certified green buildings in the United States today. Such behavior might please regulators, green consumers, and various stakeholders (Coglianese and Nash 2001).

The classic market for lemons story offers some insights about the provision of positive externalities (or reduced negative externalities) by private actors. Indeed, the market for lemons story offers a green twist in the case of ecolabels and the green building industry. For green goods, the premium qualities are attributes that involve more sustainability and less environmental harm. This perspective is critical to understanding ecolabels in this context. The information being signaled is not simply about the performance or value of the building to the buyer in the same way as a worker would want to signal their productivity to a prospective employer or a used-car owner would want to signal the car's quality to a prospective buyer. Rather, in this ecolabel perspective, the information that is being signaled refers to the external impacts or public values at stake with the premium, greener building. The greener signal can work to allow stakeholders, including buyers, to know that the building owner, and operator, and tenants,

---

[2] www.epa.gov/greenbuilding/pubs/about.htm

are members of a "green club." This version of ecolabels relies heavily on *status* in understanding the value of the green signal, although the status is presumably earned because of higher quality and better performance. In this case, the emphasis is on the signal validating claims about external environmental impacts, rather than the attributes of the good that more directly benefit the owner or user. In our used-car example, the green club perspective emphasizes the role of the signal indicating that the used car belongs in the green car category: A group of cars that have smaller environmental impacts. By contrast, the conventional quality signal for the used car is more focused on convincing consumers that the car's performance is better and brings better value directly to the owner and operator (e.g., brakes or engine reliability). In the context of buildings, the green club perspective sees a role for ecolabel certifications as signaling that green buildings have smaller environmental footprints and produce positive externalities. Buildings in the green club distinguish their quality from other "plum" buildings with premium-quality thermal controls or daylighting that benefits owners and tenants alone. The superior quality of buildings in the green club is due to the public benefits it provides, such as using sustainably sourced materials or renewable energy sources.

Learning and "peer effects" represent another major source of market failures in the green building context. Innovating greener building approaches can benefit society more broadly, beyond the innovator who undertook the costly experimentation and learned greener techniques. We will tend to underinvest in the presence of these positive spillovers from learning (Gerarden et al. 2017). Many will "free ride" and let others take on the costs of experimentation, of learning-by-doing, and of research and development (R&D). The positive externalities of R&D suggest that learning spillover and peer effects can play a major role in shaping a green building revolution. Knowledge of innovative green-building technologies functions as a public good, with potential benefits to the world yet important private costs to searching for and learning it. More adoption of green buildings entails diffusion of that knowledge. Accelerating adoption and learning can also help reverse the behavioral tendencies to underinvest in greener technologies from imperfect information (Allcott and Sunstein 2015). Arguably, this information-as-a-public-good problem constitutes the biggest barrier to adopting energy efficiency improvements (Giraudet 2020). See Chapter 6 for a more thorough discussion of the positive spillovers from demonstration projects. More learning spill-overs and peer effects then catalyze additional adoption in a virtuous cycle that mitigates the free-riding tendency that left us under-developing greener building technologies. Chapter 8 features this race-to-the-top dynamic.

Imperfect Competition

A final market failure issue in connection with green buildings is that of market power and scale issues. If the green building label helps a firm expand its market share, then green building certification schemes may actually invite monopoly power. The possibility that green building certification programs or green building mandates can, even inadvert-ently, impose a barrier to entry for other competitors should raise some concerns that green buildings may gain some of their advantage and premium from market power. For instance, research has shown how Walmart can use its scale advantages to optimize energy use more effectively than their smaller competitors (Kahn and Kok 2014). The adverse welfare consequences of (green) market barriers excluding competitors (e.g., in the form of overly expensive real estate, underpaid labor) may be at least partially offset by restricting the supply of polluting, traditional buildings that are likely already being overbuilt due to unpriced negative externalities. Moreover, the prospects of monopoly power can even induce firms to adopt stronger environmen-tal practices (with their attendant benefits for society) in a sort of "race to the top" in a competitive market (see Chapter 8 for more). Holding out the carrot of market power as a prize to those who innovate green might even incentivize greener products more than conventional incen-tives like carbon taxes (Aghion et al. 2020).

Policy Approaches to Green Buildings

The numerous market failures in the building sector have generated a call for programs to correct environmental externalities and incentivize better building practices. This has been answered not only in the form of several certification programs on the local and international scale, but also via policies promoting the adoption of specific green building tactics or certifications. These policies range from building codes to watershed management coalitions to certification programs, all at scales ranging from the local to the national. We focus here on whole-building certifications across these levels of governance. Though there has been a proliferation of changes to building codes and standards that also promote particular green technologies or practices (see Sun et al. (2015) for a review), we highlight policies that encourage flexible adoption of whole-building green upgrades to reduce lifecycle externalities of the built environment.

Table 2.1 provides a summary of these policies and their affected populations in the United States. It is intended to show the quantity of policies existing at each level of governance, in what form, and the population affected by each type of policy. It should be noted that the figures in the state, county, and city columns represent the number of policies at that level (i.e., there are 46 requirement policies at the state level, *not* 46 states with requirement policies). Many states have multiple policies in place, which raises questions of overlap and the efficacy of similar policies. The types given in the USGBC Public Policy Library[3] are requirements, which mandate some sort of action; non-binding policies, which call for action but without an enforcement mechanism; incentives, which provide rewards for certain behavior; encouragements, which symbolically promote green building; and enabling legislation, which clears red tape to allow for future green building policy action. Examples of each of these policy types are given for illustrative purposes. Table 2.1 indicates that there are a diverse variety of green building policies at the various levels of government. Requirements are the most common policy type, followed by incentive programs. Seventy percent and 50 percent of the US population are covered by these policy types, respectively, which shows how prolific green building policy has been in recent decades. Most of this legislation was passed between 2005 and 2015, with a significant slowdown in the last five years.

Federal Green Building Policies

Unlike local programs, federal green building policies have been scarce. Still, several acts and executive orders have implemented public procurement policies for high-performance buildings. Voluntary guidelines resembling LEED criteria for high-performance green buildings

---

[3] USGBC Public Policy Library, https://public-policies.usgbc.org/

Table 2.1. *Summary of US green building policies*

Policy type	Number of Policies	US Population Affected			
	State	County	City	Total	% of Total
Enabling legislation	7	4		60,943,089	19
Granting authority to make policy					
Authorizing program implementation					
Encourage	5	4	25	74,591,909	23
Publicly acknowledging green building benefits					
Raising awareness of LEED					
Incentive	27	27	146	160,720,399	49
Property tax abatement, exemption, credit, rebate, or refund					
Fee reduction or waiver					
Expedited permitting					
Density/height bonus					
Nonbinding	18	8	64	118,363,353	36
Mandate without enforcement					
Call for sustainable building program support					
Goal-setting					
Requirement	46	35	228	228,794,177	70
LEED or equivalent required					
LEED checklist required for permit					
LEED AP required on design team					

were published in a memorandum of understanding (MOU) under the Bush administration (Keller 2011). Later, President Bush signed Executive Order #13423, requiring all new federal building projects to adhere to the MOU. However, public procurement policy implementation across agencies is a mixed bag. Our analysis of existing policies reveals that public procurement policies typically hold LEED as a building standard, though policy strength varies. Important variation also exists among agencies and its potential impacts: LEED Silver is mandated for all new constructions in the Department of Agriculture, but the standard for the Department of Energy is LEED Gold. By contrast, the Departments of Defense and State recommend building to LEED standards without strictly mandating a certain certification tier.

Newly built federal buildings were required to reduce their energy use under the Energy Independence and Security Act of 2007. Under this law, federal agencies are recommended to adhere to either Green Globes or LEED standards. The American Recovery and Reinvestment Act of 2009 (ARRA) allocated $31 billion to green buildings and conservation. These costs have the potential to provide benefit beyond the public sector. Public procurement policies can spur on additional private-sector green building (Adekanye et al. 2020; Brusselaers et al. 2017; Lindström et al. 2020; Simcoe and Toffel 2014). This effect works at the local level for policies and has the potential for broader, national policy spillovers as well. If norms shift toward more green building practices, shrinking search and information costs and economies of scale in green materials production can make green building practices more affordable. (See Chapter 6 for more on the power of demonstration projects.)

State and Local Green Building Policies

A myriad of local policies have been adopted in states and cities to require or encourage whole-building sustainability measures. A collection of policies noted by the USGBC were matched against other lists of whole-building policies from the International Energy Agency and Database of State Incentives for Renewables & Efficiency to complete listings of existing state and local policies from available resources. These requirements, incentives, and symbolic gestures often direct builders to LEED or a similar certification program as a set of guidelines for compliance, though not all require certification.

Common green building policies include mandates of LEED certification or equivalent design and performance for a particular sector. Most often these requirements apply to government buildings, as is the case for 26 states, 29 counties, and 175 cities in the United States. While government procurement requirements are common at the state level, requirements for the commercial sector tend to be found at municipal or county levels. Only Connecticut requires major commercial developments to achieve at least LEED Silver through its State Building Code, though over 60 cities have similar requirements. Qualifying as a "major" can vary widely, such as the lower limit of 50,000 square feet in Boston, MA, or 25,000 square feet in San Jose, CA (Lewyn 2014). Requirements that target the residential sector often do so through affordable housing programs, as is the case in Minnesota, Washington, Maryland, and nearly 90 cities and counties. These policies do not always require certification but may simply require design teams to utilize green strategies sufficient for certification if the builders were to apply. To verify the noncertifiers' compliance, 18 municipalities such as San Francisco require a LEED Associated Professional (AP) (an individual licensed by the USGBC in the LEED certification process) as part of the design team to attest to the building's green quality.

Though about half of all states have some LEED requirement for at least some buildings (usually public buildings), incentive programs are also common among states. Eight states, including New York, offer limited grants to cover certification costs, while seven states (e.g., Nevada) offer some form of state tax relief for certifying firms. Kentucky is among a few that offer only symbolic gestures promoting certification (without financial, human, or information resources to incentivize green building). The municipal level exhibits much greater diversity in incentive structure. Over 70 cities have development density bonuses, such as exceptional height or floor-area ratio permissions, whereas over 90 cities have permitting incentives that expedite construction administration processes or reduce fees. Finally, 25 cities have approved modest financial incentives in the form of grants and tax relief. Though these cash incentives can be thought of as the most direct form of incentive, funding limitations greatly limit the effectiveness of these programs (Kingsley 2008).

These forms of whole-building policies, rather than technology-specific policies, play directly into the strategy of the Green Building

Movement. Mandates requiring green building for some building sectors, sizes, or districts promote spillovers or norm shifts for other buildings. Policy incentives for green building certification compound incentives for certification from market premiums on green real estate.

While green building policies tend to be mandates or incentives, within these categories there is significant heterogeneity in the strategies promoted by states and municipalities. Twenty-four states and 47 cities explicitly address energy efficiency or renewable energy in the language of their policies, reflecting the importance of energy to the built environment and Green Building Movement. By comparison, few specifically address water in their green building policies. Though most policies target public or commercial buildings, five towns target rapidly growing local industries including hotels and medical facilities.

Many incentive programs are tied to the building's characteristics. The most common means of dividing incentives by category is through the LEED certification level itself, a policy present in nearly 50 jurisdictions to encourage higher tier achievement in green building. Five states and 15 cities vary incentives with the size of the proposed building, providing more incentives for green activity in larger developments. By contrast, the cities of Portland, ME and Wilmington, OH structure their policy levels by the vintage of the building, targeting renovations of old and potentially less-efficient structures.

Many county and municipal governments have employed a variety of innovative policy designs and incentives including property tax reassessment moratoriums, green funds, parking incentives, electric bill discounts, green roof mandates, recertification requirements, and mandatory investment in any tactic with a positive return on investment. A few cities offer contractor training or technical assistance. Fort Worth, TX and Nashville, TN have generated their own "LEED-inspired" certification programs as part of a broader city greening goal.

The text of these policies points toward the motivations for green building. Goals are not limited to environmental externalities. Green building policies are often linked to other urban planning goals that address market failures in other parts of the built environment. Several towns and counties emphasize green building certification as a route to smart growth, community planning, and a general "public benefit." Others (such as several counties in the Southeast) pursue green building policies for job creation or economic stimulus opportunities. In other regions, policies have been created to mitigate problems related to affordable housing and the need to retrofit existing buildings. Three jurisdictions pair green education with publicity of certified buildings as a policy goal.

Finally, only a few jurisdictions have green building policies that add specific technology requirements to their whole-building mandates. For example, Chattanooga, TN, focuses on high-density planning for sustainable growth. These policies are especially interesting because the improvements addressed are normally incorporated through building codes, rather than voluntary programs, labels, and incentives.

Not all subnational policies pursue similar approaches or goals. At least two states have effectively banned LEED certification in public buildings. The governors of Georgia and Maine, in separate executive orders, have banned LEED certification for use in state-funded public buildings due to the program's failure to recognize multiple forms of sustainable wood products.[4] These orders explicitly seek to protect local timber interests and were later codified by state legislatures. North Carolina, Florida, Mississippi, and Alabama also followed suit. Notably, only nine municipalities have any form of incentive that encourages certification without mentioning LEED.

The breadth and variety of green building policy adoption in the United States did not happen overnight. The diffusion of these green building policies follows the well-established S-curve pattern where adoptions are initially slow and limited to a few early adopters, then undergo a period of rapid expansion when the policies "catch on," and finally taper off as most interested jurisdictions have already adopted them. In the case of green building policies, the biggest expansion occurred between 2006 and 2013, with states following a slightly less clear ramp-up and taper-off pattern. Figure 2.1 shows these S curves for the state, county, and city levels. The figures make clear that requirements and incentives are by far the most popular policy types. They are also more meaningful than symbolic gestures and encouragements without enforcement.

---

[4] USGBC now recognizes the Sustainable Forestry Initiative (SFI) as an alternative compliance path, though states have not rolled back their policies aimed at blocking LEED certification.

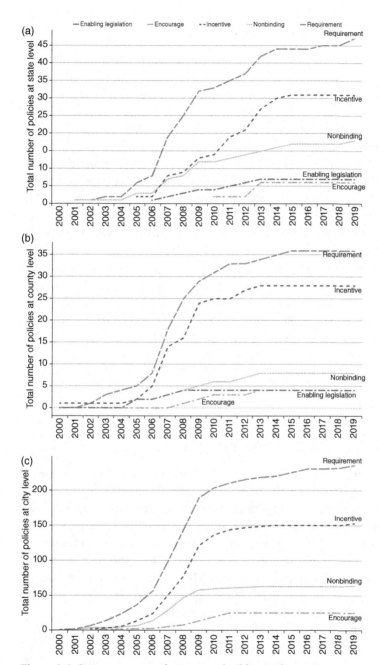

Figure 2.1 State, county, and city green building policies over time

International Green Building Efforts

The Green Building Movement has global reach. Organizations certifying green buildings across the globe have settled on similar sets of criteria that span multiple categories. Chapter 4 provides a more detailed account of the international green building landscape, but Table 2.2 summarizes some of the most well-known of these programs.

Though each program is unique, similarities exist across the certifiers. Many green building certification schemes are networked via the World Green Building Council (WGBC), including LEED, BREEAM, Green Star, CASBEE, and the Living Building Challenge. This international federation of green building practices promotion demonstrates similar building standards tailored to local markets. Although they are privately operated and independently financed through local green building councils or other certifiers, these programs often have sustainability goals or language used in their literature in common, and most have tiered certification schemes. In addition to the nongovernmental organization (NGO) certifiers connected via the GBC network, Taiwan, Singapore, and China operate public, government-run programs. Some certifications are awarded only in the label's country of origin, while other programs like LEED and BREEAM certify abroad extensively.

Diffusion of Green Building Practices

The Green Building Movement has been gaining considerable steam in the United States over the past few decades. In looking at just one of the popular green building standards in the United States – LEED – we can see its rapid rise since the turn of the century in Figure 2.2. We discussed this rapid escalation in popularity over the past 15 years in Chapter 1, and we revisit it in Chapter 8 to appreciate how this diffusion is both wider and deeper. More and more green buildings are being built (and existing buildings retrofitted) even as the green standards themselves continue to raise the bar.

While many forces combine to drive this wave of green building adoption, a critical feature of this diffusion is that the bulk of it is "voluntary." Decision-makers are increasingly choosing to build green. Though some mandates exist (see Table 2.1), and they can be

Table 2.2. *International green building labeling programs*

Labeling Program	Sponsor	Primary Country	Start Year	Number Certified
BEAM (Building Environmental Assessment Method)	BEAM Society Ltd.[a]	Hong Kong (100%)	1996	1,600
BREEAM (Building Research Establishment Environmental Assessment Methodology)	Building Research Establishment (BRE)[e]	UK (48%)	1990	22,733
CASBEE (Comprehensive Assessment System for Built Environment Efficiency)	Japan Sustainable Building Consortium[a]	Japan (100%)	2005	435
DGNB (German Sustainable Building Council)	German Sustainable Building Council[b]	Germany (89%)	2007	1,741
EDGE (Excellence in Design for Greater Efficiencies)	International Finance Corporation / World Bank[f]	Colombia (24%)	2014	307
EEWH (Ecology, Energy Saving, Waste Reduction, and Health)	Ministry of the Interior[a]	Taiwan (100%)	1999	2,155
Green Globes	Green Buildings Initiative[c]	US (89%)	2000	1,810
Green Mark	Building & Construction Authority[a]	Singapore (95%)	2005	2,166
Green Star Australias	Green Building Council of Australia	Australia (100%)	2002	2,811

Table 2.2. (*cont.*)

Labeling Program	Sponsor	Primary Country	Start Year	Number Certified
Green Star South Africa	Green Building Council of South Africa[c]	South Africa (98%)	2007	500
HQE (High Quality Environmental Standard)	Cerway[e]	France (86%)	2005	705
IGBC (Indian Green Building Council)	Confederation of Indian Industry	India	2001	7,128
LEED (Leadership in Energy and Environmental Design)	USGBC[c]	US (83%)	1998	74,840
Living Building Challenge	International Living Future Institute[c]	US (88%)	2006	107
Pearl Rating System	Abu Dhabi Urban Planning Council[a]	UAE (100%)	2010	260
Three Star	Ministry of Housing & Urban Affairs[a]	China (100%)	2006	1,358
WELL	International WELL Building Institute[d]	US (38%)	2014	5,735

Note: Number certified circa 2020. Percentages indicate the percentage of the label's certified buildings that are located within the primary country.

Sponsors are [a] government, [b] industry group, [c] nonprofit, [d] public benefit corporation, [e] privately held corporation, and [f] international organization.

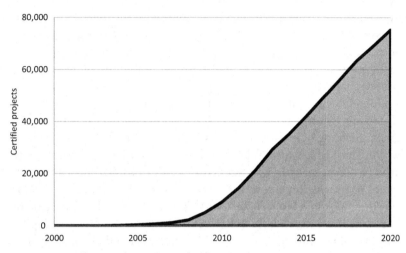

Figure 2.2 Diffusion of LEED certified buildings over time

pivotal, the vast majority of green buildings arise as a result of decision-makers deliberately opting to join the Green Building Movement in the face of conventional alternatives. The booming market in materials for green building construction, expected to grow to over half a trillion dollars by 2027 with a robust 11% annual growth rate, offers carbon emission reductions and better durability.[5] When a green building appears in an area, spillover and peer effects influence neighbors to build green as well, causing clusters of green buildings to appear in urban areas and states with stronger environmental tastes (Cidell 2009; Kahn and Vaughn 2009).

Empirical research on subnational green building policies has largely focused on state level policies. Spillover effects from local public procurement mandates have been a key promoter of private green building practices, shifting norms in the building industry. While this result is confirmed by other works, others note that this spillover may be limited to mandates and administrative incentives (Choi 2010; Fuerst et al. 2014), such as expedited permitting. Still, other factors may promote green building certification. Higher education levels, affluence or willingness to pay for luxury goods, and market growth all positively impact LEED adoption rates. Stakeholder activity may also predict green building market penetration. Stronger green sentiment

[5] www.reportsanddata.com/report-detail/green-building-materials-market

in a region predicts green-building adoption even more than carbon emissions (Braun et al. 2017). Moreover, strong interest groups, state energy agencies, gubernatorial agency power, and construction sector lobby groups also predict more widespread adoption, alongside high commercial-sector energy consumption (May and Koski 2007).

Despite the prevalence of conditions that support LEED adoption, it is difficult to simply characterize the extent of market penetration of green building due to differences in definitions and heterogeneity within the LEED label. When considering total building stock, only around 1 percent is LEED certified (Fuerst et al. 2014). This portion jumps to nearly 20 percent in offices, measured by floor area in major US cities (Kok and Holtermans 2014). There has been dramatic growth in certified real estate since 2005, with certified real estate growing by an order of magnitude. In fact, some estimates claim that almost half of new, commercial constructions are built "green" in regards to energy or resource efficiency.[6] The spillover effect observed from green government buildings to other sectors could be a sign that certification can help shift norms in the building industry. Green building practices can increasingly be adopted in noncertified buildings as builders follow the lead of initial certifiers (Matisoff 2015).

Around the world, green building adoption has already achieved a sizable footprint. Led by adoptions in the United States, the Green Building Movement is clearly underway and spanning the globe. Figure 1.1 shows the spread of certified green buildings across the six continents. Though BREEAM remains the oldest ecolabel for green buildings, it never took off the way that LEED has – which is arguably driving the global market transformation. Yet different regional contexts recommend tailored ecolabels for different regions and countries. Thus, we see different national systems (often with limited coordination among them) and, obviously, different take-up rates around the world. Progress around the world has been rapid in the past decade or so. Over time, new countries and markets have opened to green buildings as green standards get translated to local language and codes. Building codes in some markets continue to advance, making green buildings that much easier to justify. Further, demand for new construction increasingly prioritizes risk management and, in some case,

---

[6] Green Market Size. 2012. McGraw Hill Construction (McGraw Hill Financial).

marketing sustainability, helping to drive adoption of green buildings around the world.

Conclusion

This chapter introduces and reviews the key elements of what makes a green building, what factors play into the decision to "go green," the market failures that the Green Building Movement seeks to overcome, and the array of relevant public policies and certification systems around the world. At their heart, green buildings focus on holistic designs to reduce negative environmental impacts and improve efficiencies. While greener buildings can yield improvements in cost, performance, or other factors, those benefits alone may not be sufficient to overcome higher costs and uncertainties. Market failures such as environmental spillovers (externalities) and information problems pose substantial barriers to the Green Building Movement. Though policies abound at the local and regional levels, green building certifications are the most visible (and perhaps most potent) approach to overcoming these market failures. Ecolabels for green buildings can be found around the world, and a robust growth in the number of green buildings has followed in recent years. These ecolabels position themselves in a pivotal role in promoting green building because they directly address the informational problems that plague the green building market *and* they help builders capture the benefits from greener designs. Thus, builders often see certifying green as a key instrument in realizing the gains from "going green."

References

Adekanye, Oluwatobi G., Alex Davis, and Inês L. Azevedo. 2020. "Federal Policy, Local Policy, and Green Building Certifications in the US." *Energy and Buildings* 209: 109700.

Aghion, Philippe, Roland Bénabou, Ralf Martin, and Alexandra Roulet. 2020. "Environmental Preferences and Technological Choices: Is Market Competition Clean or Dirty?" *National Bureau of Economic Research*, Working Paper Series no. 26921.

Akerlof, George A. 1970. "The Market for 'Lemons': Quality Uncertainty and the Market Mechanism." *The Quarterly Journal of Economics* 84, no. 3: 488–500.

Allcott, Hunt and Michael Greenstone. 2012. "Is There an Energy Efficiency Gap?" *Journal of Economic Perspectives* 26, no. 1: 3–28.

Allcott, Hunt and Cass R. Sunstein. 2015. "Regulating Internalities." *Journal of Policy Analysis and Management* 34, no. 3: 698–705.

Asensio, Omar Isaac and Magali A. Delmas. 2017. "The Effectiveness of US Energy Efficiency Building Labels." *Nature Energy* 2: 17033.

Braun, Thomas, Marcelo Cajias, and Ralf Hohenstatt. 2017. "Societal Influence on Diffusion of Green Buildings: A Count Regression Approach." *Journal of Real Estate Research* 39, no. 1: 1–37.

Brusselaers, Jan, Guido Van Huylenbroeck, and Jeroen Buysse. 2017. "Green Public Procurement of Certified Wood: Spatial Leverage Effect and Welfare Implications." *Ecological Economics* 135: 91–102.

Chegut, Andrea, Piet Eichholtz, and Nils Kok. 2014. "Supply, Demand and the Value of Green Buildings." *Urban Studies* 51, no. 1: 22–43.

2019. "The Price of Innovation: An Analysis of the Marginal Cost of Green Buildings." *Journal of Environmental Economics and Management* 98: 102248.

Choi, Eugene. 2010. "Green on Buildings: The Effects of Municipal Policy on Green Building Designations in America's Central Cities." *Journal of Sustainable Real Estate* 2, no. 1: 1–21.

Cidell, Julie. 2009. "Building Green: The Emerging Geography of LEED-Certified Buildings and Professionals." *Professional Geographer* 61, no. 2: 200–215.

Coglianese, Cary and Jennifer Nash. 2001. *Regulating from the Inside: Can Environmental Management Systems Achieve Policy Goals?* Washington, DC: Resources for the Future.

Cooremans, Catherine. 2011. "Make It Strategic! Financial Investment Logic Is Not Enough." *Energy Efficiency* 4, no. 4: 473–492.

Deng, Yongheng, Zhiliang Li, and John M. Quigley. 2012. "Economic Returns to Energy-Efficient Investments in the Housing Market: Evidence from Singapore." *Regional Science and Urban Economics* 42, no. 3: 506–515.

Deng, YongHeng and Jing Wu. 2013. "Economic Returns to Residential Green Building Investment: The Developers' Perspective." *Regional Science and Urban Economics* 47, no. 1: 35–44.

Ding, Grace K. C. 2008. "Sustainable Construction – The Role of Environmental Assessment Tools." *Journal of Environmental Management* 86, no. 3: 451–464.

Eichholtz, Piet, Nils Kok, and Erkan Yonder. 2012. "Portfolio Greenness and the Financial Performance of REITs." *Journal of International Money and Finance* 31, no. 7: 1911–1929.

Eichholtz, Piet, Nils Kok, and John M. Quigley. 2013. "The Economics of Green Building." *Review of Economics and Statistics 95*, no. 1: 50–63.

Fuerst, Franz, Constantine Kontokosta, and Patrick McAllister. 2014. "Determinants of Green Building Adoption." *Environment and Planning B: Planning and Design* 41, no. 3: 551–570.

Fuerst, Franz and Patrick McAllister. 2011a. "Eco-Labeling in Commercial Office Markets: Do LEED and Energy Star Offices Obtain Multiple Premiums?" *Ecological Economics* 70, no. 6: 1220–1230.

2011b. "Green Noise or Green Value? Measuring the Effects of Environmental Certification on Office Values." *Real Estate Economics* 39, no. 1: 45–69.

Gerarden, Todd D., Richard G. Newell, and Robert N. Stavins. 2017. "Assessing the Energy-Efficiency Gap." *Journal of Economic Literature 55*, no. 4: 1486–1525.

Giraudet, Louis-Gaëtan. 2020. Energy Efficiency as a Credence Good: A Review of Informational Barriers to Energy Savings in the Building Sector. *Energy Economics* 87: 104698.

Jackson, Jerry. 2010. "Promoting Energy Efficiency Investments with Risk Management Decision Tools." *Energy Policy* 38, no. 8: 3865–3873.

Juttner, Uta, Helen Peck, and Martin Christopher. 2003. "Supply Chain Risk Management: Outlining an Agenda for Future Research." *International Journal of Logistics: Research & Applications* 6: 197–210.

Kahn, Matthew E. and Nils Kok. 2014. "Big-Box Retailers and Urban Carbon Emissions: The Case of Wal-Mart." *National Bureau of Economic Research*, Working Paper Series no. 19912.

Kahn, Matthew E., Nils Kok, and John Quigley. 2014. "Carbon Emissions from the Commercial Building Sector: The Role of Climate, Quality, and Incentives." *Journal of Public Economics* 113, issue C: 1–12.

Kahn, Matthew E. and Ryan K. Vaughn. 2009. "Green Market Geography: The Spatial Clustering of Hybrid Vehicles and LEED Registered Buildings." *B.E. Journal of Economics Analysis & Policy: Contributions to Economic Analysis & Policy* 9, no. 2: 1–22.

Kats, Gregory H. 2003. *Green Building Costs and Financial Benefits.* Cambridge, MA: Massachusetts Technology Collaborative.

Keller, Kaleb. 2011. "LEEDing in the Wrong Direction: Addressing Concerns with Today's Green Building Policy." *Southern California Law Review* 85: 1377–1412.

Kingsley, Benjamin S. 2008. "Making It Easy to be Green: Using Impact Fees to Encourage Green Building." *New York University Law Review* 83: 532–567.

Kok, Nils and Rogier Holtermans. 2014. National Green Building Adoption Index 2014. Maastricht University and CBRE.

Kotchen, Matthew J. 2006. "Green Markets and Private Provision of Public Goods." *Journal of Political Economy* 114, no. 4: 816–834.

Lewyn, Michael. 2014. "How Environmental Review Can Generate Car-Induced Pollution: A Case Study." *Sustainable Development Law & Policy* 14, no. 1: 16–22, 64–66.

Li, Weilin, Guanyu Fang, & Yang, Liu. 2021. "The Effect of LEED Certification on Office Rental Values in China." *Sustainable Energy Technologies and Assessments* 45: 101182.

Lindström, Hanna, Sofia Lundberg, and Per-Olov Marklund. 2020. "How Green Public Procurement Can Drive Conversion of Farmland: An Empirical Analysis of an Organic Food Policy." *Ecological Economics* 172: 106622.

Mason, Charles F. 2012. "The Economics of Eco-Labeling: Theory and Empirical Implications." *International Review of Environmental and Resource Economics* 6, no. 4: 341–372.

Matisoff, Daniel. 2015. "Sources of Specification Errors in the Assessment of Voluntary Environmental Programs: Understanding Program Impacts." *Policy Sciences* 48: 109–126.

May, Peter J. and Chris Koski. 2007. "State Environmental Policies: Analyzing Green Building Mandates." *Review of Policy Research* 24, no. 1: 49–65.

Nelson, Phillip. 1970. "Information and Consumer Behavior." *Journal of Political Economy* 78, no. 2: 311–329.

Patel, Chitral and Pawan Kumar Chugan. 2013. *Consumer Behavior and Emerging Practices in Marketing.* Mumbai, India: Himalaya Publishing House.

Prakash, Aseem and Matthew Potoski. *The Voluntary Environmentalists: Green Clubs, Iso 14001, and Voluntary Environmental Regulations.* Cambridge: Cambridge University Press, 2006.

Reichardt, Alexander. 2014. "Operating Expenses and the Rent Premium of Energy Star and LEED Certified Buildings in the Central and Eastern U.S." *The Journal of Real Estate Finance and Economics* 49, no. 3: 413–433.

Rivera, J. 2002. "Assessing a Voluntary Environmental Initiative in the Developing World: The Costa Rican Certification for Sustainable Tourism." *Policy Sciences* 35: 333–360.

Saha, Monica and Geoffrey Darnton. 2005. "Green Companies or Green Con-panies: Are Companies Really Green, or Are They Pretending to Be?" *Business and Society Review* 110, no. 2: 117–157.

Sen, Sankar and C. B. Bhattacharya. 2001. "Does Doing Good Always Lead to Doing Better? Consumer Reactions to Corporate Social Responsibility." *Journal of Marketing Research* 38, no. 1: 225–243.

Simcoe, Timothy and Michael W. Toffel. 2014. "Government Green Procurement Spillovers: Evidence from Municipal Building Policies in California." *Journal of Environmental Economics and Management* 68, no. 3: 411–434.

Singh, Amanjeet, Matt Syal, Sue C. Grady, and Sinem Korkmaz. 2010. "Effects of Green Buildings on Employee Health and Productivity." *American Journal of Public Health* 100, no. 9: 1665–1668.

Steelman, Toddi A. and Jorge Rivera. 2006. "Voluntary Environmental Programs in the United States: Whose Interests Are Served?" *Organization & Environment* 19, no. 4: 505–526.

Sun, Xiaojing, Marilyn A. Brown, Matt Cox, and Roderick Jackson. 2015. "Mandating Better Buildings: A Global Review of Building Codes and Prospects for Improvement in the United States." *Wiley Interdisciplinary Reviews: Energy and Environment* 5, no. 2: 188–215.

Turban, Daniel and Daniel Greening. 1997. "Corporate Social Performance and Organizational Attractiveness to Prospective Employees." *Academy of Management Journal* 40, no. 3: 658–672.

Verma, Saurahb, Satya N. Mandal, Spencer Robinson, and Deepak Bajaj. 2020. "Diffusion Patterns and Drivers of Higher-Rated Green Buildings in the Mumbai Region, India: A Developing Economy Perspective." *Intelligent Buildings International* 51: 1–21.

Vining, Aidan R. and David L. Weimer. 1988. "Information Asymmetry Favoring Sellers: A Policy Framework." *Policy Sciences* 31, no. 4: 281–303.

Wood, Donna J. 1991. "Corporate Social Performance Revisited." *The Academy of Management Review* 16, no. 4: 691–718.

Yeganeh, Armin Jeddi, Andrew Patton McCoy, and Steve Hankey. 2019. "Green Affordable Housing: Cost-Benefit Analysis for Zoning Incentives." *Sustainability* 11, no. 22: 6269.

3 | *Choose Your Own Adventure!*
The Landscape of Ecolabel Design

Introduction

Ecolabels and sustainability certifications typically involve reducing fundamentally multidimensional notions of sustainability to a single-dimensional signal. This leaves the signal noisy. It also poses a challenge for consumers in interpreting how ecolabels differ from one certification scheme to the next. This chapter explores how green certification design for various products affects the types of goods that are incentivized by certifications and ecolabels. We complement the green buildings example of this book by drawing parallels to another case – ecolabels for agricultural commodities. We offer a theoretical framework to understand the variation of ecolabel design. Drawing upon green clubs and signaling theories, we suggest that ecolabels vary based on the stringency of the certification program, measured by the number and criticality of required standards, and the extent to which the requirements of these certifications incentivize the provision of public goods. Looking across over 50 different agricultural ecolabels shows the important variation in factors like types of requirements, stringency, and institutional processes that govern the labels. Perhaps unsurprisingly, broader stakeholder engagement is associated with more emphasis on public benefits, while more surprisingly industry sponsorship does not tend to be found among the more lax labels with less public benefit. Of course, certification of quality for products with great private benefits can be important and valuable. Our toaster's Underwriters Laboratories (UL) certification gives us some confidence that it will not burst into flames, and we might find genuine comfort in our medical practitioners or taxi drivers being licensed. Whether the ecolabel certifies public benefits, private benefits, or mix of both, there is clearly a lot of variation in the design of these ecolabels.

A Landscape of Ecolabels

Multidimensionality of Sustainability

Ecolabels have become increasingly popular in recent decades among both consumers and producers as an informational policy approach governing the production of goods and services. Ecolabels seek to certify the sustainability of a good or service. Producers are motivated to certify their goods for many reasons, including improved product quality, price premiums, enhanced efficiency of operations, and demands from corporate and individual buyers. Consumers have demonstrated a growing concern for the sustainability characteristics of their purchases including how the goods they purchase are produced. These production processes are difficult to observe, and ecolabels serve as a governance tool that can be used by a producer to signal information to stakeholders about sustainability characteristics of products. Because sustainability is a multidimensional concept, substantial variation can exist across labels, with different labels incentivizing the supply of different environmental, economic, and social characteristics of products. We term these "multidimensional ecolabels." With a proliferation of hundreds of multidimensional ecolabels, the rigor of the labels and the sustainability characteristics certified by a label are often unclear. This chapter develops a framework to understand variations in multidimensional ecolabel design, as reflected by their design, context, and the processes used in their generation.

At their heart, ecolabels are about signals. Signaling is a mechanism to help a consumer separate high- and low-quality services and products. Ecolabels are a signal designed to communicate sustainability characteristics of a product or service with stakeholders, typically to reduce information asymmetry between a producer and a consumer. Producers adhere to process, product, or performance standards in order to gain access to a proprietary product label. Increasingly, firms, governments, and nonprofits have sought to send "green" signals, certifying environmental behavior or performance. The proliferation of ecolabels in recent decades has come to encompass a multitude of products and processes in global and local settings around the world. The International Trade Centre (ITC) tracks sustainability standards and certifications around the world, currently logging over

270 standards in its detailed database.[1] These standards certify everything from energy-efficient production to biodegradability, sometimes
with a focus on a single characteristic and sometimes focusing on
multiple dimensions of product (including production process) quality.

In principle, ecolabels can be used to signal the nature or quality of a
very wide variety of attributes. High-quality products might consume
less water or energy, improve indoor air quality, reduce or eliminate
the use of toxic emissions, or do other things to improve its user's
experience. Many green-certified goods bundle together attributes that
directly benefit the user with attributes that benefit the public or society
at large. These public benefits might involve reduced pollution or
externalities associated with the production or consumption of the
product or service. For example, ISO (International Standards
Organization) certification relates to the establishment of environmental management systems in a facility, as opposed to the traits of the
products produced. Similarly, Fairtrade ensures fair trading practices
between producers and businesses. Organic labeling certifies a production process without pesticides or fertilizers, while Rainforest Alliance
labeling certifies the forestry practices surrounding coffee plantations
and production. Each of these labels certifies hard-to-monitor qualities
that can only be observed long before consumption. Certification
might also signal more abstract qualities, such as quality of management, or a firm's environmental commitment. For these qualities,
credible signals from ecolabels rely on less able or less committed
owners finding it more costly to successfully implement a certifiable
product or practice (Mason 2013). Sometimes ecolabels compete with
one another, emphasizing different attributes or aspects of the product.
For example, four separate ecolabels in the coffee industry are distinguished by particular practices, many of which prioritize the economic
sustainability of the farmer rather than just the environmental impact
(Giovannucci and Ponte 2005).

Certifying Sustainability As a Design Problem

Across all of these dimensions, an organization designing an ecolabel
must make a number of design choices. Given the complexity and
multidimensionality of sustainability, a core question for ecolabel

[1] www.standardsmap.org/standards

A Closer Look: GreenCo Certification in India

India has emerged as one of the fastest growing economies in the world since the initiation of market reforms in the early 1990s. The strong economic growth, however, is also accompanied by deteriorating environmental quality – urban air pollution, poor water quality, exploding solid waste, deforestation, and so on. While India has had a legal framework to regulate pollution since the early 1970s, the enforcement has been hampered by weak institutions, leading to ineffective policy implementation. It is in this context that the demand for nonstate-driven, market-based programs has arisen. One such initiative, launched in 2011, is the GreenCo certification, designed and implemented by the Green Business Centre (GBC), an arm of one of India's largest industrial advocacy bodies, the Confederation of Indian Industry (CII).[2]

The CII-GBC drew its inspiration for GreenCo from its own successful green ratings program for buildings, called the Indian Green Building Council (IGBC) rating system, which was launched in 2001 and claims to have registered a green building footprint of 8 billion square feet from 7,128 building projects, making India one of the top countries in green building footprint. IGBC rating systems address various elements of the built environment including commercial, residential, affordable housing, industrial, healthcare, cities, villages, transit systems, data centers, and many more. GreenCo rates firms on their environmental performance, measured by 10 parameters,[3] designed to capture both the traditional resource efficiency indicators as well as the broader system-level environmental concerns, such as supply-chain sustainability and product stewardship. The performance on various parameters have different weights, with energy efficiency receiving the highest weight (15%). Depending on the points a firm receives, it can fall into any of the five categories of certification (see Figure 3.1): Certified (lowest), Bronze, Silver, Gold, and Platinum (highest). The scoring system recognizes the sectoral variations in the additional costs of achieving greater resource efficiency and sets the standards accordingly. For example, an engineering firm would have to achieve greater energy efficiency to receive the same score on that parameter than a petroleum refinery.

[2] https://igbc.in/igbc/redirectHtml.htm?redVal=showAboutusnosign
[3] www.greenco.in/gco/aboutgreencorating.php

(cont.)

A steering committee constituted by CII-GBC designed the first version of the rating scheme in a process that involved 120 experts representing the industry, academia, consulting, and a few government agencies. A GreenCo Review Committee with broad expertise in industry and the environment is involved in reviewing the rating scheme biannually and suggesting updates, if necessary. The process of rating the industries is governed by an elaborate organizational structure. At the core of the process is an independent assessment team, the GreenCo Expert & Assessors Panel, comprising the industry and environmental experts with an in-depth understanding of the GreenCo process as well as sector-specific knowledge. A GreenCo Execution Team coordinates the activities between the industry and the assessor panel and also provides training on GreenCo to industries that applied to receive ratings. A GreenCo Assessment Standing Committee reviews the evaluation and recommendations of the assessor panel and releases the final rating for any industry. A GreenCo Apex Committee, headed by the Chairman of the GreenCo Council and a few nominated eminent personalities (outside GreenCo), oversees the overall GreenCo certification process.

A company volunteering to participate in the GreenCo rating program usually forms a team, with representation from the top management as well as other important functions in the organization. The team undergoes a two-day training program organized by the GreenCo Execution Team to understand the requirements – for example, the assessment parameters and the nature of data to be produced – and prepare to participate in the process. The rating is valid for three years, with an annual review by GreenCo. The company pays a fee to GreenCo, depending on its size (measured by annual turnover). GreenCo retains the right to recall the ratings if any of the terms of the agreement are violated. For example, a regulatory violation by the rated company could automatically lead to the recalling of the rating.

In less than eight years since the first rating, GreenCo has 340 rated firms across sectors and geographies as of March 2020, with a plurality (42%) receiving a Gold rating.[4] More encouragingly, approximately a quarter of the certified firms are small and medium enterprises, which form one of the backbones of the Indian economy but tend to be highly pollution intensive. Although there has been no independent evaluation, the rated industries have reported an average payback period of 1.9 years on the investments made as part the GreenCo process

---

[4] www.greenco.in/gco/publication/GreenCo%20Annual%20report%202019.pdf

(cont.)

according to the preliminary interviews by GreenCo. Apart from the environmental benefits such as reductions in water and energy consumption, emissions of greenhouse gases, and waste generation, GreenCo estimates aggregate monetary benefits of up to $353 million[5] to the rated companies.

Going forward, the GreenCo team aims to expand to 1,000 Indian industrial units certified by 2022. To achieve its target, GreenCo has allocated a team to market to target industries, it hosts an annual summit that showcases the case studies of rated firms, and it provides city-level forums to enable information sharing. GreenCo is also making efforts to popularize its certification program internationally. For example, in 2019, the ITC had inducted GreenCo into its Sustainability Map program.

Despite its impressive beginnings, GreenCo has faced a few important challenges. First is the inherent conflict of interest involved in an industrial advocacy body certifying the performance of its own members (although the certification is open for nonmember industries as well). In order to address this concern, GreenCo is modifying its governance structure in accordance with ISO 17065 standards that specify processes for certifying bodies. Second, while it has strong engagement with industry stakeholders and, to a lesser extent, regulators and academia, civil society groups are largely excluded. In a business environment in which the conflicts between industry and local communities is rising, a lack of engagement with civil society groups can potentially undermine the legitimacy of the certification process. Finally, persuading small-scale industries, which lack the capital and expertise, to invest in environmental improvements and participate in such certification processes will be a significant challenge.

The case of GreenCo certification is consistent with environmental management literature that suggests that in the context of weak state regulations, voluntary, market-based approaches such as GreenCo have the potential to incentivize industries to pursue low-hanging opportunities and improve their environmental performance. It is not clear, however, if such voluntary programs have the ability to incentivize the industry to address the more complex and costlier environmental challenges such as climate change and biodiversity loss.

[5] www.greenco.in/gco/publication/GreenCo%20Annual%20report%202019.pdf

GreenCo Rating Levels

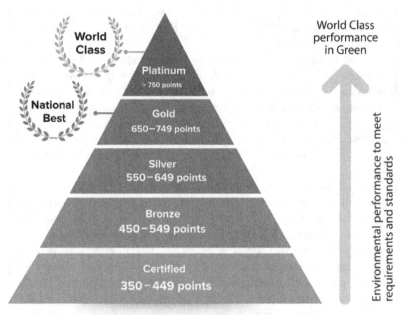

Overall rating: 1,000 points

Figure 3.1 GreenCo rating scheme.
Adapted from www.greenco.in/gco/aboutgreencorating.php

design is their scope: What do they cover? These choices get made in a particular context, too, where the ecolabel might be the only certification in play. Some ecolabels will address some parts of sustainability in a given market, while other ecolabels cover other parts, and there can be an imperfect overlap among them. This complicates comparisons across ecolabels. Further, because ecolabels typically do not operate in a vacuum, the competitive context of an ecolabel is another important consideration (Li 2020). Designers of ecolabels must consider their choices carefully across these many dimensions in light of other ecolabels which might complement their design or compete with it.

The design of an ecolabel matters in many crucial ways. We focus on two, interdependent ways here. First, ecolabel design influences the environmental performance that it fosters. Ecolabels can focus more or less on environmental impacts and those that benefit the broader public beyond the producers' or users' own immediate environments. One ecolabel might be designed for improved workplace conditions or reduced toxins in durable products, while another ecolabel might emphasize biodiversity or carbon emissions. Second, ecolabel design affects how well it competes against the status quo (i.e., no labels) or other ecolabels. Some ecolabel designs can help it grow in popularity, while others reduce its salience or make it unwieldy or redundant. Ecolabel design may need to strike a balance between these two dimensions – environmental performance and competitive appeal – in being able to meaningfully achieve environmental goals. Without some competitive advantages, even the greenest of ecolabels achieves little if it is disregarded. Conversely, ecolabels with low standards and plenty of self-serving qualities to certify may invite greenwashing as the price paid for broader appeal.

In this chapter, we develop a framework to understand the general landscape of how certifying organizations provide multidimensional ecolabels. This framework helps us characterize the enormous variation from one ecolabel to another. To demonstrate this kind of variation, we take a detour into the world of agricultural ecolabels to explore another rich setting for green certifications. We see a great many agriculturally related ecolabels in operation today. The diversity of these ecolabels is instructive about the many different dimensions of ecolabels – something also evidenced in the green building setting. We emphasize a few of these dimensions (e.g., publicness, flexibility) as central to the ultimate impacts of a certification approach. Reviewing the ecolabel landscape for green buildings (Chapter 4) offers more details about the variety, overlap, and design choices that different certification schemes take. These design choices point to features that are critical to ecolabels' ability to help catalyze market transformation.

A Framework for Thinking about Ecolabels

In understanding the role of signaling and information provision in green buildings, we introduce some basic principles. We begin with two fundamental reasons for signaling regarding green products such as buildings. First, there is the conventional and traditional notion of signaling through certification. A signal is an indicator of or proxy for some costly-to-observe or difficult-to-observe attribute or quality of the product or service. Common uses for certifications as signals would be the type of training a service provider has received, the manner in which a good was produced, or some aspect of its quality that would be hard or impossible to discern prior to purchase. In our case, we can imagine a building's energy efficiency as one critical aspect of its quality. This example is an excellent one at the heart of many buildings' value with major implications for maintenance and operation costs to future operators and owners. Despite its importance, the efficiency of the building is quite difficult to observe if you are not the current user or utility bill payer. Even if you have access to the utility bills, a multitude of factors, such as past weather, complex time-variant energy rates, and building usage patterns, are likely to impact the actual energy bills, further obscuring the quality of the building itself. The buyer of a building simply cannot easily or comprehensively observe the efficiency of the product that they are considering purchasing. Sellers can try to disclose this information to prospective buyers, but trust in the accuracy of that information will inevitably be imperfect. Sellers have all the incentive to exaggerate, fabricate, or portray their efficiency information in the best possible light. And like a certification, a third-party audit of a building's energy efficiency (if feasible) still entails substantial cost.

Second, appreciating ecolabels as a special kind of signal requires another perspective. The basic, canonical approach to the information problem in the market – providing a signal of quality – is detailed in Chapter 2 (see A Closer Look: Signals and a Market for Lemons), but it can only take us so far with ecolabels. In the case of ecolabels, we also need a mechanism to incentivize the provision of "greener" public goods. The ecolabel must address not just product quality, but also the overall environmental performance of the product or process by which it was created. An ecolabel that can signal that a firm or product belongs in a "green club" – the group of greener products and practices that the market can value and reward based on this membership – allows firms to accrue returns from their investment in improved environmental performance (Potoski and Prakash 2005). For more on green clubs, see Chapter 2. Thus, the effectiveness of an ecolabel depends on how well it does as a signal (does it provide value?) and on its environmental performance (does it foster sustainability?). An effective ecolabel needs to foster better environmental performance while also providing a valuable signal. Designing an ecolabel involves aligning and balancing environmental performance and competitive performance in the sense that the ecolabel's standards outcompete alternative "business as usual" or other ecolabels.

In some ways, the classic signaling approach tends to emphasize private goods with private, internal benefits. After all, the market for lemons narrative is one that appeals to the seller and buyer of a private good with hard-to-observe quality. It is when we start thinking of public, environmental goods, that the green club approach of Potoski and Prakash enters and gives us additional insight. Thus, we base the initial part of our framework for thinking about labels on these two core approaches. We focus on the importance of credibility, cost, and stringency, and the type of information being disclosed, which comes from the traditional signaling literature. This perspective emphasizes the information asymmetries (see Chapter 2). We supplement that with the public and private nature of the good's qualities and the broader market contexts, inspired by the Potoski and Prakash (2009) emphasis on these signaling mechanisms to support the voluntary provision of green public goods. Effective ecolabels must address these dual issues of providing a valuable signal – revealing information about quality to buyers that allows sellers to recoup their costly investments in quality – while also fostering greener products and practices. Without the former, the ecolabel gets ignored. Without the latter, the ecolabel is just "label" with no "eco." Thus, these two perspectives (signaling value, green impact) prove vital for appreciating the breadth and depth of an ecolabel's effectiveness. Ecolabels need to convey a valuable signal while also fostering greener outcomes (Rivera 2002).

This may be easier said than done, because often tradeoffs exist. Ecolabels can cover a mix of attributes with private and public benefits. An ecolabel that prioritizes conventional "private" benefits to users or owners, rather than broader public or social benefits, may find it easier to appeal to consumers. A label that certifies a more reliable heating system should confer a price premium as consumers pay more for a product with superior performance. A label that certifies that heating system's production as being carbon neutral, however, might not accord a similar premium if consumers do not fully pay to improve the public's environment (i.e., "free ride"). Ecolabels can also include attributes that offer both private and public benefits. Improved energy efficiency, for example, stands to save users on energy costs while also reducing environmentally harmful energy production in the first place.

An ecolabel that exclusively covers attributes providing only private benefits might be more popular, but that limits its green impacts. Conversely, ecolabels requiring costly attributes that predominantly benefit the public might undermine their popularity if the market does not sufficiently reward such environmental goods. These kinds of tradeoffs facing ecolabels highlight the importance and interdependence in how the ecolabel provides both signaling value (to buyers and sellers) that can sufficiently reward greener practices.

Yet a lot more goes into determining the effectiveness of ecolabels than just how it balances private and public benefits. Publicness of a label is just one aspect. How it provides signaling value depends on its credibility, how it competes with other ecolabels, how it conveys information about product quality, and much more. Similarly, an ecolabel's green impact depends on the nature of attributes being fostered, systems for compliance and improving standards, regulatory context, and more.

The Dual Core Elements of Effective Ecolabels

We begin our framework for understanding the ecolabels landscape with these two fundamental, core elements. First, how "green" is the ecolabel? Certification schemes can, in principle, send a signal about all manner of qualities or attributes. What sets ecolabels apart from more conventional certification systems is their signaling pro-sustainability, environmentally friendly qualities. This ties directly into the core problems of externalities in the built environment. Yet, as any "triple-bottom-line" sort of approach will tell you, there are private gains to be had for pursuing sustainability goals. Some green investments have positive *private* returns to investment while also benefiting the environment. Thus, ecolabels need not exclusively signal around qualities with external, public benefits. In fact, there is a great deal of variation in the degree to which ecolabels focus on more internal or private benefits versus more external or public benefits. Variation along this public–private continuum reflects the breadth of values that ecolabels can serve. Ecolabels that concentrate on qualities that benefit society at large may promise the greatest environmental impacts, but they also risk their popularity and diffusion by appealing only to the most charitable, altruistic among us.

Second, how does the ecolabel compete against the status quo (or other labels)? This core element refers to the value provided by the signal. The ecolabel needs to accomplish the essentials of a credible signal by conveying enough relevant information about quality and appealing to producers with favorable returns for investing in the ecolabel. The credibility and design of the certification system is important for attracting participation, just as its publicness is key to achieving green results. An ecolabel's signal has value in overcoming information asymmetries but its success also depends on its diffusion and attractiveness in the face of other competing ecolabels.

There many important dimensions of an ecolabel or eco-certification scheme over which the designer and manager of the ecolabel has varying degrees of control. These can be broken down into several broader categories of *content* (what the label covers, what info it conveys), *governance* (operations and implementation), and *context* (industry structure, other labels, external factors). The middle of Figure 3.2 lists these main elements. Ecolabel designers and managers have varying degrees of control over these aspects. Each element also plays some role in determining the effectiveness of the ecolabel in addressing the core challenges of externalities and information

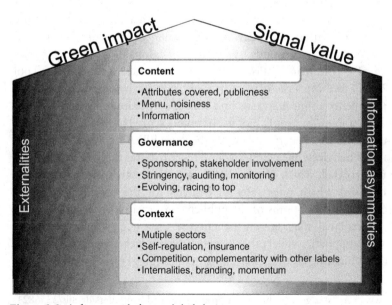

Figure 3.2 A framework for ecolabel design

asymmetries. The two sides of the house in Figure 3.2 reflect these dual core challenges for ecolabels and thus the two core elements: how green is it and how much value does the signal provide? Many design elements – like a focus on public benefits or use of a menu-based approach – largely concern just one of those core challenges. Some concern both externalities and information asymmetries. For example, involving environmental groups in the design and management of the ecolabel can lead to labels with more stringent environmental performance standards while also lending more credibility, making the ecolabel both greener and a more valuable signal. We summarize these major elements in turn.

Content of Ecolabels

A basic design choice for an ecolabel concerns its scope. Important limitations follow from these design choices (Darnall and Aragón-Correa 2014). What sorts of attributes or features are going to be certified by the label, and which will be ignored? Some ecolabels are narrowly focused on one of a handful of aspects of the product or process. Others are much more holistic or sweeping in terms of the many attributes under consideration. For instance, the Energy Star ecolabel focuses on energy efficiency, while other ecolabels look more broadly. The Apple iPad 12.9" tablet is EnergyStar certified[6] solely on energy efficiency grounds, whereas the global Green Electronics Council's Electronic Product Environmental Assessment Tool (EPEAT) tool rates the iPad in its Gold Tier for having met dozens of requirements about materials and waste, corporate reporting and dis-closure, and more.[7] Only 3 of its 40 points scored in EPEAT's optional criteria owe to its energy efficiency, because EPEAT considers so much more. When drawing a circle around the attributes that are in the scope of the ecolabel, which of those attributes offer benefits primarily to the public and which ones refer to benefits for the producer or user? Ecolabels differ in terms of the publicness of their scope. Some aspects of an ecolabel may largely benefit the user (e.g., Apple providing service support), while other aspects may largely benefit the public (e.g., eliminating chlorine bleaching in packaging) rather than the user.

[6] www.energystar.gov/productfinder/product/certified-computers/details/2356821
[7] www.epeat.net/product-details/895ab20c79d7422c9a2820209460ffa7

Some attributes offer more of a mix, such as energy efficiency, which helps with energy conservation to save users on energy costs while also reducing emissions association with energy production.

A second related issue for an ecolabel – and anything involving sustainability – is the extent to which the signal offers a more holistic or a more narrow and limited measure of green quality. Many ecolabels tend to favor the more holistic, noisier approach. Labeling programs usually require participants to surpass some threshold for quality to obtain a certification for green signaling. Many signals are awarded in lumpy categories of tiers, yet they refer to product quality that is measured on a continuous scale. They take a complex, multidimensional thing like "sustainability" or "environmental impact" and reduce it down to a single "score" or even a binary designation like "green" or not. The most basic example of this phenomenon is binary certifications, where products or organizations are rated simply pass–fail, or (non) compliant, though underlying these binary determinations is a continuous measure of product quality. Similarly, tiered signals, including bond and credit ratings, restaurant safety ratings, and numerous multitier ecolabels typically have some underlying continuous score (Farhi et al. 2013; Fischer and Lyon 2014).

For that reason, another important dimension involves the nature of the certifiers' evaluation approach, specifically whether certification is based on qualifying by achieving a specified set of conditions, or whether a more flexible menu-based approach is offered. The menu-based approach, which gives flexibility to the producer pursuing the certification but also then offers a noisier signal of green quality, because buyers cannot tell what specific qualities a product has simply by noting it has the ecolabel. When there are many paths to the same ecolabel under a menu approach, we refer to this as a "noisy" signal. Because certification allows for flexibility and does not entail specific technological requirements, and because each form of green building or energy efficiency label is unique, some authors have referred to green certification as a "noisy" signal of product quality (Fuerst and McAllister 2011; Jaffee et al. 2012; Kok et al. 2011).

Relatedly, there may be tradeoffs in the design of an ecolabel between advantages from structure and narrowing the choice set and disadvantages from inflexibility. Because green product certification programs are flexible, there is a question of which characteristics are being certified, especially when particular improvements are not typically publicly disclosed. Too noisy a signal and there is essentially not enough signal there for it to work effectively. An ecolabel can essentially shape the "language" or "operating system" of production in its market. Setting "the standard" can yield great dividends in that it gives the relevant agents a common set of terms, design principles and techniques, processes, training, and metrics. This can enable more effective communication among firms, consumers, and investors; economies of scale in training, new product development, and marketing; and lower-cost adoption of well-known techniques. Getting everyone on the same standard can be invaluable, especially when a market or practice is first starting out and the potential for a sea of confusing, inconsistent, and incompatible approaches is greatest. In that sense, an ecolabel can play a critical role in the early stages of transforming markets by establishing common standards not unlike the standard-setting power of computer operating systems, languages, and technology interfaces like keyboards. But setting standard-setting is not without potential drawbacks, especially if those standards are ill-advised or too rigid. Restrictive standards set through an ecolabel can constrain innovation if the system is so inflexible that it cannot reward novel approaches and improvements. For example, the LEED building standard does not yet measure or reward the embodied carbon in the building itself. While further iterations of the label may consider mass timber (see Chapter 5 for more discussion on mass timber), it is plausible that promising technologies not included or credited in the ecolabel may be overlooked. One-size-fits-all rigidness raises adoption costs while limiting innovation. Flexibility to experiment and to adopt greener approaches tailored to individual circumstances can be critical to an ecolabel's efficacy and popularity. Thus, ecolabel designers must balance between advantages to standard-setting, while also avoiding overly prescriptive schemes.

A related aspect of ecolabel schemes includes the information content of the signal or label itself. Often, this comes down to design choices over using a tiered or categorical approach, whether there is an underlying continuous "score" and a threshold needed to attain a particular tier, and whether the public label includes the score, just the category, or both. The scoring-along-a-continuum approach gives a more graduated measure of green quality with more detail or precision, whereas the categorical or tier-based approaches report information in a lumpier fashion. Some labels might be just a continuous measure, such as someone's credit rating or an automobile's miles-per-gallon estimate. Other labels might include just the category or tier, such as a Better Business Bureau rating or bond ratings. Sometimes – as in the case of some restaurant hygiene grading systems – both the underlying score and the category are included in the label. Although including the raw score obviously contains more information than a categorical approach, there are interesting advantages of a categorical and threshold-based approach. For one, sometimes reducing the amount of information conveyed can make it easier for consumers to process (Sejas-Portillo et al. 2020). The tiers or categories help shoppers economize on information and certification providing a low cost way for consumers to judge the overall quality of a green building that is associated with building performance benefits. Also, some of the ambiguity implicit in a more categorical approach can actually motivate producers to try to achieve a higher category of quality (Harbaugh and Rasmusen 2018). They seek to take advantage of the noisiness in the label's system by "upgrading" their quality.

Governance of Ecolabels

How an ecolabel is governed – its operations and implementation over time – also plays a critical role in its effectiveness. Governance concerns range from involvement of stakeholders to how strict its standards are set and enforced, and how those standards change over time. Sponsorship of an ecolabel is a key element of the governance dimension. In addition, the extent to which different stakeholders are involved in the design and implementation of the ecolabel can matter as well, as can the business model of the labels and their sponsors themselves. Relying on membership dues, auditing fees, donations, or government funding for revenues presents different incentives and constraints for ecolabel managers. Most ecolabels mix across these revenue sources, with fees for receipt of the ecolabel a common practice (Minkov et al. 2020). Ecolabels funded by fees paid by producers (like "user fees") stand to pressure the ecolabel managers to expand adoption. Conversely, donation funding may support more public benefits and government funding might encourage alignment with policy agendas. Evidence on business models across the ecolabel landscape remains scarce.

Ecolabels differ with respect to sponsorship. The type of entity that sponsors an ecolabel can greatly affect its signaling value, credibility, and effectiveness (Carmin et al. 2003). Ecolabels are primarily sponsored by three main groups of actors: Industry associations, independent organizations, and governments. Of course, who sponsors an ecolabel often draws a lot of attention. Industry associations are organizations founded to promote the best interest of members of a specific industrial sector, such as the American Forest & Paper Association. Research has shown that various factors incentivize industry associations to create and sponsor ecolabels, including aspirations to address environmental issues associated with the industry, reduce public criticism, preemptively avoid or affect government regulation, and improve the reputation of the industry (Carmin et al. 2003; Lenox and Nash 2003; Potoski and Prakash 2013). However, industry associations are beholden to the firms that comprise their membership; considering the costliness of modifying business practices in the interest of improving environmental or social conditions, firms are likely to pressure industry associations to create weaker standards that are easier to abide by (Darnall et al. 2017). Consequentially, an industry-sponsored label may be a mechanism for greenwashing.

Independent groups, including nonprofits and nongovernmental environmental organizations, also sponsor ecolabels. Due to their independence from government and industry, these labels have historically been considered the most credible and trusted by consumers (Carmin et al. 2003). These independent sponsors are often environmental advocacy groups who serve as societal watchdogs and seek to improve environmental performance in areas where regulation is lacking or another ecolabel is not perceived as satisfactory. Environmental NGOs may have the greatest incentive to create strong ecolabels. The implementation of a popular and successful ecolabel could help NGOs differentiate themselves among other environmental groups and prove their group's legitimacy to present and future stakeholders (Darnall et al. 2017). At the same time, NGOs that sponsor ecolabels are often dependent upon fees charged for certification in order to sustain their business. Given this constraint, NGOs walk a fine line between offering a credible and stringent ecolabel and making the label accessible enough that it attracts enough adherents to sustain the sponsoring organization.

Lastly, government-sponsored ecolabels have emerged as an alternative to current government environmental regulatory processes, such as traditional command-and-control regulations. By sponsoring a voluntary ecolabel, governments can avoid costly political gridlock that often comes along with regulatory reform while simultaneously providing public goods. They can also reduce administrative and enforcement costs associated with traditional policies (Carmin et al. 2003). Governments arguably face more pressure to balance the competing interests of the public as well as industries. Furthermore, the success of a government program may be measured by a label's ability to attract a large number of participants. If those numbers, however, come at the expense of program quality and less substantial environmental or social improvements, it may generate public mistrust of the program (Darnall et al. 2017). Research has shown that government-sponsored labels tend to fall between independent and industry sponsors (Fischer and Lyon 2014). Government-sponsored labels have been accused of being disproportionately influenced by industry representatives while limiting NGO involvement (Carmin et al. 2003).

Research shows mixed evidence in regarding the relationship between sponsorship and ecolabel design. Some elements of ecolabel design may be unaffected by sponsorship. For example, one study by Darnall and Carmin (2005) evaluated the signaling accuracy of ecolabel programs in the United States and found no significant difference among sponsors. The three categories of requirements used to assess ecolabels were environmental requirements, administrative requirements, and conformance requirements. The study finds no statistically significant differences among program sponsors by each of these requirements. A report by Carmin et al. (2003) that examined 61 US ecolabels finds no statistical difference among program sponsors in "implementation requirements for designating responsible individuals within the participating organization" (p. 16) or in monitoring requirements. The report highlights the impact of sponsorship in areas such as program rigor, general benefits, stakeholder involvement, and, in contrast to Darnall and Carmin's (2005) study, administrative and environmental performance requirements. It is important to note that these studies solely consider ecolabels in the United States, and the results of these studies may not reflect international trends in ecolabels. Other studies have concluded that sponsorship *does* impact the design and implementation of ecolabels (Darnall et al. 2017; Fischer and Lyon 2014; Potoski and Prakash 2013). These discrepancies demonstrate the complexity and ambiguity in the relationship between governance characteristics of ecolabels and their other design elements and performance. Reality here resists hard-and-fast generalizations.

Finally, the stringency of ecolabels is an important dimension in how we think about ecolabels. How costly and difficult it is to attain a particular credit for a particular quality attribute or to become certified overall is central to the signaling logic underpinning certifications. If it was just as costly for low-quality or nongreen products to receive the certification, then the ecolabel will not work as an effective or credible signal. Labels with very limited stringency may be expected to have little influence in the marketplace. Moreover, the frequency and nature of auditing or monitoring can be an important aspect of stringency as well. Some ecolabels involve recurring and costly audits or routine monitoring by third parties, while other ecolabels simply certify at the outset and conduct little or no subsequent follow-up (Rivera et al. 2006).

Other elements of ecolabel design and implementation have received less attention in the research literature, yet might be important to the governance of the label, its credibility, and its ability to deliver environmental benefits. Specific implementation practices, such as auditing, inspections, or third-party verification, are thought to increase the stringency of a label (Darnall et al. 2017). Other governance practices, such as the inclusion of multiple stakeholders in the design and implementation process, have not received attention in the literature, though a variety of scholars have speculated that careful consideration of the roles of stakeholders in the design and implementation of ecolabels can have a meaningful effect on their impact (Darnall and Aragon-Correa 2014).

Ecolabels are also described by how they are managed during their implementation. A major issue, for instance, involves whether the standards and thresholds set for an ecolabel vary over time. The static or dynamic nature of the ecolabel standards can greatly affect whether the ecolabel engenders a race to the top (see Chapter 8 for more discussion on this). Of course, highly unstable and always varying ecolabels would likely undermine their credibility and usability.

Context of Ecolabels

Lastly, the third major element characterizing ecolabels involves its economic and political context. This is not always something that the designer of an ecolabel gets to choose, but it certainly interacts with the ecolabel's other dimensions. Some ecolabels may be the first or only ecolabel in their market, while others engage in a more crowded landscape. An ecolabel may see other ecolabels as substitutes (competitors) or complements. The ecolabel landscape might get carved up by geography (i.e., where some ecolabels operate only in certain jurisdictions), by functions or attributes being certified (e.g., energy versus water, production processes versus recyclability). Overlapping ecolabels might find competition or complementarities, depending on compatibilities in satisfying alternative sets of standards. Even nonoverlapping ecolabels can still complement one another if compatibilities exist (e.g., reducing energy use also reduces water use). Another major issue to consider for an ecolabel is the extent to which it is on the leading edge of relevant regulation. The interaction between formal governmental regulation and ecolabel standards can be quite important. For instance, the possibility of preemptively self-regulating via an ecolabel, in anticipation of future government regulation along those same attributes, can be a boon to the popularity of the ecolabel. Preemptive self-regulation is a powerful force in environmental management generally. Ecolabels that can tie into this force may find much greater catalytic effectiveness. Similarly, the extent to which the ecolabel has a scope that involves supply-chain issues and actors in multiple sectors may also affect its ultimate catalytic power. Some ecolabels work only on very limited sectors, such as a basic commodity like electricity or diamonds, while others involve global supply chains and many different actors from different sectors. The ability to spillover across markets and affect several sectors of the economy will naturally depend on the scope of the ecolabel affecting a broader sector of the economy. Effective ecolabels can spur investment in the ecolabel system itself. People – as individuals or through their firm or agency – may invest in training, develop management processes, and create brand value – around the ecolabel as strategic investment. These investments can pay long-term dividends and shape future adoption decisions well after the short-term certification decision for a particular product.

The structure of the industry or sector likely matters as well. For example, we might expect consumer-oriented certification systems and labels to differ from labels that certify primary agricultural products for supply-chain management. Consumer-oriented product labels might focus more on product quality and other private-good provision. Conversely, it is possible that these labels focus more on signaling public-good provision associated with the production process in order to take advantage of a consumer market that is willing to pay for the provision of public. As another example, more concentrated product markets (i.e., those with consolidation and fewer producers) might differ from markets that are more competitive. Concentrated product markets provide monopoly power and might allow for more stringent labels, due to lower transaction costs to negotiating the labels to begin with, and an increased ability to pass through increased production costs to consumers. Third, heterogeneity in geographic scope might also shape label requirements and design. Labels that operate in areas with weak environmental regulations may serve as a substitute to traditional regulation; whereas labels operating in stronger regulatory regimes may serve as supplemental to traditional regulation. A variety of requirements such as adherence to existing labor and environmental laws means very different things depending on regulatory context. Labels that operate across a wider range of countries might also be weaker, similar to international environmental agreements that face a classic tradeoff between breadth and depth. In order to have a broader geographical reach, these labels might need to be more general or pursue very different requirements than labels that are more region- or country-specific and, thus, have more specific requirements based on local conditions.

A Closer Look: Agricultural Ecolabels

Voluntary environmental programs first emerged in Japan in the 1950s and have since proliferated around the world (Potoski and Prakash 2013). These programs certify across a wide range of industries and sectors, including chemicals, paper, manufacturing, and agricultural commodities. An Organization for Economic Cooperation and Development (OECD) study finds a five-fold increase in the number of ecolabels from 1998 to 2009 as the global ecolabel marketplace grew crowded.[8] But it is not just a matter of more labels. Their take-up has boomed as well. In recent decades, ecolabel use in certifying agricultural commodities has increased significantly. In just six years,

---

[8] www.oecd-ilibrary.org/environment-and-sustainable-development/a-characterisation-of-environmental-labelling-and-information-schemes_5k3z11hpdgq2-en

(cont.)

the area of land certified by the Roundtable on Sustainable Palm Oil increased nearly 30-fold. Between 2010 and 2014, UTZ – a certification that covers coffee, cocoa, tea, and rooibos – increased its certified area nearly seven-fold (Fiorini et al. 2016).

Several factors drive this increased uptake of ecolabels. Consumers have expressed an increasing awareness and concern for environmental and social wellbeing. Many firms have detected this shift in consumer preferences and have responded accordingly. Financial stakeholders have also pressured firms to enhance their image through displays of corporate social responsibility, thus increasing the procurement of sustainably produced goods. Due to complex global value chains, firms are now responsible for insuring that their suppliers satisfy safety and quality requirements while simultaneously meeting increasingly strict social and environmental norms (Fiorini et al. 2016). Ecolabels can help producers validate unobservable quality of their products to customers, thus enabling firms to signal their green qualities to their consumers.

Dozens of ecolabels can be applied to agricultural products. Agricultural ecolabels tend to be binary; when producers go through certification audits, they can either pass and become certified, or fail. Agricultural ecolabels also require some type of audit to affirm that the producer is meeting the program's requirements. However, many differences exist between labels. First, ecolabels differ in their *content* or areas of focus. While some labels, such as Fairtrade, emphasize the social impact of the trade of commodities, others focus the environmental impact of agricultural practices. Some even take a more holistic approach and emphasize economic incentives for producers as well as promoting environmental and social wellbeing. The ecolabel designs also differ in how they address the provision of public and private goods. For example, ecolabels that cover quality enhancements or improved operational efficiency will likely generate more private, directly appropriable benefits for farmers. In contrast, a label that focuses on environmental and ethical issues (e.g., responsible use of agrochemicals, improved water quality, ensuring the protection of workers' rights) will certify farmers who provide more public goods and societal benefits. Farmers would be unable to reap any returns on investments from those public benefits unless the ecolabel confers a price premium or attracts more demand only to members of that "green club." Fairtrade is an ecolabel that helps producers provide (environmental) public goods and overcome competitive market forces that make investing in higher quality products unprofitable. By offering farmers

(cont.)

private rewards through price premiums for their crops, Fairtrade incentivizes the provision of public goods in the form of ethics requirements and the protection of biodiversity. Second, agricultural ecolabels also differ markedly in terms of their *governance*, especially their sponsorship. Some agricultural ecolabels are essentially industry-led efforts to better communicate or market their qualities. Other agricultural ecolabels are established and run by governments, although their independence from private actors – industry groups or environmental advocates – is unclear. Most agricultural ecolabels, however, are sponsored and operated by an NGO.

Comparing across ecolabels is a difficult task, especially given the enormous breadth of domains that the hundreds of ecolabels cover. But if we look at just agricultural ecolabels, we are able to strike a balance between capturing a large number of ecolabels while also narrowing the scope to something more coherent and comparable. Of course, enormous differences exist even if we limit ourselves to looking only at *agricultural* ecolabels. In a sense, we are still making apples-to-oranges comparisons, which is at least more coherent than apples-to-skyscrapers comparisons. Nonetheless, some interesting patterns do emerge. For instance, we might expect that industry-sponsored labels will predominately provide private benefits to firms (farmers). These industry-sponsored labels will tend to offer a label that certifies increased operational or labor quality and efficiency. That consumers may not be able to distinguish between industry-sponsored labels and those sponsored by NGOs or governments also supports this narrower emphasis on more self-interested qualities from industry labels. These labels will resemble more conventional labels to signal higher product quality with private benefits. We should also expect these labels to have weaker overall standards with less costly compliance, consistent with a narrower focus on private benefits and a propensity to greenwash. In contrast, we expect NGO-sponsored ecolabels to have the most requirements. We also expect these labels to provide more of a mix of public and private goods. Many NGOs will balance the public benefits of environmental improvement with the economic viability of producers and their employees. Considering the pressure that governments face from both industry as well as the public, we expect that government-sponsored programs will tend to fall between independent and industry-sponsored labels.

Another aspect of governance – involving stakeholders in the development and implementation of an ecolabel – may also shape other aspects of ecolabels. We expect that labels that provide more opportunity for participation from a wider range of stakeholders will have more stringent

(cont.)

requirements and will provide more public goods. More stakeholder involvement could lead to requirements covering more environmental spillovers – arguably for structural reasons as more third parties are relevant and engaged. Further, certification processes that build in more involvement of third parties, thus involving more potential monitors and more heterogeneity in interests, can support a more stringent ecolabel design. Conversely, an ecolabel with few stakeholder groups involved in its governance may simply assess product performance in a narrow range of dimensions and may appeal to few or no third parties.

How do these expectations stack up against reality? To test these expectations, we look at data from the International Trade Centre's Sustainability Standards (also known as Standards Map) database.[9] The database covers more than 200 standards across 80 sectors and 180 countries.[10] Ecolabel organizations voluntarily share information about their label's structure to the Sustainability Standards website administrators. Details of the scheme are then uploaded into the database. Details include governance characteristics and standard requirements across five sustainability areas: Environmental, Social, Economic, Quality, and Ethics. Governance characteristics refer to the processes involved in the design of the ecolabel itself, including stakeholder engagement, auditing, monitoring, and enforcement procedures, and other institutional support features. The many dimensions in the Standards Map underscore just how complex and highly variable ecolabels truly are.

The ITC shared with us data on the 51 agricultural ecolabel schemes contained in their dataset. We examined their many different requirements and collected them into four sets of variables: Stakeholder engagement processes, institutional capacity, monitoring and enforcement, and sponsorship. In addition, we counted the total number of requirements and whether each requirement was a trait that indicated the provision of a public good or private good. (Some attributes, like that of energy efficiency, which reduces operating costs and emissions, offer both private and public benefits.) An overview of these 51 agricultural labels shows both diversity and consistency among ecolabels.

---

[9] Sustainability Standards is managed by the International Trade Centre and is sponsored by the German Federal Ministry for Economic Cooperation and Development and the Swiss Consideration's Federal Department of Economic Affairs, Education, and Research.

[10] www.standardsmap.org/standards_intro

(cont.)

- *Label stringency*: Even when we limit ourselves to *just* agricultural ecolabels, a great deal of diversity remains. Assessing things like an ecolabel's "overall stringency" is a messy business when comparing across ecolabels. Our straightforward approach of simply counting up requirements proxies for stringency. It might not do justice to a particular label's stringency but it is a useful starting point. Among the 51 ecolabels, the average number of requirements is 127. Substantial variation exists in the number of requirements across ecolabels, with the total requirements in these labels ranging from 19 to 387. The average number of standard requirements for government-sponsored labels (122) and for NGO-sponsored labels (132) resembles the typical agricultural ecolabel. Industry- and for-profit-sponsored ecolabels tend to have somewhat fewer requirements (108), but there is considerable variation in the number of requirements, and this difference is not statistically significant.
- *Public good provision*: There is significant variation in the amount and proportion of the ecolabels' requirements for public goods provision. The share of total requirements that can be characterized as public goods ranges from 30 percent to 78 percent across these labels. Many agricultural ecolabels have around 50–60 percent of their requirements reserved for public benefits, irrespective of how "stringent" or how many requirements the label contains. Clearly, there is a strong tendency for agricultural ecolabels to strike a balance between certifying attributes with private benefits and those with more public orientation. Having particularly many or few total points does not give much indication of whether it is a predominantly public- or private-oriented ecolabel. This can be seen in Figure 3.3, where less-stringent (in terms of number of requirements) ecolabels exhibit the same tendencies in terms of their emphasis on public goods as those with very many requirements. On the surface at least, more stringent ecolabels in our sample tend to share the same balance in public-orientation as others.
- *Stakeholder engagement processes*: Engaging with stakeholders in the governance of the ecolabel ought not be taken as a given. Only half of the labeling organizations report that they engage stakeholders in the design and implementation of the ecolabel. On average, they report engaging with five or six stakeholder groups, though never more than seven. Thirty out of 51 ecolabels offer technical support, and 16 percent offer financial support. Three quarters of the agricultural ecolabels required their certification or verification body to be legally independent. Interestingly, less than a third of them had explicit written procedures for monitoring and evaluation, and 69 percent of them had established dispute-resolution policies.

(cont.)

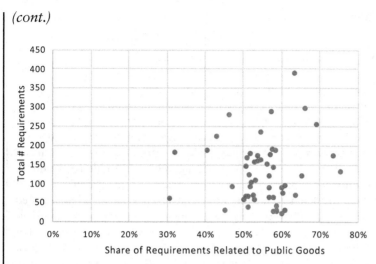

Figure 3.3 Total number of requirements versus percent related to public goods across agricultural ecolabels

- *Sponsorship*: NGOs sponsor most (35 out of 51) agricultural ecolabels, leaving industry and governments to roughly evenly split the remainder. Interestingly, the degree of publicness for these agricultural ecolabels does *not* vary based on the type of sponsoring organization. NGO-sponsored ecolabels appear to be just as public-oriented as the industry-sponsored ecolabels. There is also a tendency of the for-profit- and industry-sponsored ecolabels to engage with more stakeholder groups (average of six) than the NGO-sponsored labels (average of four). The NGO-sponsored ecolabels are also less likely to offer financial support to participants.

These agricultural ecolabels are instructive in other regards as well. They let us test our priors, whether our expectations about some key aspects of ecolabels – such as NGOs being more public-goods oriented – are well-founded. The results are surprising and important in several regards. First, when we look at ecolabels' levels of stringency as measured by the sheer number of requirements, we do *not* see a meaningful difference depending on the type sponsors. NGO-sponsored ecolabels tend to have just about the same number of requirements as industry-sponsored labels do. Moreover, these industry-sponsored ecolabels do not have an appreciably different emphasis in terms of their private benefits versus public benefits. Whether industry-, NGO-, or government-sponsored, all the ecolabels tend to have just over half of

(cont.)

their requirements addressing public benefits rather than more conventional attributes that should bring private gains.

Although overall stringency and publicness of agricultural ecolabels appear independent of sponsor, some of our other expectations are borne out in the data. The extent to which stakeholders have decision-making authority has a strong, positive influence over the publicness of the ecolabel's requirements. This is as expected, given that broader sets of constituents for an ecolabel should lead to a label reflecting a broader set of concerns. In addition, the ecolabel designs tend to institutionally support their objectives. Ecolabels that provide technical support to their participants also tend to have more public-oriented requirements. When they ask for more, they support more. Further, those ecolabels that emphasize publicness also tend to be those that conduct performance audits (rather than no audits or audits only of production processes). Relying on internal audits or requirement process-oriented audits is unrelated to the publicness of an ecolabel. Instead, those ecolabels that audit actual performance are also those that favor more public and environmental benefits (over private benefits). This is consistent with our expectations, as societal benefits may tend to be more aligned with outcomes and performance rather than farming processes themselves.

What are we to make of it when the agricultural ecolabels did not live up to our expectations? For one, we should take care in generalizing away from agricultural ecolabels to cover *all* ecolabels. Even within agriculture, ecolabels are a diverse bunch. These 51 labels cover a wide variety of agricultural products ranging from flowers to cotton to coffee to wild forest products, which in turn may be scoped at the individual country level or have global reach. Lastly, this should reinforce our belief about the complexity and messiness of the ecolabel landscape. It resists easy simplifications and generalizations. For instance, we cannot even say that industry-sponsored ecolabels actually emphasize private goods provision over public goods, at least based on this data. This aligns well with recent research that shows that industry and nonprofit ecolabels can interact in the context of their markets and actually yield greener, pro-environmental outcomes (Li 2020).

Ecolabel Challenges

In making sense of the variety in the landscape of ecolabels, we have focused on describing the design features that go into particular labeling schemes without emphasizing those features' impacts. Evaluating all the features is beyond this chapter's scope. Yet surely an ecolabel's impacts will depend on whether it is stringent but static, operates in a crowded marketplace of ecolabels, emphasizes environmental externalities over private benefits, provides very limited information, is sponsored by an industry association or a particular for-profit firm, etc. The diverse landscape of ecolabels offers many possible combinations of features in ecolabel design. Though the research literature cannot thoroughly evaluate all these combinations' impacts, scholars have shed some light on the implications of a few ecolabel design elements. One such feature – who sponsors the ecolabel – points to concerns about both stringency (Darnall et al. 2017) and credibility among consumers (Darnall et al. 2018). This research shows industry-sponsored ecolabels tend to have weaker rules and elicit less trust than ecolabels from other sponsors. More generally, this underscores the important reality that ecolabels have widely varying degrees of effectiveness. Ecolabels can fail to induce meaningful (environmental) change or fail to generate credible signals. And characteristics of the ecolabel scheme itself, as outlined in this chapter, can account for this.

To someone designing an ecolabel scheme, some elements may be more discretionary than others. Someone developing an ecolabel may not easily get it sponsored by a government but might readily select the scope of which attributes or products it will certify. Many contextual elements (e.g., geographic coverage, composition of the market, presence of competing ecolabels) of an ecolabel may be beyond the designer's control in the short-term, while more discretion exists for other operational aspects (e.g., how much information to provide, how stringent the standards). Essential decisions over the content of the ecolabel, however, entail inevitable tradeoffs and limitations, such as obscuring other environmental impacts and possibly confusing stakeholders (Darnall and Aragón-Correa 2014). How rule structures are established can make the difference between ecolabel success and failure (Darnall et al. 2017). While business associations lack discretion to become, say, a government or independent sponsor of their ecolabel, they can consider pursuing third-party certification (Darnall et al. 2018). More research is needed into the business models adopted by ecolabel designers and their implications.

A common criticism holds that ecolabels reflect only symbolic distinction with no material difference in environmental performance.

Perpetuating a myth or assumption that an ecolabeled building has superior sustainability attributes requires more than just a firm's PR department; it involves many actors who interact to create and maintain that symbol (Bowen and Aragon-Correa 2014). The context in which an ecolabel operates matters for how we connect its signals of symbolic values and environmental performance. Those managing ecolabels face the ongoing challenge of ensuring that the ecolabel is used as a tool to foster pro-environmental behavior rather than as a (symbolic) end in itself.

As we think about the landscapes of ecolabels out there – for agricultural products, for timber, for financial products, etc. – we do well to keep in mind the interdependencies and complexities within and among the ecolabels themselves. Just as their contexts may differ markedly, ecolabels exhibit enormous diversity themselves. They are not all created equally. This chapter introduces a framework to help think about important dimensions of ecolabels and how their content, context, and governance all combine to influence the value of their signal and the certification's impact on environmental performance. Each of these three core aspects of ecolabels has received attention before in the literature, although much research remains to be done to unpack each of their impacts and interrelationships. The complex and diverse ecolabel landscape also faces challenges and criticisms over ineffectiveness, symbolic rather than substantive qualities, and more. Our closer look at agricultural ecolabels illustrates the wide diversity and general messiness of the ecolabel landscape. Thus, structuring our approach to ecolabels can be useful. We can apply that framework in thinking about other crowded landscapes of ecolabels, such as certifications for green buildings. We next turn our attention in Chapter 4 to surveying that green building ecolabel landscape.

References

Bowen, F. and J. A. Aragon-Correa. 2014. "Greenwashing in Corporate Environmentalism Research and Practice: The Importance of What We Say and Do." *Organization & Environment* 27, no. 2: 107–112.

Carmin, Joann, Nicole Darnall, and Joao Mil-Homens. 2003. "Stakeholder Involvement in the Design of U.S. Voluntary Environmental Programs: Does Sponsorship Matter?" *Policy Studies Journal* 31, no. 4: 527–543.

Darnall, Nicole and J. Alberto Aragón-Correa. 2014. "Can Ecolabels Influence Firms' Sustainability Strategy and Stakeholder Behavior?" *Organization & Environment* 27, no. 4: 319–327.

Darnall, Nicole and Joann Carmin. 2005. "Greener and Cleaner? The Signaling Accuracy of U.S. Voluntary Environmental Programs." *Policy Sciences* 38, no. 2–3: 71–90.

Darnall, Nicole, Hyunjung Ji, and Matthew Potoski. 2017. "Institutional Design of Ecolabels: Sponsorship Signals Rule Strength." *Regulation & Governance* 11, no. 4: 438–450.

Darnall, Nicole, Hyunjung Ji, and Diego A. Vázquez-Brust. 2018. "Third-Party Certification, Sponsorship, and Consumers' Ecolabel Use." *Journal of Business Ethics* 150, no. 4: 953–969.

Farhi, Emmanuel, Josh Lerner, and Jean Tirole. 2013. "Fear of Rejection? Tiered Certification and Transparency." *The RAND Journal of Economics* 44, no. 4: 610–631.

Fiorini, Matteo, Bernard M. Hoekman, Marion Jansen, Philip Schleifer, Olga Solleder, Regina Taimasova, and Joseph Wozniak. 2016. "Exploring Voluntary Sustainability Standards Using ITC Standards Map: On the Accessibility of Voluntary Sustainability Standards for Suppliers." *International Trade Centre Series*, ITC Working Paper Series WP-04-2016.E.

Fischer, Carolyn and Thomas P. Lyon. 2014. "Competing Environmental Labels." *Journal of Economics & Management Strategy* 23, no. 3: 692–716.

Fuerst, Franz and Patrick McAllister. 2011. "Green Noise or Green Value? Measuring the Effects of Environmental Certification on Office Values." *Real Estate Economics* 39, no. 1: 45–69.

Giovannucci, Daniele and Stefano Ponte. 2005. "Standards As a New Form of Social Contract? Sustainability Initiatives in the Coffee Industry." *Food Policy* 30, no. 3: 284–301.

Harbaugh, R. and E. Rasmusen. 2018. "Coarse Grades: Informing the Public by Withholding Information." *American Economic Journal: Microeconomics* 10, no. 1: 210–235.

Jaffee, Dwight, Richard Stanton, and Nancy Wallace. 2012. "Energy Factors, Leasing Structure and the Market Price of Office Buildings in the US." UC Berkeley Fisher Center Working Papers.

Kok, Nils, Marquise McGraw, and John M. Quigley. 2012. "The Diffusion over Time and Space of Energy Efficiency in Building." *Annals of Regional Science* 48, no. 2: 541–564.

Lenox, Michael and Jennifer Nash. 2003. "Industry Self-Regulation and Adverse Selection: A Comparison across Four Trade Association Programs." *Business Strategy and the Environment* 12, no. 6: 343–356.

Li, Y. 2020. "Competing Eco-Labels and Product Market Competition." *Resource and Energy Economics* 60: 101149.

Mason, Charles. 2013. "The Economics of Eco-Labeling: Theory and Empirical Implications." *International Review of Environmental and Resource Economics* 6, no. 4: 341–372.

Minkov, Nikolay, Annekatrin Lehmann, Lisa Winter, and Matthias Finkbeiner. 2020. "Characterization of Environmental Labels beyond the Criteria of ISO 14020 Series." *International Journal of Life Cycle Assessment* 25, no. 5: 840–855.

Potoski, Matthew and Aseem Prakash. 2005. "Green Clubs and Voluntary Governance: Iso 14001 and Firms' Regulatory Compliance." *American Journal of Political Science* 49, no. 2: 235–248.

2009. *Voluntary Programs: A Club Theory Perspective*. Cambridge, MA: The MIT Press.

2013. "Green Clubs: Collective Action and Voluntary Environmental Programs." *Annual Review of Political Science* 16, no. 1: 399–419.

Rivera, J., 2002. "Assessing a Voluntary Environmental Initiative in the Developing World: The Costa Rican Certification for Sustainable Tourism." *Policy Sciences* 35: 333–360.

Rivera, J., P. de Leon, and C. Koerber. 2006. "Is Greener Whiter Yet? The Sustainable Slopes Program after Five Years." *Policy Studies Journal* 34, no. 2: 195–224.

Sejas-Portillo, Rodolfo, David Comerford, Mirko Moro, and Till Stowasser. 2020. "Limited Attention in the Housing Market: Threshold Effects of Energy-Performance Certificates on Property Prices and Energy-Efficiency Investments." *CESifo Working Paper Series 8669*, CESifo.

4 | The Labeling Building Challenge
The World of Ecolabels for the Built Environment

Mapping the Landscape of Green Building Labels

After overviewing the extent and variety of ecolabels in the agricultural sector, we now return to green building labels. The landscape for green building certifications may not be quite as extensive as for food products, but it is no less rich and varied. The ecolabel framework introduced in the A Framework for Thinking about Ecolabels section in Chapter 3 gives us some structure for our review of green building labels. We start this survey of the building ecolabel landscape with a short overview of many of the prominent ecolabels around the world.

Introducing Some Prominent Building Ecolabels

The LEED ecolabel was developed by the US Green Building Council (USGBC), an independent nonprofit organization composed of building and construction companies and sustainability nonprofits. The component organizations of the USGBC work together to move the building and construction industry in a more sustainable direction. Since the USGBC was established in 1993, more than 70 other green building councils have sprung up around the world. These country-level green building councils work in coordination with the World Green Building Council and receive support from it. Many of the most popular building ecolabels are affiliated with a country-level green building council in some way, whether directly or through funds and support. Other systems are run by various international green building organizations or government agencies. Here we survey 14 of the most well-known of these ecolabels and some of their attributes. Regardless of a green building label's affiliation, they all tend to share common goals, which are evident in the categories of requirements to be fulfilled to earn the label. All the programs to some extent require the provision of public goods to the greater community, except WELL, which is specifically focused on the health and wellbeing of building occupants. Common categories in these programs include energy efficiency, water efficiency, and materials and resource use. While the building owners and occupants may also benefit from having more efficient energy and water systems or safer materials, these categories also convey some greater environmental benefit to the public. Therefore, we classify the standards in these categories as intended for public benefit. While most systems prioritize environmental protection above all else at least, three systems have multiple or competing aims. Let us dig deeper into each of these ecolabels.

LEED

Leadership in Energy and Environmental Design (LEED)[1] is a US-based international program that is often regarded as the industry standard for green building certification. Its stated aim is to push the boundaries on how buildings can do better for people. Established in 1998, it is the most successful green certification system, with around 100,000 registered buildings worldwide and continually increasing standards of environmental stringency. Five out of its six main categories are meant to convey benefits to the public: location and transportation, sustainable sites, water efficiency, energy and atmosphere, and materials and resources. These are considered public goods because their positive effects are dispersed publicly to individuals whether they own or use the building or not. Only indoor environmental quality is intended to convey private benefit to the building owner by attracting more tenants to a building that is healthy for occupants to spend time in. LEED has attracted media attention throughout its multiple vintage releases, with some environmental advocates questioning if the flexibility of the program may compromise its environmental mission. In comparison with similar schemes, however, LEED stands tall as a major system providing public environmental benefits through the built environment. It also acts as an industry leader by continually raising the bar for excellence in the built environment. Many other certification schemes have modeled themselves on LEED principles.

---

[1] www.usgbc.org/leed

BREEAM

The Building Research Establishment Environmental Assessment Method (BREEAM)[2] was established in the United Kingdom in 1990 as the world's first sustainability assessment method used to masterplan buildings. The system has certified over 22,000 buildings worldwide, with over 10,000 in the United Kingdom and a significant presence throughout Europe. This makes it the second most popular ecolabel worldwide after LEED. BREEAM evaluates building development based on performance benchmarks across seven categories: management, energy, water, materials, pollution, waste, and health and wellbeing. The management and health and wellbeing categories provide private benefit to the owners and users of the building, while the remaining five categories are intended to publicly provide environmental benefits. Buildings are certified in a tiered system based on the percentage of benchmarks fulfilled. BREEAM places great emphasis on energy efficiency, with 43 percent of the final score coming from this category. Like LEED, BREEAM offers different types of certification for in-use versus new construction buildings, as well as different project types beyond buildings, such as communities and infrastructure. Many subsequent green building ecolabels have adopted elements of the LEED and BREEAM models by offering different certifications based on the stage of the building lifecycle and type of building. In this way, BREEAM and LEED have set many of the standards for how ecolabels all around the world function.

WELL

WELL[3] is a building certification scheme that measures the performance of building features with the goal of creating healthy buildings. Although not formally administered by the USGBC, WELL was founded in 2014 by investors with experience developing the LEED label and utilizes the same third-party credentialing body as LEED, Green Business Certification, Inc. (GBCI). WELL has over 5,700 buildings, with over 2,000 in the United States and others in the United Kingdom, China, Australia, France, and Canada. The certification is offered at the Silver, Gold, and Platinum levels based on the percentage

[2] www.breeam.com/   [3] www.wellcertified.com/

of optimizations achieved. WELL was developed and is managed and administered by the International WELL Building Institute, a public-benefit corporation whose mission is to improve human health and wellbeing through the built environment. As opposed to the public or environmental benefits incentivized by certification programs like LEED, WELL focuses on features of the built environment that impact human health and wellbeing, including air, water, nourishment, light, movement, thermal comfort, sound, materials, mind, community, and innovations. This health and wellbeing focus conveys private benefit to the building owner by creating a more pleasant environment inside the building and earning a certification that signals the building's quality to the market to attract tenants. Although the improved building quality and health benefits offered by the certification are public in the sense that users of the building benefit from them, the goal of the certification scheme is not to provide a public good to the whole community or environment, only to the private users of the building. The improvements encouraged by the program, such as better air quality, creating daylit spaces, and allowing access to nature, only benefit tenants or users of the building. Additionally, building owners can expect returns on their investment in WELL in the form of greater worker productivity, lower absenteeism, and lower health insurance premiums. Therefore, WELL is a very different shade of "green" certification scheme, as its market signal is a different understanding of quality based upon people as opposed to buildings. It is intended as a complement to, not a substitute for, LEED.

Green Star Australia

Green Star Australia[4] was established in 2002 and is run by the Australian Green Building Council. Its stated purpose is to lead the sustainable transformation of buildings, cities, and communities. The program only certifies buildings in Australia, and over 2,800 had been certified as of 2020. The ecolabel is broad in scope, with eight scoring categories: management, indoor environmental quality, energy, transport, water, materials, land use and ecology, and emissions. Six of these benefit the public, while management and indoor environmental quality benefit the building owner and tenants. The categories are

---

[4] https://new.gbca.org.au/

weighted relatively equally, with energy being slightly emphasized. Green Star has attracted some criticism because the members of its founding GBC are mostly property development corporations. Detractors argue that stakeholder interests may be more focused on increasing profits than achieving true environmental quality and transforming the built environment. This case points out that local GBCs may not all share the same goals and priorities as they can be composed of various sponsor groups.

Green Mark Singapore

Green Mark Singapore[5] is a certification system established by the Singapore Building and Construction Authority in 2005. The program emphasizes the environmental impact and performance of the built environment. Green Mark has over 2,000 projects in Singapore and several other southeast Asian countries including Malaysia, Brunei, Philippines, and Indonesia. There are five scoring categories: energy efficiency, water efficiency, environmental protection, indoor environmental quality, and other green features. Four out of Green Mark's five categories are environmentally focused and provide public benefits, with the private benefits category "indoor environmental quality" counting for only 4 percent of the total score. Energy efficiency is by far the most heavily weighted category in the system, with 61 percent of the certification based on these aspects, such as the air-conditioning system, renewable energy, and natural ventilation. For the flexible "other green features" category, example enhancements include a pneumatic waste-collection system and a carbon footprint of development. Green Mark has gone through several vintages since its inception, similar to LEED. This system is an example of a certification scheme outside of the WGBC network that strongly prioritizes publicly provided environmental benefits. The relatively narrow scope of the ecolabel emphasizes environmental quality over a more holistic approach.

Green Globes

The Green Globes[6] building certification scheme is sponsored by the Green Building Initiative. The stated goal of the program is to

[5] www.bca.gov.sg/greenmark/green_mark_buildings.html
[6] www.greenglobes.com/home.asp

accelerate the adoption of building practices that result in resource efficient, healthier, and environmentally sustainable buildings. The certification system was developed on the basis of BREEAM Canada in 2000, but with no prerequisites and incremental recognition for partial achievement of targets. This makes the certification a bit laxer and more achievable for businesses hoping to achieve a green signal. A completely online assessment makes it even more accessible. Green Globes certifies in the United States and Canada and has certified about 1,800 projects. Of the seven assessment areas, energy, water, indoor environment, materials and resources, project management, site, and emissions, five offer public environmental benefits, while management and indoor environmental quality convey private benefits to the building owners and users.

DGNB

The German Sustainable Business Council, or DGNB,[7] is a certification scheme that focuses on all-around building quality, with a lesser focus on environmental protection. Since 2007, the DGNB has certified over 1,500 building projects in Germany, with others in Austria, China, Denmark, and Luxembourg. It involves six scoring categories: environment, economic, sociocultural and function, technical, process, and site. Of these, environment and site are clearly meant to mitigate the negative environmental impacts of the building, while the remaining four signal other aspects of building quality. In addition to sociocultural and functional, which is mainly intended to promote wellbeing, the categories economic, technical, and process are intended to assure purchasers and tenants that the building is of sound quality. Economic criteria include lifecycle cost and commercial viability, which are clearly factors that convey private benefits to the building owner. Technical criteria focus on the physical integrity of the building, which ensures a high selling or rental price for the owner and conveys the benefit of safety to building tenants. Process quality includes some environmental aspects such as documentation for sustainable management, but the overall goal seems to be high-quality management in general, as shown by points including construction-quality assurance

---

[7] https://static.dgnb.de/fileadmin/dgnb-system/downloads/criteria/DGNB-Criteria-Set-New-Construction-Buildings-Version-2020-International.pdf

and systematic commissioning. Overall, four out of six categories seem clearly intended to convey private benefits to the owners and tenants of the certified buildings, and the environmental impact is only a small facet of overall quality. However, some of the noisiness of the signal given by the DGNB is mitigated because a project cannot rely only on technical quality to certify. There are prerequisites to be met in each category, including environmentally focused ones.

BEAM

The Building Environmental Assessment Method (BEAM)[8] is an environmental assessment tool for buildings. The BEAM Society Limited in Hong Kong operates the BEAM ecolabel (also known as HK-BEAM, now BEAM Plus). The system mainly certifies buildings located in Hong Kong and uses a four-tiered system of Bronze, Silver, Gold, and Platinum based on the percentage of requirements fulfilled. BEAM uses six scoring categories, of which five benefit the public. The categories, in order of weighting, are energy use, health and wellbeing, integrated design and construction management, sustainable sites, materials and waste, and water use. The health and wellbeing category is intended to convey private benefits to building users. The integrated design and construction management category is significant in that it is more environmentally beneficial to the public than to the building owner; credits in this category include measures to reduce site emissions, construction and demolition waste recycling, and construction that is considerate to the surrounding community. As an older ecolabel, BEAM was established in 1996 and has since registered around 1,600 projects.

Three Star China

Three Star China[9] is a building certification standard operated by the Chinese Ministry of Construction. Established in 2006, the program has certified around 1,300 buildings. The system includes three types of requirements: required, optional, and most difficult. The system grants three tiers of building certification or three "stars." Unlike other

---

[8] www.hkgbc.org.hk/eng/main/index
[9] http://chinagreenbuildings.blogspot.com/2009/02/ministry-of-construction-green-building.html

certification systems, Three Star can only certify a building after one year of operation, when it is proven that operational predictions have been met. There are six scoring categories: land saving/outdoor environment, energy saving, water saving, material resources saving, indoor environmental quality, and operation management. Four of these offer clear public environmental benefits, while indoor environmental quality and operation management mainly offer private benefits.

HQE

Haute Qualité Environnementale (HQE)[10] is a French certification scheme that has about 600 certified buildings in France and around 100 others throughout Morocco, Colombia, Luxembourg, and elsewhere. Established in 2005, the rating system is based on four equally weighted categories: environment, energy, health, and comfort. While the first two categories clearly offer public environmental benefits, the latter two specifically focus on improving the quality of the building for its users. Therefore, the mix of public and private benefits is equal in this ecolabel. HQE is split into three certification bodies based on building project type. Certivea is the certifying body for local planning and nonresidential buildings, Cerqual certifies multi-family residential buildings, and Cequami certifies detached houses. For projects outside of France, Cerway is the certification body that supports stakeholders during their project.

Green Star South Africa

Green Star South Africa[11] is a certification system operating in southern Africa. Based on the Green Star Australia system, the rating scheme was established in 2007 and rewards environmental leadership in the property industry while signaling quality in design, construction, and operation. Unlike the Australian GBC, the South African GBC claims to be a nonprofit, not an industry group. Most of its 500 certified projects are in South Africa, with a few in Namibia and Kenya. The system has three tiers of certification and eight scoring categories, of which six are focused on public benefit to the environment: management, indoor environmental quality, energy, transport, water,

---

[10] www.behqe.com/   [11] https://gbcsa.org.za/certify/green-star-sa/

materials, land use and ecology, and emissions. Management and indoor environmental quality contribute more to the private benefit of the building owner, while the other categories convey public environmental benefits. The certification process is hands-on, with a Green Star Associated Professional required to submit documents on behalf of the design team as a sort of intermediary for the certifier.

CASBEE

The Comprehensive Assessment System for Built Environment Efficiency[12] is a Japanese building certification label under the Japanese Ministry of Land, Infrastructure, Transport, and Tourism. Established in 2005, it is directed by the Japan Sustainable Building Consortium. The ecolabel has certified over 400 Japanese buildings and maintains a goal of improving quality of life while reducing lifecycle resource use and environmental loads associated with the built environment. Its unique approach to ranking green buildings reflects this. The score is based on the building's environmental quality versus its environmental load, a fraction that is equivalent to environmental efficiency. Environmental quality includes indoor environment, quality of service, and outdoor environment. These are positive externalities provided by the building. On the other hand, environmental load includes negative externalities, like energy use, resource and materials use, and off-site environmental impacts. The higher the quantified quality is over the load, the better the grade received. The final CASBEE score is given as S, A, B+, B−, or C based on this ratio. Separately, CASBEE also assesses lifecycle CO_2 to demonstrate a building's climate change impact. The four factors considered in CASBEE are energy efficiency, resource efficiency, local environment, and indoor environment. Therefore, three out of four categories provide public benefit and indoor environment provides more private benefits.

EDGE

Excellence in Design for Greater Efficiencies (EDGE)[13] is a green building certification scheme focused on making buildings in developing economies more resource efficient. The system was developed by

---

[12] www.ibec.or.jp/CASBEE/english/index.htm   [13] https://edgebuildings.com/

the International Finance Corporation in 2014 and currently receives funding from the UK government. EDGE certifies in many countries, with the greatest project concentrations in Colombia, Vietnam, Indonesia, Mexico, India, and Peru. As opposed to a menu-based approach, EDGE is a simple system based on three categories: energy, water, and materials. A project can be EDGE certified as long as it can demonstrate a 20 percent reduction in energy consumption, water consumption, and energy embodied in materials. Higher tiers are awarded when more reduction is demonstrated. The simple environmental focus of the categories clearly demonstrates the public-good provision of the EDGE rating system. As one of the newest ecolabels, only around 300 buildings had been certified as of 2020.

Living Building Challenge

The Living Building Challenge[14] is a rigorous sustainable building certification system established by the International Living Future Institute in 2006. It differs from other certification programs in that it does not allow as much flexibility. It requires applicants to fulfill all 20 requirements in order to be "living building" certified. However, there are multiple certifications offered by the Living Building Institute that may send different marketing signals. In addition to the very stringent Living Building Certification, a project can earn a Petal, Core Green Building, Zero Energy, or Zero Carbon certification, which have varying requirements. Therefore, this ecolabel is unique in not pursuing a tiered, menu-based approach while still giving some flexibility to project design teams choosing a certification to pursue. Many projects across the globe are pursuing certification, but as of 2020 only around 100 buildings have achieved the status of "Living Building." Most of these are in the United States, for now. The certification's scope covers seven "petals," of which five contribute direct benefits to the public. The other two, health/happiness and beauty, provide direct (private) benefit to the building users. Five out of the 20 imperatives relate to building materials, followed by place (four imperatives), health and happiness (three), and water, energy, equity, and beauty (each with two). Chapter 5 contains much more detail on

---

[14] https://living-future.org/lbc/

the Living Building Challenge as well as a closer look at a Living Building project.

An Overview of Prominent Ecolabels

Now that we have been introduced to the 14 prominent ecolabels around the world, let's take an overview of the whole landscape. We survey these labels more holistically to demonstrate their differences and similarities. Many ecolabels are either structured around or inspired by the environmental principles of the World Green Building Council. So, they share many focus areas and verbiage about the importance of green building in evolving the built environment. We start by exploring their common focus areas and the extent of their "publicness." Here, ecolabel focus areas are considered to be "public" if they provide some public good, even if there are also private benefits at play. For example, energy and water efficiency both contribute to a more sustainable environment outside the building, so they are here classified as public, even though the building owner will also profit from increased building efficiency. Figure 4.1 shows that some ecolabels, such as Green Mark Singapore and EDGE, have a very narrow environmental focus, and therefore their focus areas are highly public in nature. On the other hand, DGNB and WELL include focus areas that benefit only building inhabitants or investors, like health and comfort or management quality. This figure displays the "shades" of green emphasized by varying goals of ecolabel systems. Figure 4.2 shows what they have in common, and particularly that most of these ecolabel programs share five of the same categories. It is the categories in excess of these five, as well as the weights of each category in determining the score, that sets some programs apart from others in terms of their publicness.

Overall, the global landscape for building ecolabels reflects substantial coverage and diversity among those top ecolabels. However, Figures 4.1 and 4.2 only reflect the content of those building ecolabels. Table 4.1 shows some governance and context aspects of these same labels, summarizing the narratives in the previous section. These ecolabel programs reflect a wide range of sponsors, from government to private corporations, and are located in a range of host countries that span different sizes, levels of economic development, and regions. (See Table 2.2 for additional details.) Many of these programs are very

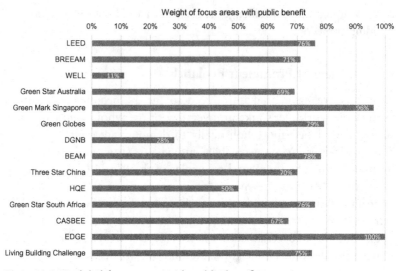

Figure 4.1 Ecolabel focus areas with public benefit

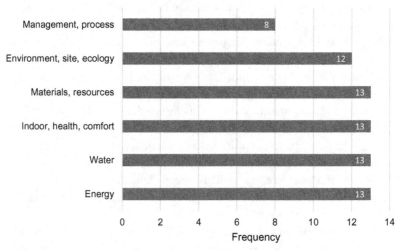

Figure 4.2 Frequency of common focus areas in ecolabels

comparable to LEED or BREEAM, often explicitly so, with each using tiers in some way and all relying on a single-indicator sort of "noisy" signal. Nonetheless, there are interesting distinctions. Some programs appear designed to complement or compete with existing ecolabels, while others feature distinctive design elements to enhance or weaken

Table 4.1. *Design elements of international green building labeling programs*

Labeling Program	Sponsor	Certifications per Capita	Notes
BEAM	Government	213.9 (Hong Kong)	Includes a random site auditing process
BREEAM	Private corporation	162.3 (UK)	Undergone major changes in standards since 2014
CASBEE	Government	3.5 (Japan)	Classifies building features by beneficial output (quality) versus environmental "load"
DGNB	Industry group	18.6 (Germany)	Rating system has minimal standards in every category
EDGE	International organization	1.4 (Colombia)	Targets developing countries with limited prescriptive requirements
EEWH	Government	96.6 (Taiwan)	First standard designed for subtropics
Green Globes	Nonprofit/ NGO	4.9 (US)	Markets as lower-cost or simpler alternative to LEED
Green Mark	Government	361.9 (Singapore)	Narrower in scope, not as holistic
Green Star Australia	Industry group	109.4 (Australia)	Sponsorship not uniform – green building council composition varies locally
Green Star South Africa	Nonprofit/ NGO	8.3 (South Africa)	Requires a third-party AP to submit documentation for each project
HQE	Private corporation	9.0 (France)	Uses third-party auditors to verify performance requirements
IGBC	Industry group	5.2 (India)	System of many certifications for built environment (see Chapter 3).
LEED	Nonprofit/ NGO	188.5 (US)	See A Closer Look: LEED

Table 4.1. (*cont.*)

Labeling Program	Sponsor	Certifications per Capita	Notes
Living Building Challenge	Nonprofit/ NGO	0.3 (US)	Must fulfill all 20 imperatives to qualify
Pearl Rating System	Government	26.3 (UAE)	All developments must achieve at least one pearl
Three Star	Government	1.0 (China)	Certification only after 1 year of operation – based on performance
WELL	Public benefit corporation	6.6 (US)	Focus on health as a complement to LEED

Note: Per-capita certifications are based on number certified in primary country (see Table 2.2) in 2020 divided by that country's population (1,000,000s).

stringency. Obviously, contextual factors like the regional economy and governmental control also vary markedly from regions like Colombia and China to Germany and the United States.

A Closer Look: LEED

We key in on one ecolabel in particular, LEED, in this book. LEED has already catalyzed so much of the building industry, and its potential for more remains great. Yet how does it fit into the diverse landscape of ecolabels? In terms of the framework introduced in Chapter 3, we place LEED as follows:

Content: We reviewed the basics of LEED earlier in this chapter. LEED covers both public and private attributes of buildings. It offers a flexible approach, allowing firms to select from a menu of credits. LEED is also a quintessentially "noisy" signal in that its menu-based approach combines with a category-based approach, with multiple tiers with an underlying score (which is not generally advertised).

Governance: LEED is sponsored and run by an independent non-profit that gains considerable credibility from inclusion of various stakeholders from across the industry. Its stringency involves

(cont.)

many requirements across many building elements, mitigated by its menu-based approach. Historically, LEED has emphasized certification and auditing at the initial outset of the building, not monitoring its ongoing performance after its launch. That much is changing, as monitoring ongoing performance takes on a more prominent role in LEED. This, along with numerous and intermittent updates to new versions over the years, reflects the ongoing and deeper evolution of the LEED standards themselves. See Figure 4.3 for a review of the timeline of some major LEED updates. LEED keeps changing over time in order to support or induce a race to the top. (See Chapter 8 for an extended look at this race.) Although the full costs for building a certified green building (including search and design costs in addition to engineering and construction costs) can be substantial (Chegut et al. 2019), lower-tier green buildings may cost only marginally more than tradition construction. This is consistent with hypotheses from Li and van 't Veld (2015) and Fischer and Lyon (2014), indicating that tiered certification schemes like LEED will keep entry-level certification costs very low in order to attract many builders with low willingness-to-pay for green attributes.

Context: LEED centers on green buildings, yet buildings are crucially not a commodity but rather the end product of production from sectors including architecture and construction as well as the owners and the ultimate tenants' own industries. This multisectoral nature is key to the impact of LEED, and its attention to supply-chain issues (e.g., sustainable sourcing of building materials) envelops other sectors in its certification system. Vitally, also, LEED (and other building ecolabels) has close relationships with building codes and other building regulations. This puts LEED in the position of allowing participants to preempt regulatory oversight as well as letting LEED indirectly and implicitly shape future regulation. The overview of other green building labels in this chapter implicitly makes clear that these labels rarely compete with one another geographically. With buildings being fixed in location, they typically face little "competition" among alternative ecolabels. The existing ecolabels, when there are more than one, tend to be complements (e.g., LEED and WELL) rather than competitive alternatives. In that regard, LEED has achieved market dominance and can exert that power to achieve other ends. This has included its acquisition of other ecolabels (e.g., GRESB – a global real estate

(cont.)

and real asset sustainability benchmark) just like other ratings agencies (such as S&P Global and Morningstar) have done. Beyond this sort of consolidation, the predominance of an ecolabel like LEED is important for its lasting impact on those in the industry. Its impact reaches further than any one particular LEED-certified building project. The idea of LEED-certified buildings lives on when the people involved, the organizational processes, or other factors give more momentum to the green-building enterprise. When the effort to get a building LEED-certified involves people learning or organizations altering their decision-making processes, the movement within organizations or the sector can gain momentum. Additionally, if the ecolabel develops a brand value – as LEED has done – then past successes in this context give rise to future successes because the brand value builds on itself and past adoptions foster future adoptions. Organizations can learn about the benefits of ecolabeling through participation in the ecolabel, which leads to more interest in and adoption of the ecolabel. LEED certainly benefits from this learning and positive feedback loop.

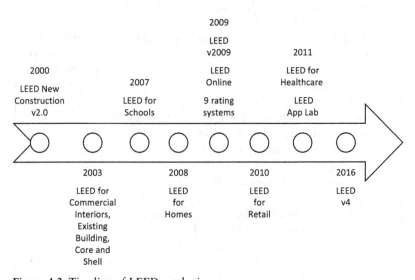

Figure 4.3 Timeline of LEED ratcheting up

Looking Ahead: Designs to Promote Market Transformation

This chapter and Chapter 3 focus on the limited question of the design of the ecolabels themselves. They say nothing about who participates in the label, how they participate in the label, or what the impacts of participation are. It seems likely that the design of the label affects the types of producers that choose to participate. Producers might join labels to acquire private benefits, or to signal social or environmental commitments to a wide range of stakeholders. Because most of these labels allow flexibility by producers, the types of goods produced and certified through the labels may be quite different across producers, both across labels and within an individual label. And the environmental, social, and economic outcomes of participation are even more difficult to assess. Linking the design of the labels to participation, how producers choose to participate, and eventual environmental, social, and economic outcomes of participation is both incredibly important yet near impossible to do with existing data. It is a complex landscape and we still have much to learn.

When seen through the lens of the two core elements of ecolabels – *green impact* and *signal value* (Figure 3.2) – we can start to see how ecolabels like LEED can play a crucial role in catalyzing market transformation. Many aspects of the LEED label's design support just such a catalytic role. The LEED ecolabel accomplishes its core functions in certifying green and predominantly public-goods-providing attributes of buildings. And it does so in a credible fashion that provides value in many ways to those who use the label. Rather than taking a purist approach or requiring something inflexible and costly, the menu-based approach of the LEED ecolabel combines a mixture of public *and* private benefits to those who adopt the label. Flexibility offers builders and other users a variety of ways to participate in and benefit from the certification program, as we discuss in more detail in Chapter 5. In addition, the LEED approach of structuring in tiers, with a fairly low-cost entry threshold, encourages builders to join and learn the program – and also to upgrade to the next tier whenever feasible. Add in an ongoing process of ratcheting up the standards over time, and you get a LEED ecolabel that is driving a race to the top. We see this in Chapter 8.

Other important contextual factors also play a role in LEED's catalytic success. By certifying the green quality of buildings, the ecolabel approach combines high visibility for the label and brand. Its focus on buildings entails multisectoral, supply-chain issues, and that brings greater potential for spillover across sectors and within a sector. Joining the Green Building Movement can be "contagious," where adopters "infect" their competitors, their suppliers, and their customers, who in turn spread the adoption. The peer effects of learning from one another and racing to "keep up with the Joneses" are strong drivers of the ecolabel's success and diffusion. Further, the scope of the label includes many aspects of the built environment that are already regulated by conventional public policy means and that look to be areas for increasing regulatory stringency in the future. Combined with the promise that energy- and water-efficient buildings can reduce firms' dependency on volatile input prices, adopting LEED can also help builders reduce regulatory risk. Green buildings – especially those with a prominent ecolabel – can preempt regulation, get ahead of the regulatory curve, and even receive favorable attention from regulators. For example, the City of Atlanta energy benchmarking program exempts reporting requirements from LEED 4.0 participants. For major investments in very durable capital, the prospects of reducing future risks for long-lived investments carries great appeal. Further, the US Green Building Council and its extended family of related green-building certifications have created an atmosphere where there are positive returns to individuals' investments in learning the tricks of the green-building trade. The business case for many green-building attributes is ever easier to make in this kind of environment with organizational learning. Larger organizations can use the ecolabel to realize efficiency gains. Realizing those gains make future adoption all the more likely. Moreover, as individuals gain (transportable) expertise in green buildings, organizations that implement processes to support investing in a particular green building may find future green building to be easier even after the current green building project is complete. Pay the one-time costs to learn the standards and join the green building "club," and subsequent green building projects become easier to fund. The LEED system has a kind of momentum-building investment for both organizations and individuals. Marketing benefits become more apparent and recognizable to a variety of stakeholders when there is a strong, visible, and stable brand (and collection of standards) such as LEED's. This helps create the conditions for continued growth and diffusion in the industry.

References

Chegut, A., P. Eichholtz, and N. Kok. 2019. "The Price of Innovation: An Analysis of the Marginal Cost of Green Buildings." *Journal of Environmental Economics and Management* 98: 102248.

Fischer, Carolyn and Thomas P. Lyon. 2014. "Competing Environmental Labels." *Journal of Economics & Management Strategy* 23, no. 3: 692–716.

Li, Yuanhao and Klaas van 't Veld. 2015. "Green, Greener, Greenest: Eco-Label Gradation and Competition." *Journal of Environmental Economics and Management* 72: 164–176.

5 | The Public and Private Benefits of Green Building
Many Shades of Green

Introduction

Green buildings distinguish themselves from conventional buildings by their superior green designs, construction, and performance. But what does it really mean to be a better building in green terms? The essence of the LEED certification and of "greenness" generally is not a unidimensional or simple concept. It is a multidimensional, complex menu of various attributes all bundled together. Even something as simple as being a "bigger" building is not so simple. Bigger might be in terms of interior square footage, cubic footage, lot size, height, or something else. And "greener" is far more complex than that. It entails a variety of environmental impacts, building performance, and better experiences for those inside the building and beyond.

There are many different shades of green buildings. Their superior environmental performance can include things like energy efficiency or water efficiency; using cleaner and lower carbon energy sources; sourcing construction materials with sustainable practices; or site selection for the buildings so as to reuse and rehabilitate brownfields or encourage use of public transportation or bicycles. The range of different environmental impacts of green building construction and operation, and thus fall under the broad umbrella of an ecolabel like LEED, is very, very wide. A green building standard like LEED incorporates these very different dimensions into a single, unifying standards and incentive system. The multidimensional nature of "greenness" for green building is an essential feature of these ecolabels and the Green Building Movement more broadly. The holistic approach to greener buildings embraces flexibility, diversity, and innovation over strictly prescriptive or one-size-fits-all approaches. Yet with this multidimensionality and flexibility comes great variety and potential confusion about what green building means.

Green buildings are about much more than the building's "footprint." They also include environmental qualities and amenities for those who are inside the building and those who contributed to its construction. On the inside of the building, indoor air quality, daylighting, better air and water emissions, and other factors contribute to the experience of the users. This is distinct from the "footprint" or spillovers (externalities) created by operating a building. Yet the LEED design principles encompass both internal and external issues in the same system. People on the outside of the building may never know about or directly benefit from the cleaner indoor air that tenants enjoy, but that greener building still yields important benefits to its users and owners.

Established in 2014 by the International WELL Building Institute, WELL is a building certification scheme that represents its own unique shade of green in the ecolabel sphere by measuring the performance of building features with the goal of creating healthy buildings in which people spend most of their time. This health and wellbeing focus conveys private benefits to the building owner by creating a more pleasant environment inside the building and signaling the building's quality to the market to attract tenants. Although the improved building quality and health benefits offered by the certification are public in the sense that users of the building benefit from them, the goal of the certification scheme is less to provide a public good to the whole community or society and more to provide private benefits to the users of the building. WELL demonstrates the diversity of pathways to green building while still adhering to the Green Building Movement's goal of creating more positive impacts from the built environment.

We note the many different approaches available as we start to categorize the various ways that an ecolabel like LEED incentivizes and certifies elements of green design. One approach might be to separate out energy, water, air, land, and materials and rate the green design in terms of its impact on these different environmental media. One could also take different parts of the construction and operation processes to differentiate among the various activities that are creditable as "green" and those that are not. Of course, there are other approaches to structuring the multidimensional nature of green buildings. We focus on two main dimensions of green building attributes.

First, we consider the *publicness* or spillover (externality) nature of the green attributes. Some of the greenness of a building is experienced only by the owners, users, visitors, etc. There are other LEED credits which reflect green attributes that people can enjoy regardless of whether they own the property or go on-site, because they might share the same watershed, the same airshed, or other aspects of the building's external or public footprint. Accounting for this public-versus-private distinction is crucial for many reasons, including the social impact of a building, marketing and ownership issues, or corporate social responsibility. Publicness in an ecolabel involves a role for the certification signal for attributes that are not confined to the property and users. We explore this key, unconventional dimension in the next section.

The second main dimension of interest to us here refers to the extent to which the buildings' performance attributes are visible. It can be hard for outsiders – those who do not build, own, or occupy the building – to observe or verify the green qualities of a building. This lack of visibility gives rise to the importance of ecolabels (see Chapter 2) while also inevitably making some amount of "noise" or imprecision in that signal. Building designers and owners can take advantage of that imprecision to demonstrate more abstract qualities like management quality and environmental values, even if the building's tangible performance features are not as impressive. Noisiness and lack of visibility allow some projects to prioritize a *marketing signal* over verification of actual building performance indicators.

Most stakeholders cannot tell the difference between a "marketing" project and a "performance" project. There might well be two "green" buildings with the same level of green certification, but the certification alone does not tell the market about the distinct paths the building designers took in constructing the project. In an extreme example, one "upgrading" building might have done the bare minimum to achieve the signal, taken advantage of cheap options, and claimed credits for attributes that would have been present anyway. At the other end of the spectrum, a similarly rated "performance" building might have invested far more in more effective green technologies, overperformed in reaching its certification level, and so on. Despite the first building being at the bottom end of its tier, both buildings receive the same marketing advantages, even though the buildings have very different environmental performance characteristics. These buildings may be experientially similar and observationally identical to the investor, employee, or occupant of the building who only observes the ecolabel sticker on the outside.

The core issue for this second dimension involves going beyond minimum requirements in ways that the designer and investor do not take credit for. This "undue modesty" has been explored in other settings (Kim and Lyon 2015). In Chapter 8, we argue that participation in ecolabel programs can create a race to the top wherein some firms go above and beyond, competing to be the "greenest," thus catalyzing market transformation toward green building as standard practice. This variety of goals and behaviors in green building certification is a direct result of the fuzzy, open "menu" approach to green building certification design discussed in Chapters 3 and 4. It allows for different degrees of greenwashing, as a direct result of the design of the certification scheme, and that becomes the focus for this second dimension of green building certification. We can think of some buildings as prioritizing the marketing signal, and other buildings as valuing the signal less and the building performance more. Whether a building falls on one end of the spectrum or another is important for appreciating the incentives and reasons for participating in the green building enterprise.

These two dimensions of greenness for green buildings – *publicness* and *marketing* – can have important interactions with one another. It is possible to have a green building that emphasizes performance but predominantly invests in credits that produce private benefits. Conversely, it is possible to have a building that barely meets minimal standards but tends to pursue credits with public and external benefits. Of course, if we see a building that is doing the minimal compliance and tending to implement predominantly private benefiting activities, then we might want to view that project as one of greenwashing. The other end of the spectrum involves a marketing orientation that tends to favor public and external benefits, something we might associate with an ideal form of corporate social responsibility. Figure 5.3 gives an example of how we might see these different combinations of these two attributes help us describe the variety of participation in green buildings.

Measuring Publicness and Marketing for Green Buildings

Of course, ecolabels themselves do not categorize the creditable attributes or activities along these two dimensions. For an ecolabel like LEED, the categories for creditable attributes are typically organized along different dimensions. Some categories – like those involving indoor environmental quality – have relatively clear and objective ways to classify the creditable attributes in terms of our two dimensions. Most other LEED credit categories, however, do not tell us much about the nature of the environmental impacts of the various credits. And the relative importance of the green signal versus the enhanced building performance is generally unrelated to specific creditable attributes because of the "menu" nature of holistic green building ecolabels. For a building that is, say, four points above the threshold for LEED Silver, we do not know which of its many green attributes were the ones that took them over the threshold (i.e., which ones were the incremental credits). Rather than review here the basics of the way that LEED structures its creditable attributes, we focus in this chapter on a different way to see the mix of activities for each building and observing what that mix can tell us. There are, after all, many shades of green when it comes to green buildings.

Evaluating whether a particular attribute or activity is more externally or internally beneficial for a particular building depends considerably on context. Many of the credit activities have both substantial internal and external benefits. Thus, this might not be a binary distinction, but rather a continuum between internal and external. For some of the activities, however, the distinction is more clear-cut. Buying renewable energy credits, for example, has no appreciable internal or private benefit, but rather simply affects, ideally, larger issues such as greenhouse-gas emissions and developing markets for lower carbon energy sources. Similarly, activities such as the sourcing of renewable materials (public) or using low-emission interior paints (private) will have fairly unambiguous impacts.

The marketing signal presents more difficulty in assessing. We start our assessment of the marketing signal by examining the extent of overperforming without pushing to the next certification tier. This certainly depends on the decisions and processes that lead to various activities being pursued. It can also involve a more holistic sense of the green building overall, rather than simply a credit-by-credit assessment. We can see that some buildings may enjoy the same LEED certification signal despite one building doing far more to earn it. Furthermore, some buildings may find it extremely easy to gain certain credits, while other buildings may find it far more costly to do the same. For instance, rural buildings often lack realistic access to certain density- and location-specific credits under LEED. When the building designer takes all the easy gains in terms of low-cost investment for LEED credit, it looks like simply smart, cost-minimizing business practice. Thus, it is even more remarkable for buildings and investors that go above and beyond the regular cost-minimizing expectations to implement something far more costly, with a low or even negative return on investment, and then earn the LEED credit but not any additional green signal. In the aggregate, we can see a diversity of approaches taken to earning LEED credits. As discussed later in this chapter, within this diversity there are distinct patterns emerging that show the prevalence of marketing to upgrade – gaining just enough credits to earn a particular ecolabel signal – while also indicating that many building projects indeed go above and beyond what is necessary for that signal. Many buildings clearly find substantial benefits from improved building performance, even if their ecolabel does not reflect those particular improvements.

From the Builders' Perspectives

From the perspective of the builder, these dimensions of greenness are important and practical to contemplate. The open menu and many possible combinations of creditable activities in the LEED system present a large set of choices for any builder seeking to certify their building as green. Of course, there are incentives for builders to invest in internal or private benefits from certain activities. They may also get the benefits of having a green label for their project. A more prosocial mission, some corporate social responsibility, or other circumstances may help builders prioritize the more public and external orientation of certain credible activities. The mere fact that these activities provide benefits to others rather than themselves can enhance the reputation of the building owners, operators, and users, with attendant benefits that have been chronicled in the research literature. (See examples in An and Pivo 2020; Eichholtz et al. 2012; Lanfranchi and Pekovic 2014; Palacios et al. 2020; Singh et al. 2010; and Turban and Greening 1997.)

Then, beyond this public-versus-private distinction, there are matters of picking the preferred tier for certification, deciding how many credits to pursue, and other marketing-oriented decisions. Some buildings certify but remain confidential. Other buildings merely register, not doing enough to earn certification. And yet some buildings become green on their own and do not seek external certification or verification of any sort. How a builder markets and takes credit for its green investments presents an important part of the decision. Our Chapter 7 on pilot projects points to an important aspect of green buildings from the builder's perspective, where some builders prioritize being seen as leaders in their sector or peer group. The interest of some builders to lead and inspire change is an important part of the above compliance dimension of some green buildings, especially those at the vanguard for their particular situation. The LEED certification system itself gives credit to projects that help service demonstrations or visible exemplars of green buildings for their communities. This marketing and promotional aspect takes several different forms and is clearly quite important. While these types of credits are often derided for not adding any sustainable features to the building, from our research the dissemination of information about LEED or other advanced buildings is incredibly important for the overall adoption patterns.

By its very design, LEED certification does not permit much credit-taking for activities that lack demonstrable and meaningful green impact. Of course, it is possible that some of the green elements to a new building would have occurred or been implemented without the LEED certification scheme. For instance, a new building may have its locations prescribed for non-LEED reasons, yet that location may nonetheless provide it with a reward in the LEED accounting system. But for the most part, the activities that LEED certifies and rewards are those that will have some positive green effect, whether it is public or private.

Importance of the Marketing Signal

Ecolabels providing a noisy signal means ambiguity in the link between building quality and the certification. These voluntary signals may fulfill a vital function in mitigating information problems, but there are limits. Allowing some flexibility in how a building attains certification creates wiggle room for building designers and owners to work strategically. Building performance is just one part of LEED certification. The Green Building Movement relies heavily on symbolic values and marketing signals to convey information about building performance, organizational commitment and competence, and other factors. (Here, and throughout this book, we use the terms "marketing signal" and "marketing value" interchangeably to refer to this concept.)

An Ecolabel for Building Performance or Marketing an Upgrade?

Our exploration of the diversity of approaches taken in building green – the many shades of green – begins with the harder question of "how important is the marketing *signal*?" The ecolabel conveys some green distinction on the building, and it generally does not (and cannot) perfectly detail all its green attributes. A LEED Platinum building may be "greener" than a LEED Silver building, but those certifications tell us little or nothing about the particulars of what makes the building green. Yet the marketing signal itself still matters. For particular ecolabels with tiers like LEED or BREEAM, which tier is achieved also matters. The marketing rewards from "going green" increase with each tier. Hence, incentives to "upgrade" and achieve certified status – or one tier better – can be important. Beyond the green attributes and the performance gains they entail, the ecolabel or certification tier matters in and of itself. Compliance with rules or stakeholder expectations may be satisfied by the certification alone, not particular creditable attributes. Some constituents may value the greenness more holistically, appreciating the overall achievement or tier attained rather than any specific green performance benefits. Some projects prioritize the marketing signal itself – not the greener building performance – in building green.

To help see this, consider a canonical competitive, profit-maximizing firm. Econ 101 tells us that a firm chooses its level of production such that its cost to produce another unit exactly equals that unit's sale price. In a slightly more complex setting where the firm can also make energy-efficiency investments, the firm jointly determines its optimal investment level and the optimal output level. If energy-efficiency investments are both costly and reduce production costs, the firm faces two simultaneous balancing acts. First, it balances the revenue it gets from another unit of output with its costs from growing its output by another unit. Second, it balances capital outlay for investment in energy efficiency with the savings it will enjoy from improved production output performance. In general, we should expect firms to invest in *some* energy efficiency and produce *some* output.

This basic model shows an efficient or cost-saving principle for investing in energy efficiency. However, outside the impacts of productivity, a firm may also gain a competitive marketing advantage from upgrading its efficiency investment. A "green" signal to the market from a green certification or clearly environmentally minded investment is thought to accrue benefit to the firm. Firms that upgrade to take advantage of this seem greener to consumers and can potentially increase demand and market share, charge premiums for their products, or otherwise influence the price they charge. Firms that can recognize that their green investments translate into increases to the sales price they command face somewhat different tradeoffs. They still equate the cost of another unit of output with their sale price on the first margin. But now in order to maximize profits, they must also balance their cost-savings *plus* their added per-unit revenue with their investment costs for another unit of energy-efficiency investment. Put another way, with a marketing impact from upgrading, the firm invests *more* in energy efficiency because it realizes the dual benefits of lower costs (productivity gains) and higher prices (marketing gains).

Hypothetically, if additional increments of investment in energy efficiency garnered no marketing gains, we would expect to see those investments stop at that point. This is especially relevant if the signal provided by green investments is only earned when some threshold level of investment has been achieved (i.e., when the firm has enough credits to certify). The discontinuous or "lumpy" price impacts of additional efficiency investments observed in green signaling mechanisms complicate the simple decision-making model put forth here. In a more realistic, lumpy setting, we expect to see that optimal energy efficiency investments rise when there are marketing gains from upgrading. But once the threshold has been passed and there are no additional price premiums to be gained from incremental investments, the firm would stop buying more energy efficiency (except for the amount that saves costs by improving productivity, as discussed earlier in this chapter). In an extreme example where there were no productivity gains and only marketing gains, we would expect firms to invest up until the thresholds where they obtain marketing gains and the revenue gains must be greater or equal to the cost of upgrading to that threshold. We would expect to see firms only invest (a) in zero units of energy efficiency or (b) in amounts right at thresholds for marketing gains. At the other extreme, where the investments only confer productivity gains and no marketing gains from upgrading, we would expect firms' investments to vary more smoothly or continuously with their production and investment costs. Likely, reality lies somewhere between these two extremes, causing some (but not perfect) clustering in energy efficiency investment values around the certification threshold(s). Many projects will have zero extra investments, some will do exactly enough to just reach a threshold to attain a particular tier, and some will go above and beyond to optimize cost savings that extend beyond marketing gains.

Moreover, while we expect that reality is somewhere between the extremes (investment in green attributes is a cost-saving investment versus green investment is an unproductive green signal), we have no strong priors about where along the continuum the empirical evidence will lie. However, given that certifying alone incurs cost (e.g., obtaining any level of LEED certification costs more than just investing in greener building without registering with the US Green Building Council), among the firms that seek some green certification we expect the threshold effects and thus clustering to be nontrivial in size.

Green building projects are often undertaken by government entities or nonprofits, where this profit-maximizing model may not apply well.[1] If we think of these agencies as maximizing output, rather than profit, then the model predictions change very little. This is largely because the intuition remains under conditions of budget constraints in these agencies. Agency directors still hope to lower costs or raise prices as long as they can increase output (as opposed to increase profit, as in for-profit firms). Nonprofits and government agencies still balance their energy-efficiency investment costs with their productivity and marketing gains. In this case, raising "prices" can be understood as obtaining greater support for their mission in the form of appropriations or donations. Perhaps the only difference is that we would expect total output and total investment in energy efficiency to simply be greater for nonprofits than for for-profit firms – assuming they possess identical production technology and face identical product demands – because of their objective to expand output as far as they can afford. In that case, we might imagine that there are some marketing thresholds out there that would be reached, and thus clustered at, by nonprofits that would not be worthwhile for for-profit firms. Thus, even more clustering might be observed for nonprofits and government agencies than for for-profit firms. If, alternatively, (marketing) upgrading gains are smaller for the output produced by a government agency, perhaps because they do not market their green

---

[1] While this chapter develops some theory and provides empirical evidence surrounding firm participation in green-building programs, nonprofit organizations and governments undertake a large portion of green building. Much less is known about the motivations for these actors to certify green-building practices. This is disappointing, especially when we see the prevalence of green buildings *outside* of the commercial, for-profit sector. Moreover, because those highly visible public investments have helped inspire and educate others, they are key player in the green building market transformation. Yet the drivers of adoption of green buildings by nonprofits and governments – aside from simple responses to regulatory mandates – remains underexplored in the scholarly literature.

signal as much or as effectively (or there are no competing firms so price is not set competitively anyway), then it is possible that, even for firms with identical technologies, an agency would invest less in energy efficiency than a for-profit firm would (and thus possibly less clustering would be observed because those threshold effects are smaller).

How Much Is Marketing for the "Upgrading" Signal versus Building Performance?

To what extent is LEED certification intended to achieve a productive input and to what extent is it intended to achieve a greener marketing signal? To test this, we observe the amount of clustering at the thresholds of LEED tiers and compare this number of firms to what we might otherwise expect from a smooth distribution of LEED scores. One advantage of LEED being a noisy signal is that the wiggle room in terms of actual credits earned and tier achieved gives a lot of flexibility to builders in how they get certified. By digging into the details on each project's certified green attributes, we can see distinct patterns in that noise. The data implicitly reveal striking patterns about how much each project prioritized reaching the next threshold – marketing for the upgrading signal – and how much they overshot the threshold with an eye to marketing for their building performance across a host of creditable attributes. Just like the model of builder decision-making described in the previous section shows, builders can – and do – take different approaches to certification and prioritize different sorts of signal values from LEED.

We unpack thousands of LEED-certified building projects to observe these different approaches taken. Public LEED project data were accessed from the USGBC website. This information included the total LEED project score and project details about the builder, location, size, and owner. To ensure the sample was consistent, the data analyzed were limited to new construction projects in the United States that utilized LEED scoring versions 2009 and v4.

Figure 5.1 shows a very distinct pattern of upgrading behavior where the total LEED score earned tends to cluster right at the minimum threshold needed for a particular certification tier. As shown in the figure, there is a very strong tendency for LEED buildings to earn the bare minimum number of credits or near the threshold number of credits to attain a certain level of certification. It is far more common to

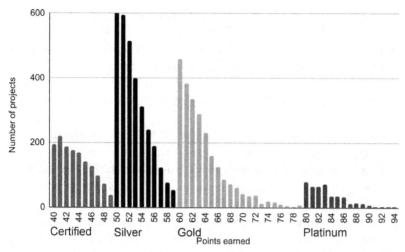

Figure 5.1 Upgrading behavior in LEED NC v2009-v4 certification scores

be at or just above the threshold to the next level than it is to be one or two credits short of the next certification tier. Taken at face value, those projects that go well above the minimum needed to obtain their certification tier, although they are fewer in number, reflect something special about their building design process and ambitions for making a green building project. More than half of all projects exceed the minimum threshold for their tier by at least two points. Clearly, there is more at play for those projects than simply the marketing signal from LEED. We would expect many projects that might naturally find themselves just shy of the requirements to go up a tier will find a way to make the investment to gain one or two extra points and improve their tier. This is reflected very clearly in the data. Also, as mentioned in Chapter 4, this additive menu-based approach in the design of the LEED certification system gives incentives to those projects to upgrade and jump up a tier. Although that might make the upgrading builder look a bit cynical in their operation and design, that upgrading behavior should bring an undeniably positive green impact and reflect the willingness of builders to make costly investments to achieve that upgraded signal. Cynical or not, these are real investments and real positive environmental gains.

Based on the values in Figure 5.1, it is apparent that more buildings earn the Silver certification than would in a smoother distribution, while fewer earn the Certified and Platinum designations. These results suggest that the Certified level does not capture sufficient marketing benefits, or that green-signaling competition drives firms toward Silver certification but not to higher levels of certification. In addition, it suggests that because costs increase as certification tiers rise, these costs may outweigh the marketing and performance benefits of higher tiers.

The data also show that there are some buildings that earn points close to the upper end of the point range within each certification level. This may indicate that some project teams seek LEED certification without paying close attention to the threshold levels, instead prioritizing building performance benefits. In contrast, prior research has indicated that project owners choose their target certification level and custom select a combination of LEED credits that will reach this level (Corbett and Muthulingam 2007). The data in Figure 5.1 demonstrate that a mix of these behaviors are at play.

Marketing benefits from upgrading play a significant role in a building owner's motivation to certify with LEED, but they impact LEED projects on the margin the most – when moving from just below a certification threshold to just above that threshold. Being able to signal via upgrading obviously plays a major role for those projects that are stacked up at the thresholds in Figure 5.1. What else can we say about how these upgrading projects differ from others? We can examine whether the tendency to pursue an upgrading strategy differs by the type of owner, the purpose or sector of the building, and even the types of credits being earned. There are indeed many shades of green here, so we do not expect to see any hard-and-fast differences between the upgraders and those emphasizing the label to market their building's performance. Yet even an arm's length analysis of the data can reveal some interesting patterns in the data. Notably, when we compare projects that are just above a threshold with those just below – say 59 points (Silver) versus 60 points (Gold) – then we do not expect to see massive differences between these projects on average. Sure, the ones just above the threshold will have earned an extra point or two, but it would indeed be strange if those upgraders were much more likely to be nonprofits, industrial buildings, or some other type.

We employ a statistical technique here that leverages this comparison – projects just above each tier's threshold versus those just below – to see if there is a sharp contrast in the characteristics of projects on either side of the threshold. This statistical technique (sometimes called the "notches" technique) is based on an approach called regression discontinuity. In regression discontinuity, an arbitrary threshold is introduced to determine whether a treatment, administered at random, produces an effect. For example, a canonical example is the "treatment" of being admitted to honors and gifted programs and its' impacts on future success. When students are taking the exam to be admitted to honors and gifted, they do not know what the cutoff will be, nor do they have any reason to do strategically worse or better on the exam. The cutoff is determined by the percentile performance of the student. Students performing above or equal to the 95th percentile are moved to a gifted track. Below the 95th percentile, students remain with the rest of the children. Yet the difference between a student at the 95th percentile and the 94th percentile is likely negligible – this difference is most certainly within the margin of error in the test, and we can comfortably assume that any difference in the performance of students at the 94th and 95th percentiles is random. Yet the students who scored in the 95th percentile are moved into the gifted program, and the students in the 94th percentile are not. While the students at the 94th and 95th percentile are identical, there has been a discontinuous treatment applied. We can evaluate outcomes of the gifted program by comparing outcomes (graduation rates; college admission; lifetime earnings; etc.) of those students who were at the 95th percentile and were treated with the gifted program against the outcomes of those at the 94th percentile and were not treated with the program.

Of course, with green building certification, the builders and ownership teams know, a priori, what the thresholds are for each certification tier. The certification tier is not applied at random after the buildings are built – the builders can take the scoring system into account as they design and build the building. We can use this knowledge of the thresholds as a way to test the impact of the certification design on the strategic behavior of the participants. If the certification tiers do not matter, or if builders only pay attention to the total amount of points accrued by the building, we would expect that there is a smooth distribution of points on either side of the threshold. That is, there should not be a big difference in the number of buildings receiving 58 or 59 points, receiving silver, and the number of buildings receiving 60 or 61 points and receiving gold. From a performance perspective, these buildings are nearly equivalent. One or two individual points may represent a very small investment in renewable energy credits or other minor building upgrade. But from a certification perspective, these couple of points move the building from the Silver certification tier to the Gold certification tier. From a strategic perspective, we believe that some building owners and building teams see it as worthwhile to invest some additional resources to upgrade to the next tier.

The challenge of course is that some buildings would have ended up in the next tier, achieving a 60 or 61 even without pursuing upgrading behavior. To this end we need to estimate a counterfactual distribution of what the distribution buildings might have looked like even without upgrading behavior. To do this, we exclude the scores around the upgrading threshold and draw a smooth distribution representing the counterfactual distribution of what we expect to have happened in the absence of the discontinuities at the thresholds. When we compare what actually happened in real life (with the pronounced discontinuities at the thresholds) to the smooth counterfactual distribution, we are able to calculate the excess number of buildings built at a higher ecolabel tier as result of the ecolabel design. (See more details about this approach in Flowers et al. (2019) and Matisoff et al. (2014).) We are looking for a sharp *discontinuity* associated with the threshold itself, an artificial feature in the design of the ecolabel rather than something that should normally be expected to create differences in upgraders and non-upgraders. After all, if green building was exclusively about building performance, then projects with 59 points would look a lot like those with 60 points. In other words, there is nothing about getting 60 points rather than 59 points that should make upgrading projects more likely to be residential or located in urban areas. The menu-based approach of LEED supports this approach of looking for discontinuities at thresholds, too, because the many paths to reach 59 *or* 60 points makes it exceedingly unlikely that we should see systematically different portfolios of credits earned at 59 points versus 60 points.[2] The only reason we expect to see significant

---

[2] A careful reader might rightly note that, of course, we do expect that – on average – projects upgrading to just above a threshold will tend to have more of *all* credit types than those just below the threshold. After all, by design, the one thing we know for certain in comparing those just above with those just below is that the upgraders have a slightly higher score. Our approach here – based on a technique known as regression discontinuity design – takes this fact into account. Basically, the analysis identifies any baseline trend across the full spectrum of

Table 5.1. *Tendencies of upgraders at various LEED tiers*

Silver upgraders	Gold upgraders	Platinum upgraders
More indoor	Less indoor	More private
More innovation	More innovation	Less indoor
Less materials	More materials	More innovation
Less sustainable sites	More sustainable sites	Less sustainable sites
More water efficiency	More for-profit	Less water efficiency
Less for-profit	Less civic	Less for-profit
More nonprofit	More commercial	More nonprofit
More civic	Less industrial	Less civic
More commercial		More commercial
More industrial[a]		More residential
Less residential		

[a] Also, more healthcare and hospitality.

differences at the threshold would be if there was, in fact, something "special" or different about those projects that prioritized marketing for upgrading.

This analysis demonstrates differences in signaling strategies used at increasing LEED certification tiers. Table 5.1 reports the results of this discontinuity analysis to observe differences in signalers compared to those who do not upgrade and reveals the green practices more commonly pursued for signaling purposes. Signalers are more likely to choose credits for indoor environmental quality and water efficiency at the Silver level and are drawn to credits with purely public benefits. Conversely, at this level buildings also tend to earn significantly fewer materials and resources credits. As the tier level increases, different

points and controls for that. So, if the baseline likelihood of a project being owned by a government agency is steadily increasing across the range of points from 40 to 90, then our examination of potential discontinuities at the thresholds is looking for sharp departures from that baseline trend right around the threshold. Thus, for example, the number of points earned for water efficiency credits is, on average, rising as we look across projects earning more and more total points. Our approach controls for that and narrows its focus on right around the threshold to see if there is a break in that trend. Perhaps those just above the Gold threshold tend to earn more water efficiency credits than those just below, much more than we would expect from the baseline. Or, perhaps more strikingly, upgraders tend to earn fewer water efficiency credits than those just below the threshold. Our approach detects these kinds of differences, ones that we can associate with projects prioritizing marketing signals for upgrading.

patterns emerge. Signalers more often take advantage of site selection credits at the Gold level, but less often make energy or cost-saving improvements. At the Platinum level, the focus shifts to more private returns via cost-saving, energy efficiency, and innovation credits. We also divide the sample by building type. Civic buildings tend to upgrade only for Silver certification. Commercial buildings dispropor-tionately tend to upgrade at all tiers, while residential and industrial buildings are especially unlikely to be upgraders at Silver and Gold tiers, respectively. These results show that organizations typically cer-tify strategically to avoid high-cost resource use, and that designers at the highest tier differ from others in their pursuit of private benefits and energy efficiency gains.

We can see the relevance of marketing or signaling effects of ecola-bels when we start looking across sectors or industries in the building sector. We might expect that highly competitive industries are ones that have less overcompliance and more performance focus. We might expect public-sector buildings to be more inclined toward performance signaling, to value public-oriented credits, or to seek to influence private markets through leadership in implementation. Yet the results in Table 5.1 suggest that such clear-cut expectations are not always borne out in the data. There is not a strong tendency for competitive sectors (e.g., commercial, hospitality, industrial) to eschew upgrading; if anything, we see the opposite. The for-profit sector appears to favor upgrading to Gold but avoids it for Silver or Platinum. For-profits disproportionately pursue signals for building performance at the high end of the Certified and Gold tiers. Public-sector buildings, conversely, are no more or less likely to bunch at any of the thresholds. This result may be among the most surprising, as we might expect a tendency toward upgrading behavior among government buildings that are more likely subject to regulations requiring certification. It appears that any upgrading tendency induced by regulation is offset by a tendency to also prioritize building performance. In practice, there is a great mix of green building practices.

Beyond the prevalence of this upgrading behavior in the pursuit of green building certifications, the importance of this upgrading signal can be seen in the importance of the symbolic value – attaining par-ticular tiers or status – on others' building behavior. We explore this more in Chapters 6–8 by examining the effects of demonstration projects and "peer effects" in the industry. Just looking at these

3,000 new construction projects, we can see evidence of strong spillovers and "contagion" in adoption of green buildings to others in the same regional market. Chiang-Hsieh and Noonan (2017) show that it is not just that green buildings tend to spatially cluster in "hot spots" where the Green Building Movement has taken root in a region. They show that the tendencies to signal for upgrading benefits also exhibit very strong spatial concentrations. Green buildings often pop up where other green building are already growing, and those projects with upgrading signals compound or drive this effect. While government-owned projects do tend to upgrade due to local regulations, the peer effects of the upgrading signaling behavior are powerful. More nonprofit-owned LEED buildings in a city leads to more upgrading behavior in the private sector in that city. Local competition and spillover promotes more green building, especially for marketing around upgrading and the green status of buildings.

Publicness of the LEED Credits Earned

Next, we turn our attention to the other dimension of ecolabels for green buildings: Publicness. In reality, green certification frequently embodies a mix of private and public good considerations, in a hybrid of these two pure signaling types. Improved environmental behavior may provide a private rate of return, in the form of improved energy and water efficiency or improved employee productivity (and retention and recruiting). These same improvements might reduce an organization's environmental footprint, providing some positive externalities. Joining the green club of the ecolabel may have some cost-savings in addition to conferring reputational benefits. Conversely, the greener production process or product itself may simply be of higher quality (i.e., private benefit) for consumers even if it also involves less environmental harm. The signal enables the market for the high-quality good, which, in turn, yields environmental benefits. Because participants vary in the mix of public and private benefits produced for certification, the type of quality signaled by certification is not uniform.

Some aspects of green buildings reduce environmental harms associated with the construction or operation of a building. These environmental harms can include local pollution, greenhouse gas emissions, increased automobile traffic, unsustainably sourced building materials, etc. These environmental harms fall on those outside of the building or property. Reducing these spillovers or externalities represents an important public benefit of green buildings. Yet not all attributes of green buildings involve reducing harm to others. Third parties do not directly benefit from cleaning the indoor air quality, improving daylighting, or ensuring thermal comfort. These benefits are referred to as private benefits because the owners or occupants of the building are the direct beneficiaries. Of course, some green attributes of buildings provide *both* private and public benefits. For instance, improvements in water efficiency allow a building to operate with less water. This saves on utility costs, a private benefit for the owner, while also reducing the building's impact on the watershed, a public benefit. Many green building ecolabels include attributes with public benefits as well as those with private benefits. The LEED green building label includes some credits thought to reduce a building's production costs and improve employee productivity, though other credits do not have such private benefits.

We categorize LEED credits as private or public based on the extent to which the improvement would provide a return on investment for building owners or tenants, regardless of certification. Credits may generate private returns when they reduce resource costs or improve productivity by enhancing occupant (user) experience. While this categorization provides a simple way to discuss public versus private credits, it is important to note that the design of the LEED system intends every credit to be associated with at least some external environmental benefit. We accept this claim as an assumption for our delineation of credits' publicness. A key feature of LEED's credit system is that it is designed to encourage public good provision first, and it is largely successful in this. By default, each credit is associated as a public point. However, when it is possible to justify a green building strategy as providing a reduction of operating costs or additional employee productivity, the credit is reclassified as private. For example, improved indoor air quality as a result of outdoor air delivery monitoring and increased ventilation is thought to improve worker productivity. We classify credits for these strategies as private points, along with credits that lower utility costs through efficiency. Taking this approach acknowledges how most creditable attributes in the LEED system confer at least some positive environmental externality and provide some public goods. Almost a quarter of all available credits in the LEED menu are "pure" public goods in the sense that they confer no direct private benefit to the building owner. The other credits offer mixes of private and public benefits to varying degrees.

Another remarkable feature of LEED, and a testament to how effective it is at encouraging public good provision, is the consistency with which these public-benefits attributes appear in certified projects. It is not like the lower-end (Certified only) projects tend to emphasize the private benefits and ignore these public-benefits credits while only the high-end projects can afford to take the prosocial stance and earn public-goods credit. Hardly. As Flowers et al. (2019) show, the share of credits earned for purely public credits is largely unchanged along the continuum of low scores to high scores. As seen in Table 5.1, there is not even a strong tendency for upgrading projects to (cynically) private-benefit credits. The only distinct pattern in terms of pursuing purely public-good oriented credits arises for those upgrading to Platinum. Here, these elite buildings actually tend to attain *more* of the private-benefit credits, largely because these are among the only remaining credits left on the menu as projects get into the rarefied air at the top of the LEED scoresheet.

We follow Flowers et al. (2019) in categorizing the many credits on LEED's menu into those with purely public benefits and those with at least some substantial private benefits. Figure 5.2 illustrates our categorizations. The use of certified wood in the construction of a building may help with deforestation or other concerns, broadly and globally, but generally would not yield a positive ROI for the building owner. Conversely, improved daylighting or using on-site renewables can easily have positive ROI upon which a builder can capitalize. Of course, other categorizations might reasonably be made, as a lot depends on assumptions being made about these attributes and considerable variation in local context matters. For example, reducing light pollution might yield public benefits without reducing (net) costs, which could justify placing it in the "purely public benefits" column. Nonetheless, the essence of this approach holds true regardless: the many creditable attributes of green buildings have varying degrees of publicness. As discussed more in Chapter 3, some attributes of sustainability have larger private ROIs while others might not be something the builder could ever (directly) capitalize on. Figure 5.2 shows one simple classification of LEED credits into a "more private" and a "pure

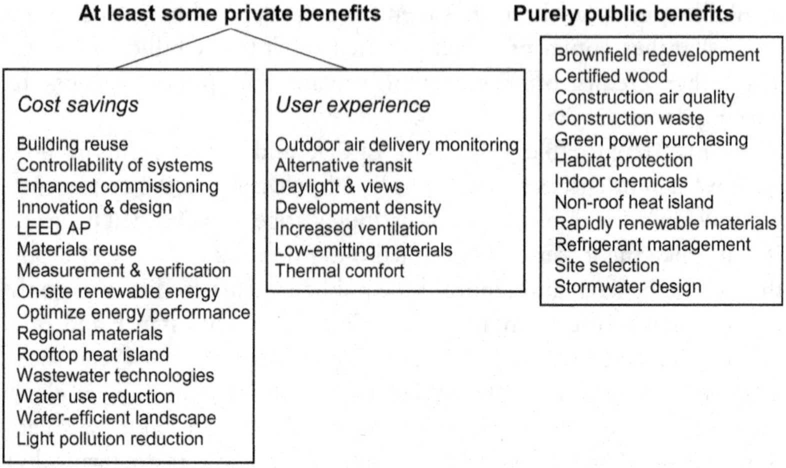

At least some private benefits   **Purely public benefits**

		Brownfield redevelopment

Cost savings

Building reuse
Controllability of systems
Enhanced commissioning
Innovation & design
LEED AP
Materials reuse
Measurement & verification
On-site renewable energy
Optimize energy performance
Regional materials
Rooftop heat island
Wastewater technologies
Water use reduction
Water-efficient landscape
Light pollution reduction

User experience

Outdoor air delivery monitoring
Alternative transit
Daylight & views
Development density
Increased ventilation
Low-emitting materials
Thermal comfort

Brownfield redevelopment
Certified wood
Construction air quality
Construction waste
Green power purchasing
Habitat protection
Indoor chemicals
Non-roof heat island
Rapidly renewable materials
Refrigerant management
Site selection
Stormwater design

Figure 5.2 LEED credit categories based on private and public benefit types

public" categorization. It bears emphasis that even credits the "private" category can provide substantial public benefits. In this sense, even our conservative approach that highlights the private ROIs to many LEED credits cannot help but implicitly emphasize that a great deal of LEED is dedicated to public good provision.

Bringing It Together: Publicness and Marketing Signal

A Typology of Certified Green Buildings

Green building behavior can be understood through a two-dimensional space that allows us to understand individual building strategies and motivations for green building certification. Firms who focus on a building's high performance who also provide public goods through the credits they earn can be considered altruists, or the ideal type. Firms that prioritize performance but also profit-maximizing private benefits are pragmatists, certifying wisely to increase business reputation. Firms that do just enough to earn the signal but do this through public good-providing benefits are green club members, who may be aiming for a green benchmark but do not feel the need to go above and beyond. Lastly, firms that just barely earn the signal and mainly collect private benefits are greenwashers, providing no extra significant environmental or performance quality but claiming a veneer of virtue through the ecolabel.

Figure 5.3 shows this typology along the two dimensions of signaling value and publicness. These dimensions align with the core elements of ecolabel design introduced in Chapter 3. Along the publicness dimension, green buildings differ in the extent to which their green attributes provide public benefits. Some projects might emphasize attributes that produce public goods and yield little or no direct benefit to the owners and operators. Other projects might still be "green" while emphasizing attributes that building users can benefit from, owners can capitalize on, and that have positive ROIs for investors. The signaling dimension refers to the signaling value being provided through the certification. Some projects use the ecolabel's marketing signal primarily for its building performance. The ecolabel helps these high-performance buildings credibly market their greener attributes that outsiders might otherwise find difficult to detect or verify. At the other end of the signaling spectrum are those that use the ecolabel's marketing signal for showing that they have upgraded to a greener status. These projects use ecolabel signals to market more symbolic values, a status reflecting pro-sustainability values that not so directly associate with particular building attributes. Figure 5.2 characterizes those projects depending on where they fit along these two dimensions of signaling value and publicness. We label as *Greenwashers* those who prioritize marketing value from upgrading status and who specialize in private-benefit green attributes. In the opposite corner, *Altruists* are those who emphasize building performance and producing pure public goods in their building. We term those who emphasize pure public-good provision while also prioritizing upgrading and symbolic status of their green buildings as *Members* of a green club. Finally, opposite from them, we have those *Pragmatists* who value signaling the building performance to recoup their investments in higher quality – both greener and productivity-enhancing attributes.

We should pause to note that this typology is loose-fitting in at least two important senses. First, though Figure 5.3 depicts quadrants in a two-dimensional graph as though they are simple categories, the fact is that there are *many shades* of green and each of these dimensions runs along a continuum. As we shall see shortly, many green building projects do not fall neatly into one of these characterizations. Many – if

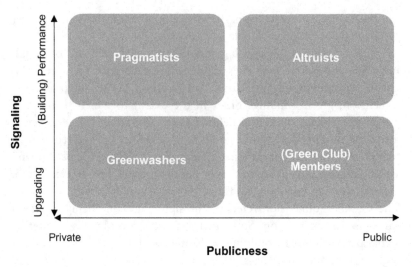

Figure 5.3 A typology of green buildings by signaling and environmental performance

not most! – projects resemble borderline cases. Second, the typology in Figure 5.2 must be taken as *relative* to the ecolabel design itself. As discussed in Chapters 3 and 4, ecolabels differ wildly in their design. Some designs, such as LEED, can skew everything toward more publicness. This would make even a Pragmatist in LEED look rather like an Altruist if they were to construct the same building under a different ecolabel regime. Similarly, the opportunity to use the ecolabel to market for upgrading value also depends on the label design.

A Closer Look: A Typology of LEED v2.2 Projects

Using proprietary data on each building's selected improvements that it earned credits for, we categorize project types based on this typology. Data on LEED v2.2 certified projects shows where different types of buildings tend to fall in the typology and trends in credits earned. For each project – the data points that give rise the sawtooth pattern in Figure 5.1 – we classify them as upgraders or not depending on whether their point total is at the threshold or just one or two points above it. This two-point allowance allows a buffer as some builders may intentionally or unintentionally overshoot their target threshold slightly.

(cont.)

Table 5.2. *Frequencies of types of LEED v2.2 projects*

		Private	Public	Totals
Marketing for	Performance	Pragmatists 526	Altruists 502	1,028
	Upgrading	Greenwashers 918	Members 1,035	1,953
	Totals	1,444	1,537	2,981

We see almost 2,000 or two-thirds of all projects fall within this two-point buffer of LEED thresholds. Next, we classify projects as being "public" if their share of credits earned from the purely public-goods attributes (see Figure 5.2) is above average. Those below-average projects, meaning more of their credits came from attributes with private ROIs, are classified on the "private" side of the typology. Table 5.2 shows the relative frequencies of projects in this typology. Given how we assign projects along the two dimensions (i.e., two-thirds are "upgraders" and half are "public"), it is remarkable to note how roughly even the distribution is across the four types. Among those signaling primarily for building performance, Pragmatists are roughly as common as Altruists. Among upgraders, Greenwashers are nearly as frequent Members.

This roughly even distribution across the typology may mask some underlying tendencies, especially for builders from different sectors. For instance, a cynic might expect buildings owned by for-profits to be more likely to fall into the Greenwasher quadrant, while nonprofits might be predisposed to be Altruists. Table 5.3 depicts the frequencies of each ownership type across the four groups in our typology. The initial takeaway from Table 5.3 is that the distribution of frequencies observed in Table 5.2 are essentially mimicked for each owner type in Table 5.3. At first glance, no strong tendency appears. But this approach crudely lumps all 2,981 projects into one of four categories. We know that many of the projects are "borderline" cases – projects that would fall in the white space in Figure 5.3. Thus, Table 5.3 also shows the frequency distribution of projects across our typology after dropping the borderline projects and retaining only the projects that more clearly distinguish themselves as belonging to one type or

(cont.)

Table 5.3. *Frequency of types of LEED New Construction by owner*

Owner	Members	Greenwashers	Altruists	Pragmatists
For-Profit	193 (31)	187 (30)	83 (8)	91 (20)
Government	592 (88)	501 (58)	303 (62)	298 (54)
Nonprofit	146 (15)	146 (21)	78 (17)	98 (11)
Other/Mixed	84 (10)	84 (12)	38 (7)	39 (6)

Note: Frequencies in parentheses represent counts of projects with borderline cases removed.

another.[3] That so many projects appear to have elements of more than one strategy (e.g., part Altruist and part Pragmatist) underscores the variety of strategies and behaviors when it comes to pursuing sustainability. In looking at the clear-cut cases – the counts in the parentheses in Table 5.3 – the distribution of ownership within each quadrant is *not* homogenous. For-profit firms differ in their frequencies compared to other ownership categories, and they appear to favor private benefits in certification. Also from Table 5.3, we note the attention government agencies pay to reducing negative externalities. Government agencies are more likely to certify in the green club Member or Altruist categories than other owner types, and on average earn more external credits as a share of the building score compared to for-profit firms and nonprofit organizations. Government agencies also build in more "cushion" to their certification compared to other owners, securing a threshold by earning on average an extra third of a credit. (This may indicate that government agencies, rather than being ignorant of the tiers, are simply more risk-averse when planning to certify at a particular level.) Interestingly, nonprofits are more likely to be upgrading – as Greenwashers or Altruists – and tend to pursue Member status much less than other owner types.

   Figure 5.4 offers another perspective on this typology across different owner types. This figure depicts the three main owner types of for-profit, nonprofit, and government as icons for skyscrapers, churches,

---

[3] Borderline cases are defined by being within one standard deviation of the vertical or horizontal axis in Figure 5.3. In this case, this means borderline cases are those whose LEED scores exceed the threshold by one point or more *or* those whose share of credits earned from public-goods credits are between 18.1 percent and 27 percent (as the mean, where the axis is located, is 22.58 percent).

(cont.)

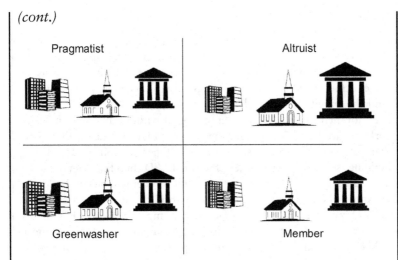

Figure 5.4 Relative frequencies of different green building strategies by owner type

and town halls, respectively. The size of the icon varies according to the relative frequency of projects in a particular quadrant. The Pragmatist quadrant serves as the baseline for each owner type: the size of its building icon in the other quadrants is proportionate to the frequency of projects by that owner group in that quadrant relative to the frequency of Pragmatists by that owner group. Thus, government buildings very frequently appear as Altruists (as indicated by the larger town hall) and nonprofit buildings infrequently appear as Members (as indicated by the smaller church). Perhaps contrary to our expectations, Greenwashers are not dominated by for-profit builders and nonprofits are not dominating the Altruist group. Rather, again, we see a wide range of approaches to green buildings being taken across the ownership spectrum.

In terms of trends observed in the types of LEED credits earned, regardless of public or private ownership and building type, LEED buildings on average earn over 70 percent of their credits from activities that yield private ROI, with very little variation. This point merits emphasis. While Figures 5.2–5.4 show wide variation in publicness for LEED green building projects, these are *relative* publicness scores. The reality is all LEED buildings rate highly in terms of providing public benefits, some very highly. (See Figure 4.1 for another

(cont.)

perspective on this.) Where there is variation, it seems that healthcare sector projects earn somewhat more public credits, while hospitality and residential projects focus more on private benefits. In terms of scores achieved, commercial buildings tend to earn more points overall, while hospitality, retail, and healthcare projects earn less. As is consistent with their priority of earning the signal without investing in costly performance upgrades, signalers tend to earn less points. Furthermore, there are distinct relationships between types of points earned and building setting. More water-efficient LEED buildings tend to be located in dense urban areas, while more energy-efficient buildings are more likely to be found in areas with high electricity prices. This shows how local and regional factors can impact which LEED credits are ultimately earned. Additionally, larger buildings tend to earn more public points, and urban buildings typically earn fewer total points, perhaps pointing to the limitations caused by additional costliness of developing in a dense urban setting.

Discussion of Certification Patterns

Differences in certification pathways across ownership categories suggest different drivers of decisions about sustainability practices. Practices that governments are likely to rely on are uncommon in for-profit firms. This suggests different procurement policies of for-profit firms or discrepancies in the way that various actors calculate returns on investment. For example, that governments are unlikely to obtain sustainable site selection credits suggests that political calculus may drive location preferences. In the private sector, firms are more likely to innovate for greater efficiency and higher performance as they obtain higher tiers of certification. While design innovation may pay off in the for-profit sector, it could be difficult to justify for government organizations. While the public and private sector appear equally disinterested in enhancing employee experience, government agencies justify efficiency investments at all tiers of certification. Differing managerial perspectives between the public and private sectors may drive the divergence in certification pathways, as public managers find ways to justify very different sustainability practices compared to firm decision-makers.

LEED has been criticized for not producing buildings that are more energy efficient than other buildings (Newsham et al. 2009; Reichardt 2014; Turner and Frankel 2008). Yet as electricity prices increase, and as projects certify at higher tiers, builders pursue more resource efficiency. At lower tiers, projects are more willing to provide public goods to meet certification requirements, potentially seeking generalized signals of quality rather than emphasizing building performance. To obtain higher tiers, builders are willing to pursue credits for which they have very high discount rates, including efficiency. Amplified general quality signals at higher tiers may help make efficiency enhancements more attractive to organizations that would not otherwise adopt these sustainability practices.

Assessing the practices organizations appear to use specifically to bump up to higher tiers of certification reveals how general marketing signals promote particular practices. For lower tiers of certification, organizations adopt practices that provide public goods in exchange for certification and its general marketing signal. At higher tiers, firms are more willing to pursue efficiency at levels not otherwise cost-effective. Government actors appear less motivated to bump up to higher thresholds, often overshooting the minimum requirement for their certification tier. By contrast, nonprofit and for-profit organizations often bump up to Platinum, barely exceeding the required number of LEED credits for that tier. This may be due to greater managerial risk aversion to potential failure to meet the requirements for a mandated tier of certification under various procurement policies (Simcoe and Toffel 2011).

Reliance on particular sustainability practices to obtain different thresholds suggests differences in the motivations organizations have to achieve a higher signal of general performance. Yet these observations of revealed preferences cannot directly explain why managers are more dependent on energy credits for upgrading but tend to avoid improving indoor environmental quality to move across the Platinum threshold. Nor is it certain why decision-makers tend to innovate for Platinum certification but seem to care less about sustainable site choice when obtaining this tier.

One plausible explanation relates firm quality, innovation, and the general marketing signal organizations sent by upgrading to higher tiers. Firms engaging in this general quality signal may be especially likely to be industry leaders and innovators, obtaining more LEED credits for innovative designs for efficiency (Lyon and Maxwell 2008). These credits have less certainty surrounding how to implement them and whether they will be approved. Comparatively, indoor environmental quality credits, awarded for sustainable practices like using carpeting and sealants with low emissions of volatile organic compounds, have extremely specific guidelines, may be easily implemented, and rarely go unapproved.

Buildings certified at the higher tiers typically have high quality independent of the green characteristics. These are owned and operated by better-managed organizations. High-quality organizations seek to send a general signal of quality that extends beyond the building itself. Additionally, these organizations tend to be innovators and industry leaders, and more capable of absorbing the potential costs of risky investments in innovation.

Conclusion

In this chapter, we have opened the black box of green certification to establish how builders systematically select green strategies to gain marketing benefits by signaling key stakeholders. Signaling can be achieved mostly through certification of private benefits, but credits benefiting the external environment are needed to signal some groups of stakeholders. A mix of certification approaches exists in the market. Unpacking the details of thousands of LEED-certified new buildings sheds light on the many approaches to green that LEED buildings reflect. Some projects appear to emphasize better building performance with less waste, smaller footprints, and enhanced quality. Other projects appear to prioritize upgrading to a particular tier – attaining the status and symbolic benefits from the ecolabel. In addition, green buildings vary in terms of the types of investments made. Some emphasize building attributes with positive private returns on that investment, while others lean more heavily toward public benefits. To help make sense of these many motivations and strategies for green building, we turn to two prominent perspectives on green signaling. From one vantage, ecolabels help overcome information asymmetries that undermine premium green building markets (Spence 1973). From another, ecolabels signal membership in a green club that consumers and investors reward (Potoski and Prakash 2005). One perspective emphasizes the Pragmatists, while the other emphasizes green club Members. Yet the green club raises the possibility or temptation for some buildings to Greenwash and seek member status through self-serving investments. Conversely, we also see more Altruistic approaches that overachieve in joining the green club. A classic signaling perspective highlights the importance of signaling and performance to customers. But more is going on here. Figure 5.1 plainly shows how upgrading and symbolic values matter. Clearly, the predominance of public benefits from greener buildings underlines the critical role of the green club and marketing rewards. As we see in the detailed data on many green buildings, certifications often represent a hybrid of different approaches to voluntary environmental certification.

The motivation for and implementation of green certification varies broadly across types of organizations. Discrepancies in attainment of certification across owner types suggest different calculus for the rate of return on building investments, or differences in procurement policies of for-profit firms. Government agencies, for-profit firms, and nonprofit organizations may all take distinct approaches to green building, in line with their respective missions and stakeholder obligations.

This analysis gives a valuable glimpse into firm and agency behavior in the pursuit of environmental certification, and a peek at the revealed preferences of firms and governments that seek to achieve these certifications. Our results show how owners undertake sustainability behavior in the hopes of earning environmental certification and how their sustainability investments vary based on ownership type, building use, and tier of the certification system. We demonstrate that organizations strategically adopt sustainability practices to avoid high-cost resource use, appeal to key stakeholders, and send signals of quality intended to extend beyond the building itself. The results underscore the importance of a mix of strategies in going green and the value of a flexible, voluntary ecolabel that can accommodate and encourage them.

References

An, Xudong and Gary Pivo. 2020. "Green Buildings in Commercial Mortgage-Backed Securities: The Effects of LEED and Energy Star Certification on Default Risk and Loan Terms." *Real Estate Economics* 48, no. 1: 7–42.

Chiang-Hsieh, Lin-Han and Douglas S. Noonan. 2017. "Strategic Behavior in Certifying Green Buildings: An Inquiry of the Non-Building Performance Value." *Environmental Management* 60, no. 2: 231–242.

Corbett, Charles J. and Suresh Muthulingam. 2007. "Adoption of Voluntary Environmental Standards: The Role of Signaling and Intrinsic Benefits in the Diffusion of the LEED Green Building Standards." *UCLA Anderson School of Management*, Working Paper.

Eichholtz, Piet, Nils Kok, and Erkan Yonder. 2012. "Portfolio Greenness and the Financial Performance of REITs." *Journal of International Money and Finance* 31, no. 7: 1911–1929.

Flowers, Mallory E., Daniel C. Matisoff, and Douglas S. Noonan. 2019. "For What It's Worth: Evaluating Revealed Preferences for Green Certification." *Journal of Environmental Planning and Management* 62, no. 5: 843–861.

Kim, Eun-Hee and Thomas P. Lyon. 2015. "Greenwash vs. Brownwash: Exaggeration and Undue Modesty in Corporate Sustainability Disclosure." *Organization Science* 26, no. 3: 705–723.

Lanfranchi, Joseph and Sanja Pekovic. 2014. "How Green Is My Firm? Worker Well-Being and Job Involvement in Environmentally-Related Certified Firms." *Ecological Economics* 100: 16–29.

Lyon, Thomas and John Maxwell. 2008. "Corporate Social Responsibility and the Environment: A Theoretical Perspective." *Review of Environmental Economics and Policy* 2, no. 2: 240–260.

Matisoff, Daniel C., Douglas S. Noonan, and Anna M. Mazzolini. 2014. "Performance or Marketing Benefits? The Case of LEED Certification." *Environmental Science & Technology* 48, no. 3: 2001–2007.

Newsham, Guy, Sandra Mancini, and Benjamin Birt. 2009. "Do LEED-Certified Buildings Save Energy? Yes, but …" *Energy and Buildings* 41, no. 8: 897–905.

Palacios, Juan, Piet Eichholtz, and Nils Kok. 2020. "Moving to Productivity: The Benefits of Healthy Buildings." *PLoS ONE* 15, no. 8: e0236029.

Potoski, Matthew and Aseem Prakash. 2005. "Green Clubs and Voluntary Governance: ISO 14001 and Firms' Regulatory Compliance." *American Journal of Political Science* 49, no. 2: 235–248.

Reichardt, Alexander. 2014. "Operating Expenses and Rent Premium of Energy Star and LEED Certified Buildings in the Central and Eastern U.S." *Journal of Real Estate Finance and Economics* 49, no. 3: 413–433.

Simcoe, Timothy and Michael Toffel. 2011. "LEED Adopters: Public Procurements and Private Certification." *National Bureau of Economic Research*, Working Paper no. 18385.

Singh, Amanjeet, Matt Syal, Sue C. Grady, and Sinem Korkmaz. 2010. "Effects of Green Buildings on Employee Health and Productivity." *American Journal of Public Health* 100, no. 9: 1665–1668.

Spence, Michael. 1973. "Job Market Signaling." *The Quarterly Journal of Economics* 87, no. 3: 355–374.

Turban, Daniel and Daniel Greening. 1997. "Corporate Social Performance and Organizational Attractiveness to Prospective Employees." *Academy of Management Journal* 40, no. 3: 658–672.

Turner, Cathy and Mark Frankel. 2008. *Energy Performance of LEED for New Construction Buildings.* Vancouver, WA: New Buildings Institute.

6 | *Tossing a Pebble in a Pond*
The Anatomy of a Demonstration Project

Introduction

The adoption of advanced energy and environmental technologies is often hindered by the risks and uncertainties associated with new technologies (Bass 1969; Bollinger 2015; Farzin et al. 1998). These risks and uncertainties are related not only to the technical feasibility of the technologies, but also to potential uptake by the markets, financial considerations, and the policy environment (Dalby et al. 2018; Harborne et al. 2007). In this regard, *demonstration projects*, or limited-scale implementation of nascent technologies, provide a way to showcase advanced technologies. Demonstration projects often occur in a setting where normal commercial considerations of markets do not apply, with the goal of reducing uncertainties, creating information or learning spillovers, acting as a focal point to shorten the concept-to-market timeframe (Buijs and Silvester 1996; Harborne et al. 2007; Hendry et al. 2010; Jacobsson and Bergek 2004; Kerr et al. 2014; Lefevre 1984). As a result, demonstration projects may promote diffusion of these technologies into the markets. Demonstration projects can also lead to the formation of networks for dissemination of information and coordination of strategies among various actors (Buijs and Silvester 1996; Kemp et al. 1998).

The effectiveness of demonstration projects in helping to diffuse technologies into markets has been the subject of many previous studies. Technologies most likely to be successful in diffusing into the markets are those that are relatively mature and ready for commercialization (i.e., no longer in the R&D phase and free of major technical problems), with the costs and risks shared with local participants (Baer et al. 1976; Bossink 2015). Being clear about the purposes of the demonstration project is also important (i.e., whether the demonstration is experimental or exemplary), as lack of clarity can result in nondiffusion of otherwise effective technologies (Macey and Brown

1990). Diffusion of technologies into the markets via demonstration projects is helped by policies in favor of innovation, as well as enabling learning (in particular, learning-by-doing) to disseminate information through the supply chain (Bossink 2015; Buijs and Silvester 1996; Hendry et al. 2010). Demonstration projects, and in particular early adopters, are important for increased adoption of energy and environmental technologies through several mechanisms (explained in more detail in Chapter 7). Demonstration projects can help lower search and transaction costs, or the costs of discovering new technologies and their suppliers. Demonstration projects help diffuse information, such as the costs and benefits of emergent technologies and the technical challenges of deploying these technologies. This information diffuses through existing professional networks, as well as through the newly formed networks that arise around a particular demonstration project (Blackburn et al. 2020; Buijs and Silvester 1996; Catalini and Tucker 2017; Rogers 2003).

The KBISD Project at Georgia Tech: Inside a Demonstration Project

In September 2015, Georgia Tech received a commitment for $30 million from the Kendeda Fund to build what was expected to become the most environmentally advanced education and research building ever constructed in the Southeast.[1] The idea was to create a building that lives, learns, and teaches, and connects Georgia Tech with the broader community. The Living Building Challenge (discussed in Chapter 4, and in more detail further in this chapter) was identified as a program structure that could help govern the sustainability of the building and provide certification.

More than just building a better building, the Kendeda Fund wanted the building to transform the built environment in the Southeastern United States. Georgia Tech was chosen as a partner, in part because of its track record and reputation in the region. Says Lauren Wallace, a Principal at the Epsten Group, "Not only is Georgia Tech a frequent builder, but it's in a major city with significant visibility. To have such

---

[1] https://livingbuilding.gatech.edu/news/georgia-tech-receives-30-million-grant-kendeda-fund

a prominent institution engage in a project like this – it really confers a lot of legitimacy to this type of a project."[2]

To generate ideas and designs for the project, Georgia Tech held an "ideas competition."[3] This aspect, interviewees noted, was unique because it created transparency into the design of cutting-edge building designs, whereas in past efforts many of the design features of advanced buildings had been kept secret, especially for designs that did not ultimately win. According to the architects, this feature was important for disseminating knowledge about the green design. Says Alissa Kingsley on the Lord Aeck Sargent design team: "Often when there are plans to build environmentally advanced buildings, the designs and plans are kept private as proprietary information. One thing that this competition did was shine a lot of light onto how different design teams were thinking about sustainable design."[4]

A team comprising of Lord Aeck Sargent, an Atlanta-based design firm; Miller Hull, a Seattle/Portland based design firm that had worked on the Bullitt Center Living Building built in Seattle five years earlier; and Skanska, a construction manager, won the bid. The design team adapted the design from the Bullitt Center, working with local engineering firm Newcomb & Boyd to adapt the electrical and HVAC systems for the hot, humid southeastern climate. This aspect was also indicative of the impact that this project might have on the region. The collaborative project team-based approach for transferring knowledge of new technologies shows significant promise. (We need further research to understand how to make this approach most effective.)

KBISD is designed to be regenerative. The Living Building Challenges requires achieving net-positive energy annually, being net-positive water (i.e., harvesting rainwater and treating wastewater onsite), and achieving net-positive waste during the construction process (i.e., diverting more waste from the landfill than sending to the landfill). It must also fulfill a number of other criteria related to beauty, equity, health, and happiness. In practice this means that the building needs to produce an annual total of 5 percent more electricity than it consumes, with combustion prohibited. For water, the building needs to use and treat rainwater and discharge these to the ecosystem. This is

[2] Interview with authors, August 21, 2020.
[3] https://livingbuilding.gatech.edu/news/team-selected-design-living-building-georgia-tech
[4] Interview with authors, February 8, 2019.

net positive because the project diverts rainwater and wastewater from the storm sewers. For waste, the project focuses on construction waste and is needed to incorporate enough recycled or salvaged materials to offset any construction waste. The strategies used to accomplish this are discussed in more detail. Altogether, KBISD contains 20 innovative or experimental technological solutions that we discuss in more detail in this chapter.

The Role of a Demonstration Project for the Building and Construction Industry

The KBISD demonstration project provides an opportunity to observe, in real time, the formation of a network around a demonstration project and how attitudes and behaviors relating to environmental technologies permeate and disseminate through the building design and construction network. In this section we present results from an industry-wide survey as well as several dozen semi-structured interviews related to the KBISD. The interviews reveal motivations, challenges, innovations, costs, and risks associated with participation in a demonstration project, as well as key differences between this living building approach and design–bid–build approaches often employed in traditional buildings. (These details address a major limitation of the arm's-length analysis in Chapter 5.) Further, the interviews highlight the role that networks have played in the construction of the KBISD building, as well as how information disseminates through networks to seed market transformation. The results of the industry-wide survey provide a baseline of the knowledge and attitudes associated with the innovative technologies in the building and construction industry. Tracking the learning and attitudes over time can reveal much about the transformative ripple effects of demonstration projects.

The KBISD project – and other innovative green building projects – need to surmount numerous obstacles related to risk and cost. Interviews with contractors are revealing. One contractor (who was not part of the project but has participated in other innovative projects near campus) noted that "nobody wants to be the first to try something." In particular, he noted a lack of experience with chilled beam cooling technology in the Southeastern United States. (See Chapter 7 for more on chilled beam.) Because Georgia Tech had piloted chilled beam cooling in on-campus buildings, it made it more feasible to implement the technology in the NCR headquarters near campus, and in the CODA building (a large private innovation ecosystem with high performance computing and data near campus, developed by John Portman & Associates). In addition, he explained that cost ends up being the largest driver in decision-making, noting that sustainability initiatives and innovative technologies are often the first cut when trying to trim the budget. Many of his clients are looking to sell their buildings in the 3–10-year time horizon, so energy upgrades that pay off in 3–5 years often do not seem particularly appealing. Others in the field have noted that developers may seek to sell off their building after just 2 years, and energy investments are not seen as providing financial return in the market.

Given these hurdles, why did contractors sign up to work on the KBISD building? Primarily, it was for the expansive project budget (the building ended up costing $397 per square foot for programmed space or $503 per square-foot for conditioned space), which represents an enormous opportunity for firms. In this particular instance, a private foundation covered the costs of the building.[5] Under normal circumstances, contractors might provide several options – a low, medium, and high performance option to a client, representing different cost points and energy performance – but because many of these decisions are made during the bid and proposal phase, there is often little appetite to pitch anything too out of the ordinary or too expensive. While there are many high-end technologies available, most of these are never seriously considered for budgetary reasons. KBISD at Georgia Tech was unique because they were looking for such aggressive options, knowing contractors would be watching the performance closely to highlight these technologies to new potential clients.

The demonstration project role was quite important to many contractors' decisions to participate in the project. Many contractors felt that this was a loss-leader, where they would be spending excess time on the project at a loss, but also a high-profile project that they could feature on their websites and learn from for future projects. This project was seen as a learning opportunity – a chance to implement new technologies and gain market experience and a differentiating market advantage for future projects. As discussed in Chapter 7, demonstration projects produce high-quality information that can help

[5] http://livingbuilding.gatech.edu/kendeda-building-innovative-sustainable-design

spur the uptake of even more projects. Markets are unlikely to provide sufficient demonstration projects because the information provided by these projects is costly and builders are not compensated for providing a public demonstration.

The design of the Living Building uses off-the-shelf and commercially available technologies in innovative ways to achieve a net energy positive, net water positive, and net waste positive footprint. In this section, we highlight the innovative features of the key building systems that are not yet widespread. The Living Building Challenge requirements (see Chapter 4) are designed across seven "Petals," designed to provide a metaphor for a flower. These include Place, Energy, Water, Materials, Health and Happiness, Equity, and Beauty. In this chapter we discuss the innovative features of the KBISD building and how they fulfill these Petals. We detail these to provide readers with a better sense of the emerging systems and technologies in the green buildings, a more concrete understanding of what market transformation might look like. For those engaged in building sustainable structures or engaging in the sustainable built environment, this in-depth look at one of the most advanced structures in the Southeast might offer some ideas about where the industry is headed.

Place

Keeping in line with goals for sustainable buildings related to their impact on the broader ecosystem, the Living Building Challenge requires buildings to minimize the impact on land. Unless there is an exception, projects must be built on greyfields or brownfields (or on land that has already been cleared for a parking lot or commercial or industrial building site), and projects must not infringe on ecologically sensitive habitats. The KBISD project is built on the site of a former parking lot. Despite fears that soil compaction over the course of decades would preclude restoration, the landscaping design team was able to restore the soil to a healthy state using minimal soil amendments and to design a landscaping plan to mimic natural hydrological flows on the site. Urban agriculture is an imperative for Living Buildings as well, with requirements that 20 percent of the area needs to be capable of producing food for human consumption. Native plants with edible fruits or flowers were chosen for the site to enable urban foraging, and a rooftop garden that houses honeybees was planted with blueberries. Fruiting vines live on the building sides. Living Building Challenge certification requires a number of other advances, including access via transit, bicycle, and by foot, and set asides and conservation easements for natural habitat through land trust organizations.

Energy Systems

The built environment, globally, is responsible for 35–40 percent of the energy use and carbon emissions, representing a major challenge for addressing climate change. How can we construct buildings in such a way that reduces this impact? The KBISD building provides some insight toward how we might substantially improve energy efficiency as well as consider the use of the built environment for energy production and storage.

The KBISD project aims to have an energy-use intensity (EUI) of 30 kBTU per square foot per year, which is 72 percent more efficient than an average building of the same size and occupancy. (The building is intended to host large events with a 176-person auditorium, and has a number of additional classrooms, teaching labs, and a maker space.) The building has an efficient building envelope, with triple-pane window glazing and continuous insulation in the walls and under slabs. The building uses shading on the south and west facades from a large solar canopy to reduce solar heat. The solar canopy consists of 917 PV panes providing 330 kW direct current (DC) solar capacity. It is expected to generate over 455,000 kWh per year that will cover building net energy demands plus an additional buffer of 15 percent to ensure a net-positive building footprint (42 EUI kBTU per square foot per year). The canopy also serves to collect rainwater and provide covered outdoor space. Automated window shades aid in solar control and daylighting optimization, and strategically planted trees help manage solar radiation as well. When the solar panel is not generating sufficient power, the building will receive electricity from the grid. When it is producing more than the building needs, it will send electricity back to the grid. A lithium ion battery system provides emergency back-up.

Radiant heating and cooling exist in the majority of the building, enabled by moisture condensation sensors. Further, a dedicated outdoor air system (DOAS) provides heated/cooled and dehumidified ventilation air to the majority of the building's spaces. A variable air volume HVAC supplements heating and cooling requirements in the auditorium.

Skylights, large windows, and clerestory windows help reduce lighting needs and provide natural daylighting. Vestibules and air curtains at entries help to prevent hot air and humidity from entering the building. Automated and operable windows allow for fresh air intake and help maintain system balance when outdoor conditions are conducive.

The building also employs a design/management technique called "deadband expansion." The deadband is the temperature at which neither the air conditioning nor heat are operating, reducing energy use. Because the primary users of the building are college students, building designers thought that students would be more likely to be flexible with clothing choices. In traditional office buildings, a 68–72°F deadband is designed to provide thermal comfort for an average man wearing a suit. In contrast to these dated approaches to comfort, the KBISD project was designed to allow temperatures to rise to 78°F in the summer, and to drop to 68°F in the winter, providing an expanded deadband zone to reduce energy demands in the building and enable the use of smaller and more efficient cooling systems. To further improve thermal comfort while reducing heating and cooling needs, the building employs 24 "Big Ass" fans, using moving air to decrease cooling requirements. In addition, the use of radiant heating and cooling from crosslinked polyethylene tubes embedded in the poured concrete floor ensures that thermal comfort is emphasized near the occupancy zone of the building (and exert less energy to heat and cool air in the high zones where there is no occupancy).[6]

Water Systems

Fresh water availability is a significant problem around much of the world. This is not the case in Atlanta. Atlanta, the location of this building, receives about 50 inches of rainfall annually, an amount greater than famously rainy Seattle, WA (~37.5 inches). However, high variability in Atlanta's rainfall patterns, rising sewer bills due to increased stormwater flooding, and limited groundwater options make

[6] https://livingbuilding.kendedafund.org/2019/01/28/concrete-pour-radiant-floor/

water management a critical regional issue. Further, 9 of 14 measured contaminants in Atlanta exceed the Environmental Working Group's recommended health limits.[7]

The Living Building Challenge certification requires 100 percent of occupant water to come from captured precipitation or closed-loop water systems. Water used on-site for drinking and irrigation must be treated on site without the use of chemicals. The building converts rainwater to drinking water through a Public Water Supply System permit issued by Georgia's Environmental Protection Division. As of this writing, the building operators are waiting (and have been for over a year) for the permit, highlighting some of the administrative and policy challenges with innovations that do not fit in to existing regulatory systems. The rainwater is collected by the PV solar canopy and the roof deck and is filtered and routed to the 50,000-gallon cistern in the building's basement. The cistern treats 41 percent of the annual rooftop runoff. The remainder is directed to on-site stormwater treatment systems.

The cistern is expected to be large enough to provide ample capacity for drought and provide water resiliency. While connections with the city water and sewer are provided, they exist mostly to fulfill regulatory requirements. As water is needed for drinking, it is pumped from the cistern, filtered, and disinfected with ultraviolet light to potable stand-ards, then piped throughout the building.

Greywater (water that does not contain organic matter) is collected from shower drains, sink drains, and water fountains and is directed to a primary tank for infiltration on-site. This recycled water is pumped to a constructed wetland and ultimately infiltrates back into the soil and recharges surrounding groundwater. *Condensate* collected from the HVAC system is used for irrigation on the green roof and for drip irrigation around the site. The building employs 12 composting toilets and four waterless urinals to separate liquids and convert solids into compost that can be taken offsite for beneficial reuse (e.g., as a fertilizing soil for uptake by plants).

Stormwater management is a major issue in Atlanta, with low-lying areas prone to flooding during storms. The Environmental Protection Agency (EPA) entered a consent decree in 1998–1999 with the city, requiring it to build massive stormwater infrastructure projects that have brought Atlanta's water and sewer rates to amongst the highest in

[7] www.ewg.org/tapwater/system.php?pws=GA1210001

the country. Living Buildings are required to have minimal stormwater runoff. All stormwater from a normal rain event in this project is captured onsite and infiltrated back into the soil using rain gardens, permeable pavers, and seepage areas. The design mimics pre-human development by mimicking the hydrological flow of the area and reintroducing native vegetation through an eco-commons project that attempts to restore a Piedmont Forest ecosystem to the area. The porch of the KBISD supports this effort by providing stormwater storage under permeable pavers, allowing the water to seep back into the hydrological system (Figure 6.1).

Materials and Net-Positive Waste

One of the biggest challenges in achieving sustainable solutions in the built environment is that construction materials themselves are manu-factured with many chemicals that have significant toxic footprints, impacting human health – and often in very inequitable ways – with toxic pollution disproportionately impacting lower income commu-nities. Further complicating the matter is that building materials do not exactly have ingredients lists – meaning that choosing a sustainable option can be challenging or impossible for the builder or client.

The Materials Petal seeks to advance construction materials and tech-nologies that are "non-toxic, ecologically restorative, transparent, and socially equitable."[8] This requirement incorporates five imperatives: (1) sourcing construction materials that do not contain chemicals banned on the Living Building Red List (including PVC, Chromium-6, and other common chemicals used in construction materials), (2) tracking carbon emission associated with construction, (3) using salvaged materials and responsibly sourced wood and stone, (4) reducing or eliminating waste during construction, and (5) sourcing materials locally.

The imperative on Red List chemicals was seen by construction managers, such as Jimmy Mitchell, of Skanska, as particularly challen-ging. The Red List is a list of 19 classes of materials or chemicals with the greatest impact to human and ecosystem health. The list is com-piled as part of the Pharos project, which aims to aggregate and catalog health risks from over 270,000 Chemical Abstract Service Registry Numbers. The Red List imperative aims to eliminate the use of these

---

[8] ILFI.org

NET POSITIVE WATER CYCLE –
LIVING BUILDING CHALLENGE STRATEGY

Kendeda Building for Innovative Sustainable Design

Georgia Institute of Technology, Atlanta, GA

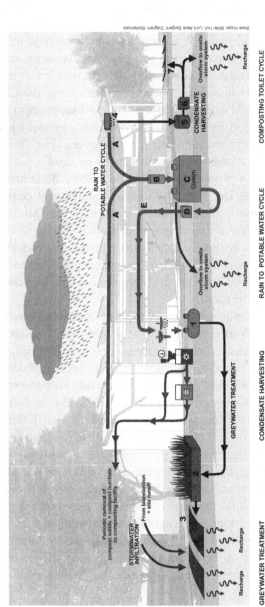

GREYWATER TREATMENT

1 Primary treatment tank–collects, settles*, digests
2 Constructed wetlands–passive ecological polishing
3 Subsurface infiltration–recharges groundwater

CONDENSATE HARVESTING

4 Condensate from building cooling system
5 Condensate storage tank
6 Filtration, UV unit, + irrigation pump
7 Site irrigation system

RAIN TO POTABLE WATER CYCLE

A Rainwater collection–piping
B Inlet Filtration from roof
C Basement cistern
D Potable water filtration + UV disinfection skid
E Distribution to potable fixtures

COMPOSTING TOILET CYCLE

① Foam flush toilet fixtures
    (compatible with composting unit)
⊗ Composter units
    (serve multiple toilets)
⊜ Compost leachate storage tank

*Periodic solids removal to biosolids/composting facility

Biohabitats

PROJECT TEAM

Miller Hull	Newcomb & Boyd
Lord Aeck & Sargent	Long Engineering
Andropogon Associates	Biohabitats
PAE	Skanska USA

Base Image: Miller Hull, Lord Aeck Sargent; Diagram: Biohabitats

Figure 6.1 Sustainable water strategy for KBISD

153

worst-in-class materials and chemicals. As such, Living Building Challenge certified projects cannot contain Red List materials or chemicals. Some commonly recognizable items on the Red List include asbestos, formaldehyde, phthalates, toxic heavy metals, and polyvinyl chloride (PVC). Because the ingredients of construction materials are not typically disclosed, contractors faced considerable search and transaction costs in seeking out appropriate materials. Construction managers reported working with students and suppliers to track down manufacturers and ensure Red List compliance by seeking Chemistry Abstract Service numbers from manufacturers. The Declare Label, Healthy Product Declaration, and Cradle to Cradle products labels assisted with this process. One outcome of the KBISD project was to contribute to the Declare Label's online database of compliant construction materials, allowing future projects to take advantage of an increasing number of listed construction materials. Another impact of the project was to encourage manufacturers to produce Red List compliant materials. For example, special efforts were made to secure sheet metal that did not contain chromium 6, a Red List chemical used primarily for aesthetics.

Another example was the electrical contractor Eckhardt's use of high-density polyethylene (HDPE) as an electrical conduit, instead of PVC. Ryan Swenson, the project manager for the electrical contractor, noted that they had always used PVC piping because it was what they were familiar with. And they did not necessarily know or recognize the damaging environmental footprint that PVC has on many communities. While HDPE had been common in many electrical applications such as solar farms and highway lighting, it had not been typically used in building construction. PVC piping, in general, was more available in the market in smaller quantities and was perceived as easier to work with by contractors. The experience with this new technology was a positive one. While the project managers expected the job to take longer because of some challenges associated with installing couplings, HDPE was more flexible – allowing it to be used for long runs, and, if anything, ended up being faster to install than the traditional PVC piping. In the future, Swenson expects to suggest HDPE piping in future project bids.[9]

---

[9] https://livingbuilding.kendedafund.org/2018/12/04/eckardt-recognized-pioneering-hdpe-electrical-conduit/

Another major concern relating to the carbon footprint of the built environment is the embodied carbon in the building materials. Concrete and steel are heavy and highly carbon intensive. In contrast, mass timber is a technology that uses wood to create a strong, light-weight building material that can replace steel and concrete and can reduce the footprint of the building foundation. KBISD was built with Glued Laminated Timber (Glulam) mass timber technology. Glulam is an approach that uses smaller pieces of wood and an adhesive to join them, creating a strong construction product that can sequester carbon from sustainably harvested forests. This technology enables the cost-effective, environmentally friendly construction of mid- and high-rise buildings that would typically be built with concrete and steel, which emit greenhouse gases during their manufacture. Many states have been revising building codes to allow construction with Glulam, Cross-laminated timber, or other mass timber products. While the KBISD project required a waiver to use Glulam (the adhesive in Glulam contains less than 10 percent phenol, which is banned in the Red List), this is a promising sustainable construction technology if the adhesive can be modified to be Red List compliant.

The Forest Stewardship Council (FSC) certified mass timber helped minimize the carbon footprint of the building construction by having only a sixth of the embodied carbon of steel or concrete. In addition, stone for the project was salvaged from the former Georgia Archives Building. Additional stone came from the local Forest Park Quarry. Other construction materials, including carpet, steel, Glulam, Nail Laminated Timber (NLT), and rigid insulation, were all manufactured or fabricated locally, minimizing carbon emissions associated with materials transport. Later in this chapter, we explore the implications for demonstrating new technologies such as mass timber.

Net-positive waste seeks to address the environmental burden associated with construction waste. To achieve the imperative, nearly all waste must be diverted from the landfill during construction. For this project, nearly 443 tons of asphalt were recycled. To make the building net-waste positive, the builder was able to reclaim 25,000 feet of two-by-four from demolished film sets discarded wood and turn this wood into Nail Laminated Timber (NLT) to create wooden ceiling paneling. This paneling was created working with the Georgia Works! workforce development program to help give people new skills, to help achieve an equity benefit. In addition, the design team utilized several campus trees that fell due to storms to create benches, countertops, and tables from the reclaimed wood. Other reclaimed materials included: slate for the interior wall finishes from the renovation of another building, granite from the Georgia Archives Building for landscaping, 1880s heart pine joists from a 2016 building renovation used as stair treads, and wood trimmed from the NLT ceiling panels used for internal stairs. Additionally, a recycling and compost program aims to minimize landfilled waste from the building's continued operation.

Health and Happiness, Beauty, and Equity

In addition to the core technological and managerial requirements for the Living Building, there are a number of requirements that seek to optimize the experience of building occupants. These include natural daylight and access to windows and fresh air. The KBISD building has functional windows – some of which open to create large indoor/outdoor spaces. The building can also utilize outdoor air to heat and cool the building. The building seeks to optimize indoor air quality by using safer cleaning products, improving ventilation rates, reducing Volatile Organic Compounds, and monitoring CO_2, temperature, and humidity.

To address equity and beauty, the building has installed public art and is open to the community for events. In addition, during the construction of the building, Skanska partnered with Georgia Works!, an organization that trains formerly homeless individuals in construction trades. Six of these individuals helped build the KBISD building by assembling the NLT ceiling panels. At least one of these individuals was hired for future projects by Skanska. Finally, the challenge requires the use of Just labels – a transparency and disclosure labeling certification for business – by at least one of the major systems component contractors. On this project, the design firms Muller Hull Partnership and Lord Aeck Sargent had Just labels.

Understanding Industry Knowledge of Advanced Building Technologies

In May 2019, during the construction of the KBISD, we conducted a survey to evaluate knowledge and attitudes related to 19 innovative technologies used in the building, as well as three additional technologies that were considered but ultimately not used in the KBISD (blackwater treatment; chilled beam heating/cooling; and geothermal

Table 6.1. *List of techniques and technologies in the KBISD survey*

Energy Systems
1 – Solar Panels
2 – Integrated Automation System
3 – DC Microgrids[2]

Water Management Systems
4 – Stormwater Management System[2]
5 – Greywater Management System
6 – Blackwater Management System[2]
7 – HVAC Condensate Collection System

Materials
8 – Living Building Materials Red List
9 – Use of Salvaged Materials
10 – Heavy Mass Timber Construction

Heating and Cooling
11 – Blower Door Testing
12 – Radiant Heating and Cooling
13 – Ceiling Fan Deadband Expansion
14 – Natural Ventilation
15 – Auto Exterior Shutters
16 – Chilled Beam Heating/Cooling[2]
17 – Geothermal Heating/Cooling[2]

Other
18 – Composting Toilets
19 – Edible Landscapes
20 – Workforce Development Plan
21 – Carbon Footprint Analysis
22 – Intensive Green Roofs

Placebo
23 – Placebo[1] (Kyber Crystal Heating and Cooling)

(1) Placebo technology; (2) Technology considered but ultimately not used.

heating/cooling), and one imaginary placebo technology (Kyber Crystal heating ventilation), designed to test the reliability of survey responses. Table 6.1 summarizes the technologies included in the survey.

Approximately 180 respondents with various organizational backgrounds completed the survey (see Figure 6.2). These included design firms, general contractors, design build firms, and associated building services firms. The survey contained several questions to identify the respondents' familiarity and relationship with the KBISD (see Figure 6.3), such as whether or not they had heard of the KBISD, whether or not they had visited the KBISD or the GT campus, or if their companies were involved in the building's construction. The survey also contained a question to evaluate the respondent's current professional network structure by asking them to list the professional organizations and networks that they are a part of.

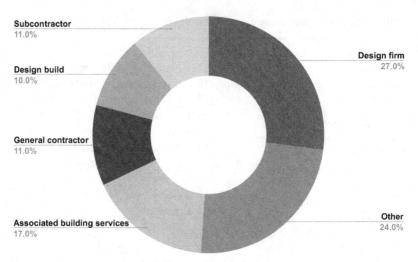

Figure 6.2 Survey respondents' organizational backgrounds

Have you ever heard of the Kendeda Building
for Innovative and Sustainable Design being
built at Georgia Tech?

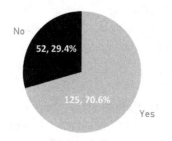

Is your company involved in the
construction of the Kendeda Building
for Innovative Sustainable Design?

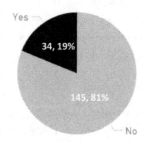

Have you visited the Georgia Institute of
Technology within the previous year?

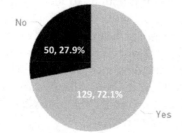

Have you visited the Kendeda Building for
Innovative Sustainable Design project
while on campus?

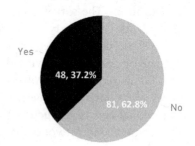

Figure 6.3 Survey respondent's familiarity and relationship with the KBISD

In addition, we interviewed several dozen individuals involved in the construction of the KBISD, as well as those participating in projects on or near Georgia Tech's campus. Survey responses ranged from those who claimed varying levels of familiarity (i.e., "moderately familiar" to "extremely familiar") with the technologies included in the survey. Those who claimed "moderately familiar" or "extremely familiar" with the imaginary "placebo" technology were excluded from the analysis, as a way to ensure high quality responses. This resulted in a final sample size of 165 respondents. We used the survey responses to calculate an index of *Technology Familiarity*, which considers only the 19 technologies used in KBISD. We calculated the *Technology Familiarity* index by assigning a score based on reported familiarity (*fs*) with the individual technologies (4 for being "extremely familiar" with a given technology, 3 for being "moderately familiar," 2 for being "somewhat familiar," 1 for being "slightly familiar," and 0 for being "not at all familiar") then summing up the scores for all technologies:

$$\text{Technology Familiarity} = \sum_{i=1}^{n} fs_i$$

Table 6.2 summarizes the variables used in the statistical model. To assess the results, we employ multivariate regression analysis to explain variation in *Technology Familiarity* across individual respondents. Multivariate regression explains variation in an outcome (in this case, *Technological Familiarity*) with variation in a number of potential explanatory factors. It determines the amount of independent variation attributable to each factor, and whether that factor has a relationship with the outcome of interest that is statistically different from zero.

Survey Findings

Figure 6.4 shows that pre-construction technology familiarity levels are variable depending on each technology. For example, respondents report high familiarity levels for relatively well-known technologies such as solar panels (#1) and stormwater management systems (#4), as expected, while they report lower familiarity levels for some of the less well-known technologies such as ceiling fan deadband expansion (#13) and DC microgrids (#3). Most respondents reported that they were not familiar with the imaginary placebo technology (Kyber Crystal Heating and Cooling Technology, which also powers light

Table 6.2. *Survey variable descriptions*

Variables	Description
Years	Numbers of years in the building and construction industry
Projects	Number of green certified building projects worked on during the past five years
Green Building Frequency	Frequency of working on green certified buildings (0 = Never, 1 = Rarely, 2 = Most of the time, 3 = All the time)
Revenue	Approximate annual revenue for company (1 = Less than $1 million, 2 = $1 million to $10 million, 3 = $10 million to $100 million, 4 = $100 million to $1 billion, 5 = $1 billion to $10 billion, 6 = Greater than $10 billion)
Green Building Knowledge	Self-reported knowledge of green certified buildings (0 = None at all, 1 = Low, 2 = Some, 3 = Moderate, 4 = High)
KBISD Familiarity	Self-reported familiarity with the KBISD; that is, whether or not survey respondent has heard of the building (0 = No, 1 = Yes)
Construct-KBISD	Self-reported firm's involvement in the construction of the KBISD (0 = No, 1 = Yes)
Visit-KBISD	Whether or not survey respondent had visited the KBISD (0 = No, 1 = Yes)
# Green Conferences	Number of green building conferences attended in the past five years
USGBC Member	Whether or not survey respondent is affiliated with USGBC (0 = No, 1 = Yes)

Table 6.2. (*cont.*)

Variables	Description
Design-Build Firm	Whether or not survey respondent's company was primarily classified as "design build" (0 = No, 1 = Yes)
General Contractor	Whether or not survey respondent's company was primarily classified as "general contractor" (0 = No, 1 = Yes)
Design Firm	Whether or not survey respondent's company was primarily classified as "design firm" (0 = No, 1 = Yes)
Technology Familiarity	Technology Familiarity Index (range = 0–92)

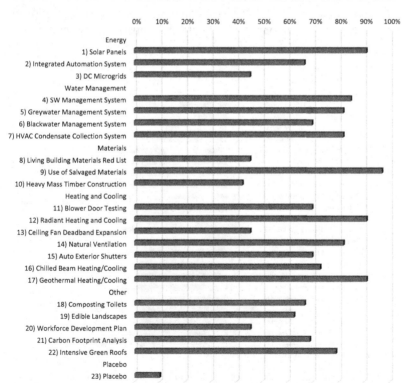

Figure 6.4 Survey respondents' familiarity with green building technologies: Percent of experts at least familiar with each technology by category

sabers in Star Wars), showing evidence that the survey respondents carefully considered their answers.

Figures 6.5–6.7 show the differences in technology familiarity between groups. For example, Figure 6.5 demonstrates the difference in familiarity levels between those who had heard of the KBISD building versus those who had not. A positive difference indicates a higher level of familiarity of those who had heard of the KBSID building versus those who had not. A negative difference shows a lower level of familiarity. Those who had heard of the KBISD were more likely to be familiar with the various technologies versus those who had not heard of the KBISD.

Figure 6.6 shows the difference in technology familiarity between those whose companies were involved in the construction of KBISD and those whose companies were not involved. The participants whose companies were involved in the construction of KBISD were more familiar with certain technologies, such as the Living Building Materials Red List (#8), but less familiar with others, such as blower door testing (#11). Perhaps surprisingly, participants whose companies

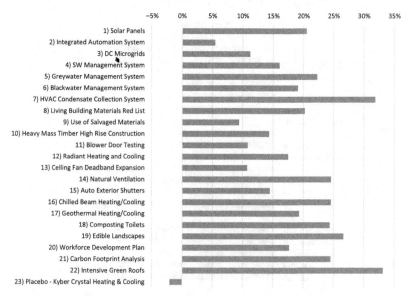

Figure 6.5 Difference in technology familiarity: Those who had heard of KBISD minus those who had not

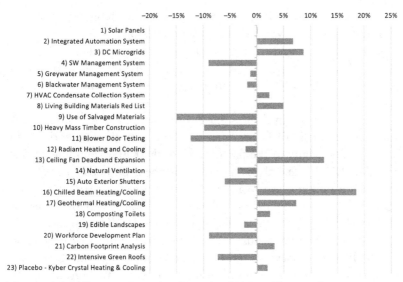

Figure 6.6 Difference in technology familiarity: Those whose company worked on KBISD minus those that did not

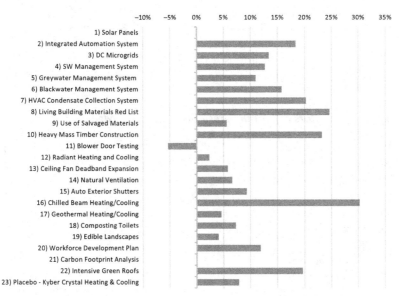

Figure 6.7 Difference in technology familiarity: Those affiliated with USGBC minus those who are not

were involved in construction did not appear to exhibit higher overall levels of familiarity with technologies in the project.

Figure 6.7 shows the difference in technology familiarity between those affiliated with the USGBC and those who are not. Those affiliated with the USGBC were more familiar with the technologies compared to those not affiliated.

The comparisons in Figures 6.5–6.7 do not enable us to understand the complex array of factors that correlate with the familiarity with technologies. Many of the participants in the KBISD building project are also USGBC members. USGBC members may also have more experience building green projects. Are workers in the construction industry learning about these technologies through networks such as the USGBC or through experience working on building projects? Or maybe learning just depends on years in the trade or the size of the firm employing them. Social scientists often attempt to sort out these complex relationships using multivariate regression. We break up the puzzle by separating general, green building knowledge from familiarity with specific technologies.

Green Building Knowledge appears to be driven by networks and experience. Table 6.3 demonstrates that the number of projects one works on and the frequency at which one works on green building projects are the most predictive indicators of green building knowledge, indicative of *learning by doing*, a theory that suggests (as titled) that people and organizations learn and innovate through on the job experience. In addition, network effects indicated by USGBC

Table 6.3. *Factors explaining green building knowledge*

Years	0
Projects	+
Green Building Frequency	+
Revenue	0
KBISD Familiarity	0
Construct-KBISD	0
Visit-KBISD	+
# Green Conferences	0
USGBC Member	+

0 = no statistically significant relationship.
+/− = strong positive/negative relationship ($p < 0.10$).

Table 6.4. *Factors explaining technology familiarity*

Years	0
Projects	+
Green Building Frequency	+
Revenue	−
Green-Building Knowledge (self-reported)	+
KBISD Familiarity	+
Construct-KBISD	−
Visit-KBISD	0
# Green Conferences	+
USGBC Member	0
Design-Build Firm	−
General Contractor	0
Design Firm	0

0 = no statistically significant relationship.
+/− = strong positive/negative relationship ($p < 0.10$).

membership help explain *Green Building Knowledge*. This highlights the role of professional associations, conferences, and communities of practice in building knowledge in an emergent sector.

As intended by the KBISD demonstration project, having visited the construction site of the KBISD building predicts *Green Building Knowledge*. These results emphasize the role of a demonstration project and associated educational events and tours in promoting familiarity and knowledge of green building techniques. Interestingly, firm size does not predict *Green Building Knowledge*. This might be indicative of the relative niche role that green building techniques have in the industry, with a significant role for smaller, specialized firms.

In contrast, Table 6.4 focuses on the factors that explain familiarity with specific new green building technologies. Similar to results for *Green Building Knowledge*, neither the number of years in the construction industry nor the company size (revenues) appear to be significantly correlated with *Technology Familiarity*. Similar to the results for *Green Building Knowledge*, we also see a strong role for learning by doing. The frequency of working on green certified buildings is positively and significantly correlated with *Technology Familiarity*. Familiarity with the KBISD is also associated with *Technology Familiarity*, highlighting the crucial role of the KBSID in promoting knowledge and familiarity with advanced green building technologies. Thus, we see both a role for learning by doing, and a role for leveraging a demonstration project like the KBISD building to educate people about advanced technologies for the built environment.

Like the results for *Green Building Knowledge*, we see a relationship between professional networks and *Technology Familiarity*. Rather than USGBC membership, we see a strong role for conferences playing a role for the dissemination of new technologies. Indeed, one key emergent technology – active chilled beam cooling and ventilation – was pioneered in the Southeast by Furman University.[10] Their experience was shared at a conference attended by the campus architect for Georgia Tech, who then iterated the technology and pushed for its diffusion on and off campus.

The negative and strong correlation between involvement in the construction of the KBISD and *Technology Familiarity* is noteworthy. While those who work on many green building projects and those who tour green building projects seem to have higher levels of green building and technology-specific knowledge, the people who actually worked on this building have *lower* levels of general green-building knowledge or technology-specific knowledge. This may be related to the "silo effect," which refers to the lack of information exchange with outside entities (or even with firms). The specialized nature of green building construction is such that specialty contractors may not be familiar with systems and technologies outside the ones with which they typically work. Thus, the siloed nature of the contractors and unfamiliarity with technologies outside of their specialty may be explained. Interviews revealed that many of the contractors were chosen solely based on cost and ability to do the work (per state law). Public procurement rules frequently require a specified bidding process to make sure that the public does not overpay for construction services. The process that produced the KBISD building therefore involved the recruitment of contractors who had less experience with these technologies. This represents a chance to disseminate green-building techniques beyond the firms that already specialized in green building. One contractor working with the electrical and plumbing systems was forced to switch from PVC, to HDPE piping, a new

---

[10] www.esmagazine.com/articles/94005-chilled-beams-win-over-the-humid-south

technology for this particular contractor. He also noted that the ease and lower cost of working with HDPE piping meant that he is likely to recommend it on future projects.

Discussion

The interviews highlighted barriers for new technology adoption that were unsurprising. Barriers cited were cost, a lack of familiarity with new technologies and their potential performance characteristics, and high discount rates associated with efficiency investments. The interviews also revealed interesting patterns of learning about new technologies or spreading information.

First, the transmission of information through project teams was particularly intriguing. The KBISD building at Georgia Tech is a direct descendant of work that was done on the Bullitt Center in Seattle, with adaptations made for the local climate. The team-based approach to the KBISD construction project has led a large number of firms to become exposed to new technologies and practices associated with the Living Building. Matt DiPiro, an engineer working on the project with Newcomb & Boyd, described the formation of a professional network working on advanced building technologies:

This project has brought together a community of firms and individuals who I didn't even know existed. It's been really interesting to interact with this community of firms that are all attempting to transition towards new and innovative technologies to address energy and environmental problems.[11]

Interestingly, while we might have expected contractors working on the building to have been selected based on prior knowledge, this is not supported by the data. Contractors came into the project with average levels or even below-average knowledge of new technologies. But they repeatedly noted in interviews how much they had learnt by being part of this process and community. This creation of a community of practice appears to be a powerful way to disseminate new information about technologies.

Second, the role of Georgia Tech in voluntarily accepting risk associated with new technologies appears to be a potentially important

---

[11] Interview with authors, April 24, 2019.

driver in subsequent technological uptake. The partnership with a private foundation allowed Georgia Tech to invest in risky and unproven technologies at high cost. It is unclear if this model is replicable across a wider range of situations. Not every university or institute has high technical capacity for demonstrating and innovating technologies, and certainly generous philanthropists are always a scarce resource. Contractors on the project joined in order to gain experience with new technologies. While the long-term impacts of this particular demonstration project are not yet known, the role of Georgia Tech in being an early adopter of innovative cooling technologies and then pushing them to the private sector was noted by contractors. One specific role that Georgia Tech played was to bring together and coordinate a wide range of actors across the green building space. Todd Mowinski, from Newcomb & Boyd, noticed that a much higher degree of coordination was required in such a unique project. "In order to make this building happen – the construction manager had to take a lot of time, work and vision."[12] One unique approach taken by Georgia Tech was to contract with the construction team and major subcontractors for a full year after the building opened to ensure everything functioned as intended.

The success and performance of the Living Building over the next several years will help determine which innovative technologies gain momentum. Much of the industry focus has been on the building envelope and its energy performance. The combination of automated shutters, outdoor air exchange, radiant heating and cooling, "Big Ass" ceiling fans, an expanded deadband zone, and triple-pane windows represents a unique and innovative approach to building energy management that will be closely watched by many of the contractors for its performance. That said, another less-heralded technology is gaining momentum in the marketplace and has been breaking down policy barriers in order to do so. That technology? *Wood.* While wood is obviously not a new product, mass timber – an engineered wood product that allows wood to be used as a structural product in mid- and high-rise construction – has been piloted and demonstrated recently. Let us dig deeper.

[12] Interview with authors, February 15, 2019.

A Closer Look: Mass Timber

We do not build a lot of commercial buildings with wood, mostly because wood structures have historically seriously constrained the upper limit on building size and scale. Mass timber, however, is a type of reinforced timber product designed for loads similar to conventional materials with a higher environmental impact, such as concrete or steel. There are several products in the mass-timber family, including Nail Laminated Timber, glued laminated timber, and cross-laminated timber. In the past 20 years, fire and structural engineering methods for these materials have been developing. Mass timber allows taller buildings to be built with a lighter low-carbon and high-quality material. There are many timber buildings over eight stories tall around the world.

Mass timber can provide environmental, social, and economic benefits. Mass timber products can be created using timber, which is a renewable resource that can be sustainably harvested, and use of sustainably grown timber contributes to climate-change mitigation. Mass timber is being used around the world to contribute to local and global climate action goals. Many jurisdictions are beginning to recognize wood as an integral part of a low-carbon future. Mass timber is also a very high-performance material. Its physical properties create extremely airtight buildings that support energy efficiency. Economic benefits to project developers include off-site fabrication, which shortens construction schedules, and limiting financing time. As wood is a lighter material, the size of footings (part of the foundation) can be reduced, leading to a reduction in costs. Additionally, mass timber often means smaller construction crews and simpler tools.

Notable Mass Timber Buildings: The Brock Commons Tallwood House at the University of British Columbia in Vancouver, Canada, was the world's tallest mass timber building upon its completion in July 2017.[13] Constructed from five-ply cross-laminated timber (CLT) panels supported on glued laminated timber columns, the student residence stands 18 stories (54 meters) high. Brock Commons includes rooms for 400 students, public amenity spaces, and a lounge. The LEED Gold-certified building is a focal point of one of the university's "hubs" that consist of student housing, academic facilities, and community amenities.[14]

---

[13] https://vancouver.housing.ubc.ca/residences/brock-commons/
[14] www.naturallywood.com/resources/brock-commons-design-preconstruction-overview

(cont.)

The Brock Commons "reflects UBC's leadership in sustainable construction and our commitment to providing our students with more on-campus housing," according to UBC president Santa Ono.[15]

It is worth pointing out that this project by the University of British Columbia, similar to the KBISD project at the Georgia Institute of Technology, was completed by a university. Another higher education institution that has recently constructed a mass timber building is Clemson University, which built a CLT fitness center in 2019.[16] The University of Arkansas was also an early adopter of mass timber technology in the United States, constructing a dormitory complex and a library annex in 2019.[17] This trend toward experimental mass timber projects among universities demonstrates that this type of organization may have a higher-than-average willingness to try out new technologies, especially environmentally friendly and quick-to-construct solutions like mass timber.

The services rendered by the building go far beyond what is immediately visible to its surrounding community. The built environment is responsible for around 40 percent of total carbon emissions due to the use of heavy manufactured materials. Wood is a sustainable material not only because it is a renewable resource, but also because it stores atmospheric carbon, unlike other building materials that emit carbon during their manufacturing processes. The Brock Commons building avoids or sequesters 2,432 tons of CO_2 by utilizing wood instead of other common construction materials. This is the equivalent of removing 511 cars from the roads for one year.[18] Paired with sustainable forestry practices, the widespread use of mass timber in construction could help significantly reduce carbon emissions in the atmosphere as a form of carbon sequestration.

Consider that the carbon in the atmosphere results from burning fossilized organic material. By sequestering carbon in buildings in the form of wood, we can transfer solar energy into stored carbon (in the form of trees and timber) and store it for long periods of time as the

---

[15] www.architectmagazine.com/technology/the-university-of-british-columbias-brock-commons-takes-the-title-of-tallest-wood-tower_o

[16] https://swinertonmasstimber.com/swinerton-in-the-news/mass-timber-on-the-rise-new-building-opens-at-clemson-university/

[17] www.archpaper.com/2019/11/adohi-hall-university-of-arkansas/

[18] www.thinkwood.com/our-projects/brock-commons-tallwood-house

(cont.)

structural components of the building. There are further benefits to mass timber as well. Because timber is lightweight, there is less energy-intensive concrete and steel required to manufacture the building. The physical flexibility of wood makes it effective for resisting earthquake damage.

The construction of Brock Commons demonstrates to the building market that wood is a viable and cutting-edge option for tall buildings in the context of recent advances in engineered timber products and building techniques. The design team behind the project is Canadian firm Acton Ostry Architects Inc., in collaboration with Fast + Epp, Architekten Hermann Kaufmann, GHL Consultants Ltd., and mass timber firm Structurlam. While sustainability may be a key value in state-of-the-art mass timber building projects, wood in construction also provides considerable economic benefit. Because of the lower weight of wood, designers can reduce the purchase of expensive, heavy-duty footings. Most importantly, mass timber buildings can be constructed very quickly thanks to offsite prefabrication. Brock Commons was completed only 70 days after the mass timber components arrived on site.[19] By displaying both environmental and economic benefits, this project inspired design teams and developers worldwide to construct tall, mass timber buildings.

Brock Commons was upstaged in March 2019 when Mjostarnet, a multi-use building designed by Voll Arkitekter in Brumunddal, Norway, was completed and earned the title of the tallest timber building in the world. Home to a hotel, residential apartments, office space, and more, Mjostarnet is also 18 stories but surpasses Brock Commons at 85.4 meters tall.[20] It is the third-tallest building in the country, boasting Glulam columns and elevator shafts made entirely of cross-laminated timber. Materials for the project were sourced locally from timber firm Moelven Limitre, as the region is home to a major forestry and wood-processing industry.[21] The building stands as proof that tall buildings can be built sustainably using local resources and as a symbol of the "green shift" in construction

[19] www.archdaily.com/879625/inside-vancouvers-brock-commons-the-worlds-tallest-timber-structured-building
[20] www.designbuild-network.com/projects/mjosa-tower-mjostarnet/
[21] www.dezeen.com/2019/03/19/mjostarne-worlds-tallest-timber-tower-voll-arkitekter-norway/

(cont.)

practices.[22] Replicating and improving upon the successes of other tall wooden buildings serves as a signal that mass timber can be adapted and implemented across the world in the future of architecture.

Cleveland, OH, will become home to the tallest mass timber project in the United States when the nine-story INTRO building is completed (scheduled for 2022). While mass timber is newer to the US building industry, the potential impacts of this demonstration project could be significant in introducing mass timber to a broader market. The building will be a multi-use development with 300 apartments, 35,000 square feet of retail space, an event venue, underground parking, and a public plaza.[23] The port authority of Cleveland provided financing for the project as a path to local economic growth. In addition, 5,000 cubic meters, or 120 truckloads, of wood will be supplied by Binderholz, an Austrian mass timber firm that commits to zero-waste timber by using every part of the tree in production. Hartshorne Plunkard is the architecture firm behind the ambitious project.

Plans for other tall timber buildings around the world are well underway as competing firms race to the top of green building construction, both literally and metaphorically. In 2018, Japanese timber company Sumitomo Forestry announced plans for the new world's tallest wooden building to be constructed in Tokyo. Named W350 in honor of the company's 350th anniversary (talk about sustainability!!), the building is planned to be a towering 350-meter, 70-story skyscraper, and the country's tallest building. The company plans to use 185,000 cubic meters of wood that will make up 90 percent of the hybrid structure.[24] Elsewhere, the Chinese/Austrian architecture firm Penda has planned the Toronto Tree Tower project, a 62-meter, 18-story apartment building made of cross-laminated timber and adorned with trees on every balcony.[25] Australian software company Atlassian hopes to build a 40-story mass timber and steel skyscraper for its new headquarters.[26] With these ambitious architectural plans sprouting up across the globe, new and innovative solutions for energy efficiency and

[22] www.moelven.com/mjostarnet/   [23] https://introcleveland.com/
[24] www.dezeen.com/2018/02/19/sumitomo-forestry-w350-worlds-tallest-wooden-skyscraper-conceptual-architecture-tokyo-japan/
[25] www.dezeen.com/2017/08/02/toronto-tree-tower-penda-cross-laminated-timber-construction/
[26] www.popularmechanics.com/science/a32971165/tallest-mass-timber-skyscraper-australia/

(cont.)

customization for various building purposes are emerging. The result of such high-profile demonstration projects is serving to further the market adoption of wood as a sturdy structural building material that could transform the built environment for greater sustainability.

Building Codes and Mass Timber: US building code provisions permit mass timber in construction, allowing for "alternate methods" of construction. Additionally, the 2015 International Building Code (IBC) began to streamline the acceptance of cross-laminated timber buildings by recognizing cross-laminated timber products manufactured in accordance with an IBC standard. The code permitted cross-laminated timber walls and floors for use in all types of combustible construction.[27]

The upcoming 2021 IBC will give mass timber a much larger boost. It will delineate three new construction types allowing for the use of CLT in businesses and residential buildings up to 18 stories tall. The IBC formed the Ad Hoc Committee on Tall Wood Buildings, composed of building and fire officials, architects, fire protection engineers, and industry experts, in 2015 to examine and propose appropriate code requirements for the 2021 IBC. Two groups of changes, Group A and Group B, have been proposed and are being reviewed and voted on sequentially. The Group A submission proposed 14 changes including three new construction types and changes related to allowable building size, fire-resistance ratings, exposed timber, and fire safety during construction. These changes were approved in January 2019. The Group B changes include three additional administrative and structural provisions related to tall mass timber buildings. They are now in the process of being approved. The three new construction types that will be included in the 2021 IBC will allow certain types of mass timber building to be 18 stories tall with nearly 1 million square feet.[28]

In a push to allow taller mass timber buildings before 2021, Oregon has preemptively approved the Group A changes through a Statewide Alternative Method, and Washington is pursuing similar allowances. Additionally, the city of Denver is considering tall wood buildings through Alternate Methods and Materials Requests or allowing

[27] www.bdcnetwork.com/mass-timber-construction-grows
[28] www.woodworks.org/experttip/current-status-tall-mass-timber-buildings-building-code/

(cont.)

builders to refer to the 2021 IBC, despite the code still awaiting formal adoption.[29]

In terms of performance standards, the American Plywood Association has published a document that serves as the US standard for cross-laminated timber. The guide offers structural grading classifications, design values, and requirements and test methods for qualification and quality assurance. In 2015, an Oregon lumber mill was certified to produce American Plywood Association compliant cross-laminated timber products.[30] The mill is the first in the country with this certification, and it is already in talks with over a dozen projects.

Certification Mechanisms and Mass Timber: In 2016, the US Green Building Council (USGBC) expanded the number of wood certification programs that could qualify for LEED credits. The LEED pilot program offers an Alternative Compliance Path credit for projects with wood verified by the FSC, Sustainable Forestry Initiative (SFI), American Tree Farm System, or the European-based Programme for the Endorsement of Forest Certification (PEFC).[31] This change applies to the existing provision for wood products obtained from responsibly managed sources in the credit "Responsible Sourcing of Raw Materials." USGBC's widening of accepted wood certification organizations may contribute to wider use of any kind of certified timber in LEED buildings, but USGBC does not yet specifically reward the use of mass timber.

In terms of other green certification systems, Green Globes recognizes timber certified by the same wide variety of organizations accepted by LEED. Several other systems including Green Star Australia, DGNB, BREEAM, HQE, BEAM, and the Living Building Challenge recognize only FSC- or PEFC-certified timber. FSC is the most widely recognized. FSC acknowledges that mass timber is an

---

[29] www.woodworks.org/experttip/current-status-tall-mass-timber-buildings-building-code/

[30] www.woodworks.org/experttip/current-status-tall-mass-timber-buildings-building-code/

[31] www.smithcurrie.com/publications/common-sense-contract-law/usgbc-announces-new-leed-credits-for-structural-wood-building-materials-the-decision-is-a-boost-to-the-expanding-use-of-wood-in-public-and-private-projects/

(cont.)

opportunity for carbon pollution reduction and the creation of a market for products from forest restoration and fuel-load reduction harvests.[32] However, the organization maintains that sustainable sourcing is their main priority, and thus wood for mass timber must come from responsibly managed forests in order to be certified. Therefore, the above building certification schemes do not reward mass timber use unless it is also certifiably sustainably harvested.

There is room for growth in mass timber in the green certification sector as a low-climate impact material. As real-estate investors and building owners increasingly prioritize the entire carbon footprint of the construction process and building footprint, we expect ecolabel rating systems to give credit for the carbon sequestered by buildings. In this particular circumstance, we are talking about embodied carbon that is sequestered in the mass timber in the project, but conceivably other emergent technologies like direct air capture and alternative cements that absorb CO_2 that could gain credit as well. These might be rewarded through official policies and subsidies that give a financial payment for carbon sequestration. It remains to be seen if and when these innovations gain a foothold through ecolabel schemes where investment in these technologies earns credits toward certification.

In Japan and the United States: Historically, many buildings in Japan have been constructed with timber, but the risk of fire greatly reduced the construction of wooden buildings after the Meiji Restoration of 1868 in favor of modern building materials. Japan has recently seen a shift from heavy construction materials back to wood in the form of cross-laminated timber. The Japanese government has actively promoted mass timber by passing the Promotion of Use of Wood in Public Buildings Act in 2010. The Act required all government buildings up to three stories high to be constructed with or to utilize wood. The Japanese Forest Agency also contributes to a national road map for integrating cross-laminated timber into the built environment. The Agency subsidizes new mass timber facilities in order to increase Japan's production capacity to supply timber in the domestic and international markets.[33]

---

[32] https://us.fsc.org/en-us/newsroom/newsletter/id/1028

[33] www.globenewswire.com/news-release/2018/11/15/1652081/0/en/Japan-Cross-Laminated-Timber-Market-Trends-Share-Size-Growth-Opportunity-and-Forecast-2018-2023.html

(cont.)

Cross-laminated timber is covered under Japan's 2016 Building Standard Act for CLT. Since the passage of the Act, mass timber has become a common building material in Japan. A modest number of two and three-story mass timber buildings have been built in Japan to date, including detached homes, staff dormitories, bus shelters, and public housing. The market for mass timber is expected to reach 500,000 cubic meters of annual production by 2024. Europe is currently the world leader in mass timber, producing approximately 700,000 cubic meters annually. Europe has been constructing 5–10 story cross-laminated timber buildings since the 1990s, and a 24-story building is currently planned in Vienna.[34] As Japan is situated on the boundaries of four different tectonic plates, its vulnerability to earthquakes makes resilient cross-laminated timber structures more attractive. Remaining barriers to greater CLT market penetration include fire-resistance regulations and the high cost of the material. The market for mass timber in Japan is currently exhibiting robust growth, but for now only consists of a few manufacturers, including Meiken Lamwood Corporation, Yamasamokuzai Co. Ltd., and Chuto.[35]

Mass timber is a relatively new construction material in the United States. Mass timber, however, is gaining momentum with the support of federal and state governments. The FY 2016 Military Construction, Veterans Affairs, and Related Agencies Appropriations bill included language encouraging the Department of Defense to collaborate with the US Department of Agriculture and its US Forest Service to design a joint plan to further the use of sustainable building materials like cross-laminated timbers. The Department of Defense has already contracted to build a hotel using only cross-laminated timber in the structure of the building. Oregon State University also plans to construct a state-funded mass timber building.[36]

The US Department of Agriculture has also encouraged the use of mass timber by establishing the US Tall Wood Building Prize Competition in 2014. Teams of architects, engineers, and developers

---

[34] https://japanpropertycentral.com/2016/01/clt-could-soon-be-incorporated-into-japans-building-code/

[35] www.globenewswire.com/news-release/2018/11/15/1652081/0/en/Japan-Cross-Laminated-Timber-Market-Trends-Share-Size-Growth-Opportunity-and-Forecast-2018-2023.html

[36] www.smithcurrie.com/publications/common-sense-contract-law/usgbc-announces-new-leed-credits-for-structural-wood-building-materials-the-decision-is-a-boost-to-the-expanding-use-of-wood-in-public-and-private-projects/

(cont.)

competed to showcase the architectural and commercial benefits of cross-laminated timbers in tall buildings. The prizes for the winners were grants of $1.5 million, awarded to "Framework," a 12-story mixed use mass timber building, and a 10-story condominium building planned to be the largest wooden structure in New York City.[37] The bipartisan Timber Innovation Act (S. Bill 2892) was introduced in the Senate in 2016 to authorize the Tall Wood Building Prize Competition to be conducted yearly for the next five years. The Act would also create federal grants for research and development on the use of wood as a structural material in tall buildings over 85 feet high, or approximately seven stories tall.[38] The Act is strongly supported by the forest products industry, but has been stalled in committee for four years. These examples of public procurement for innovative, green building hold important promise for diffusion and market transformation.

Private mass timber projects are also popping up around the country, including two multi-story buildings on the West Coast, a large pavilion on the lake in Chicago, and a building at the Oregon Zoo. An office building project called T3 (Timber, Transit, Technology) was constructed in Minneapolis in 2016, and a second project by the same team was completed in Atlanta in 2019.[39] This pattern of project teams demonstrating new technologies in different geographical locations highlights the phenomenon of project-based learning-by-doing that was articulated in the Living Building case. According to Thomas Mende, CEO of Binderholz Timber, speedy construction and prefabricated designs have the potential to make mass timber a cost-competitive choice for large, repetitive projects like chain hotels, affordable housing projects, condos and apartments, and a number of new applications. Mende explains the opportunities to innovate and improve mass timber processes: "The more that people do it – the more

[37] www.smithcurrie.com/publications/common-sense-contract-law/usgbc-announces-new-leed-credits-for-structural-wood-building-materials-the-decision-is-a-boost-to-the-expanding-use-of-wood-in-public-and-private-projects/

[38] www.smithcurrie.com/publications/common-sense-contract-law/usgbc-announces-new-leed-credits-for-structural-wood-building-materials-the-decision-is-a-boost-to-the-expanding-use-of-wood-in-public-and-private-projects/

[39] https://structurecraft.com/projects/t3-atlanta

(cont.)

competition there is, we get better at solving the little problems; the engineers get better at it and it costs less; the more costs come down."[40]

Results from new projects are promising. Lend Lease's Redstone Arsenal mass timber hotel project in Huntsville, Alabama was completed 37 percent faster than traditional steel-frame projects and was first-cost (initial capital costs) neutral. This example successfully demonstrated the benefits of mass timber and is being replicated elsewhere. Mass timber could be particularly beneficial in residential, hospitality, and office settings for mid-rise buildings between 6 and 12 stories.[41]

These mass timber projects and other forthcoming ones (see Figure 6.8) are remarkable considering that no cross-laminated timber factories existed in the United States until 2011. Components were imported from Canada or Europe, where mass timber has been a construction staple since the 1990s.[42] Lingering challenges in the industry include limitations on both the supply of mass timber in America and industry experience and data. The 2021 IBC will provide explicit support for mass timber that will boost the industry in the United States. Overcoming regulatory barriers remains difficult, but early adopters like Lend Lease are supporting fire, blast, and seismic testing to demonstrate acceptable performance parameters to regulators and authorities.[43]

Conclusion

We anticipate that the introduction of the KBISD building in Atlanta will change the regional information and behaviors related to advanced technology adoption. In a similar way, the construction of tall mass timber projects in Vancouver, Quebec City, Oslo, Minneapolis, and Cleveland are likely to spur the diffusion of these technologies by demonstrating their cost and performance characteristics. Preliminary results from our study of KBISD suggest that actors more closely connected with the KBISD, whether through a community

[40] Interview with author, October 26, 2020.
[41] www.smithcurrie.com/publications/common-sense-contract-law/usgbc-announces-new-leed-credits-for-structural-wood-building-materials-the-decision-is-a-boost-to-the-expanding-use-of-wood-in-public-and-private-projects/
[42] www.bdcnetwork.com/mass-timber-construction-grows
[43] www.usgbc.org/articles/mass-timber-tall-wood-buildings-highperformance-design-usgbc-northern-california

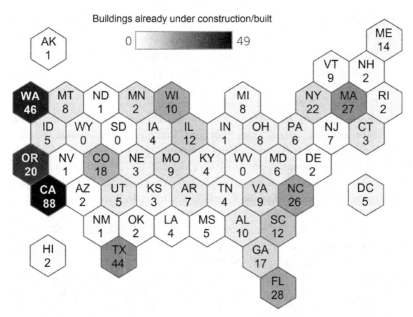

Figure 6.8 US mass timber projects in design or under construction, June 2020

of practice or through physical interaction with the space, have an increased awareness of sustainability technologies and practices for the built environment. Learning by doing and exposure to the KBISD project promotes green building knowledge and familiarity with nascent green building technologies. Network effects, facilitated through the US Green Building Council membership and the number of green building conferences one has attended in the previous five years, predict increased levels of familiarity.

Construction patterns associated with mass timber are also likely to demonstrate the performance characteristics and disseminate information in such a way that facilitates a rapid uptake of this innovative technology. The role of major universities in demonstrating these technologies also emerges from these two cases. The KBISD project at Georgia Tech and the Brock Commons project at the University of British Columbia highlight the role of major research institutions demonstrating innovative technologies and conferring legitimacy to those projects. Buildings like KBISD are important for their ability to promote both general green building knowledge and technology-specific knowledge. In Chapter 7, we take it to the next step and explore how these projects can spur market transformation.

References

Baer, Walter, Leland Johnson, and Edward Merrow. 1976. "Analysis of Federally Funded Demonstration Projects: Final Report." *Rand Corporation Report* No. R-1926-DOC (April).

Bass, Frank. 1969. "A New Product Growth for Model Consumer Durables." *Management Science* 15: 215–227.

Blackburn, Christopher, Mallory Flowers, Daniel Matisoff, and Juan Moreno-Cruz. 2020. "Do Pilot and Demonstration Projects Work? Evidence from a Green Building Program." *Journal of Policy Analysis and Management* 39, no. 4: 1100–1132.

Bollinger, Bryan. 2015. "Green Technology Adoption: An Empirical Study of the Southern California Garment Cleaning Industry." *Quantitative Marketing and Economics* 13: 319–358.

Bossink, Bart. 2015. "Demonstration Projects for Diffusion of Clean Technological Innovation: A Review." *Clean Technologies and Environmental Policy* 17: 1409–1427.

Buijs, Arjen and Sacha Silvester. 1996. "Demonstration Projects and Sustainable Housing: The Significance of Demonstration Projects as a So Called Second Generation Steering Instrument Is Examined by the Use of Case Studies." *Building Research & Information* 24, no. 4: 195–202.

Catalini, Christian and Catherine Tucker. 2017. "When Early Adopters Don't Adopt." *Science* 357, no. 6347: 135–136.

Dalby, Peder, Gisle Gillerhaugen, Verena Hagspiel, Tord Olsen-Leth, and Jacob Thijssen. 2018. "Green Investment Under Policy Uncertainty and Bayesian Learning." *Energy* 161: 1262–1281.

Farzin, Yeganeh, Kuno Huisman, and Peter Kort. 1998. "Optimal Timing of Technology Adoption." *Journal of Economic Dynamics and Control* 22: 779–799.

Harborne, Paul, Chris Hendry, and James Brown. 2007. "The Development and Diffusion of Radical Technological Innovation: The Role of Bus Demonstration Projects in Commercializing Fuel Cell Technology." *Technology Analysis & Strategic Management* 19, no. 2: 167–188.

Hendry, Chris, Paul Harborne, and James Brown. 2010. "So What Do Innovating Companies Really Get from Publicly Funded Demonstration Projects and Trials? Innovation Lessons from Solar Photovoltaics and Wind." *Energy Policy* 38: 4507–4519.

Jacobsson, Staffan and Anna Bergek. 2004. "Transforming the Energy Sector: The Evolution of Technological Systems in Renewable Energy Technology." *Industrial and Corporate Change* 13, no. 5: 815–849.

Kemp, Rene, Johan Schot, and Remco Hoogma. 1998. "Regime Shifts to Sustainability through Processes of Niche Formation: The Approach of

Strategic Niche Management." *Technology Analysis & Strategic Management* 10, no. 2: 175–198.

Kerr, William, Remana Nanda, and Matthew Rhodes-Kropf. 2014. "Entrepreneurship as Experimentation." *Journal of Economic Perspectives* 28, no. 3: 25–48.

Lefevre, Stephen. 1984. "Using Demonstration Projects to Advance Innovation in Energy." *Public Administration Review* 44: 483–490.

Macey, Susan and Marilyn Brown. 1990. "Demonstrations as a Policy Instrument with Energy Technology Examples." *Science Communications* 15, no. 3: 219–236.

Rogers, Everett M. 2003. *Diffusion of Innovations*, 5th ed. New York: Free Press.

7 | *Demonstrating Innovation in Green Buildings*
Catalyzing Market Transformation

Introduction

In Chapter 6, we explored the role of a particular demonstration project in providing the initial seeds of market transformation. Demonstration projects take on high costs and high risks and demonstrate the use of emergent technologies. Once these demonstration projects are built, however, the process by which demonstrated technologies will gain broad market uptake is far from automatic. These technologies might remain expensive, encounter operational challenges, or, due to path dependency and perhaps status-quo bias (or a number of other biases or heuristics), may fail to gain traction in the marketplace.

In this chapter, we develop a theory to explain how demonstration projects can help facilitate transformation in the marketplace. This theory is based primarily on a single economic concept: The costs of acquiring and utilizing new information. Understanding the role that pilot and demonstration projects can play in disseminating information is crucial to understanding the prospects for market transformation. These information flows occur both on the supply side and demand side of the (building) technologies market. In this chapter, we detail how information flows across supply networks and throughout markets can eventually shift standard operating practices, though these results are hardly guaranteed. To illustrate some of these concepts we begin with a case focusing on the uptake and diffusion of chilled beam technology.

A Closer Look: Dissemination of Chilled Beam Technology

Chilled beams are air distribution devices with an integral coil installed to provide space heating and cooling. This approach to heating and cooling saves an estimated 60 percent of energy relative

---

(cont.)

to variable air volume or constant air volume systems, helping reduce electricity and energy costs. It can also save costs due to the reduced need for expansive ductwork. Chilled beams reduce noise associated with the movement of air, making it particularly attractive in hospital, school, and university applications. These systems have been popular in Europe for decades, where higher energy costs justify additional upfront investment in building technologies. Nevertheless, despite the improved efficiency of chilled beams and their seemingly cost-effective deployment, they have not caught on in the United States.

A number of reasons could explain the failure of chilled beams to gain traction in the United States. First, due to different climatic conditions (mostly humidity), it was perceived that there were technical barriers to effectively installing chilled beams. More humidity requires additional investment in equipment to dehumidify the air, and systems are potentially susceptible to condensation issues. Second, because of lower energy costs in the United States, the costly upfront investments required for chilled beams may have been perceived as risky or not cost-effective for the US market. These additional investment costs may be due to additional technical expertise, the need for advanced temperature controls, and the installation of a dedicated outdoor air system (DOAS) that can help manage humidity and ventilation in the space. Third, because the building and construction industry is highly localized, there was simply insufficient expertise in passive-cooling technology in the United States. This promising technology simply failed to gain traction due to information barriers limiting learning and information transmission among regions. Recently, advancements in temperature control technology, increased attention to building energy use, and ecolabel programs have spurred new demand for the technology in the United States and around the world.

There are two main types of chilled beams: Passive and active. Passive-chilled beams are suspended from the ceiling and consist of inducted air being drawn across the coil by the buoyancy of air and gravitation (see Figure 7.1). The warm air that rises to the ceiling enters the beam from the top, passes through the coil and drops down. This makes pressure drop behind the chilled air and draws warm air through the coil. This type of chilled beam does not supply primary air, does not make use of air ducts, and avoids the need to use electric fans to move

(cont.)

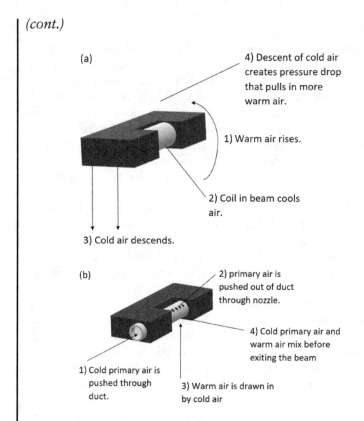

Figure 7.1 Passive- and active-chilled beams

the air to cross the coil.[1] In contrast, active-chilled beams are recessed in or suspended from the ceiling (see Figure 7.1). They have ductwork that provides the primary (dry) air that is forced into the area with the chilled beam, inducing warm air from the room up through the coil. Active-chilled beams have a higher cooling capacity compared to passive-chilled beams due to this induction process and for this reason are more commonly used.[2]

In 1975, chilled beams were developed in Norway. They rapidly spread all over Europe and became standard practice.[3] Chilled beams

---

[1] www.achrnews.com/articles/123293-chilled-beams-what-they-are-why-you-should-use-them

[2] www.trane.com/content/dam/Trane/Commercial/global/products-systems/education-training/engineers-newsletters/airside-design/adm_apn034en_1209.pdf

[3] www.ashrae-wi.org/crc/CRC_files/ASHRAE%20CRC%20Presentation%20DOAS%20WITH%20CHILLED%20BEAM.pdf

(cont.)

caught the interest of architects and engineers due to the significant energy-efficiency benefits they provide, which is important in light of the growing number of green buildings being designed and developed. Benefits of chilled beams include reducing energy costs, improving the quality of the indoor environment and occupant comfort, and reducing the size of air-handling units compared to traditional HVAC systems. Besides the benefits of chilled beams, other factors that accelerated their use in Europe include carbon emissions reduction targets, high building-efficiency standards, and regulations that limit the fan energy that can be used in relation to the building size.[4] Nevertheless, this technology did not become common outside Europe until much later. The construction industry is notoriously localized. Due to high transportation costs, regionally focused materials sourcing and construction firms are common. Expertise and innovative technologies often remain geographically siloed.

Chilled beam adoption then gained some momentum in Australia. In 2002, the Donovan Hill Architects office in Brisbane became the first building in Australia to include this technology. The technology broke through when Lend Lease developed the 30 The Bond building in Sydney, the first five-star Australian Building Greenhouse Rating and a five-star Green Star-office as rated by the Australian Green Building Council. These ratings were given, in part, due to the use of chilled beams. After 30 The Bond, developers began incorporating chilled beams into several projects around Australia, mainly because they gave a better chance of achieving a five-star green building.[5,6]

Chilled beams developed in Scandinavia in the 1970s and 1980s before rapidly spreading throughout Europe and Australia where mild humidity and temperatures made it a success, particularly in the commercial office sector. Due to higher-humidity climates, the adoption and use of chilled beams in the United States is still relatively new. When chilled beams were introduced in the US market, there were limited choices for designers and engineers, but the technology has gained popularity because of its excellent performance, high cooling

[4] www.semcohvac.com/admin/UploadedFiles/Product/7200SEMCO%20Pinnacle%20&%20Chilled%20Beam%20Application%20Guide.pdf
[5] https://inhabitat.com/30-the-bond-sydneys-greenest-building/
[6] www.architectureanddesign.com.au/news/industry-news/the-chill-factor

(cont.)

capacities, and energy-savings opportunities.[7] The Tahoe Center for Environmental Sciences in Nevada was the first laboratory in the United States to use chilled beams. The building opened in August 2006 and includes chilled beams in all of the labs except for two with intensive cooling requirements. The project was attractive because reducing the ducting, airshaft, and air handler sizes brought cost-effectiveness in the form of a $20,000 saving. However, the innovative design required additional time spent to analyze the system and then to explain and justify it to the contractors and owners.[8]

The hot and humid Southeastern region of the United States poses additional challenges for chilled beams. If the supply air is not dehumidified enough, condensation presents a problem because chilled beams only satisfy low latent loads. In 2006–2008, Furman University in Greenville, SC, was the first to install chilled beams in the Southeastern region during the renovation of a 1950s-era building complex. The main reason for adopting the technology was that chilled beams provided more space for engineers to work in buildings with little floor-to-floor height. And the decision had economic advantages as well. It was estimated that chilled beams would save the university 31 percent in energy costs and cut sheet-metal costs in half.[9]

For the chilled beams to succeed in the humid Southeast, it was critical to ensure a dry air supply. At Furman University, energy-recovery wheels were incorporated to dehumidify the air supply upstream of the chilled-water coils. The recovery wheels transfer sensible and latent energy from the incoming airstream to the supply airstream, ensuring the delivery of cool, dry air to the chilled beams as primary air. In this way, Furman demonstrated that it is possible to successfully implement this energy-saving technology in the humid southeast.[10]

The technology was later adopted by another university, Georgia Tech. Chilled beams were first considered for the labs inside Georgia Tech's new building, Clough Commons. Although the technology was implemented successfully in South Carolina, humidity in Georgia was still a concern. A side-by-side test with a conventional HVAC system

---

[7] www.priceindustries.com/content/uploads/assets/literature/tech-tips/a-bright-future-for-chilled-beams.pdf
[8] https://nepis.epa.gov/Exe/ZyPURL.cgi?Dockey=P100SKM9.txt
[9] www.esmagazine.com/articles/94005-chilled-beams-win-over-the-humid-south
[10] www.esmagazine.com/articles/94005-chilled-beams-win-over-the-humid-south

(cont.)

was set up using two labs in the Clough Commons building.[11] The building was completed in 2011 and the experiment proved that chilled beams were a viable option with no sweating or condensation issues. In 2015, the Engineering and Biosystems Building (EBB), a LEED Platinum-certified building, was completed at Georgia Tech. The EBB includes a network of 365 active-chilled beams for heating and cooling, minimizing the energy needed to distribute conditioned air through the building. This large-scale implementation of chilled beams is a key component in achieving the building's energy goals.[12,13] In January 2019, Crosland Tower, Georgia Tech's library, reopened after a three-year renovation that included the installation of chilled beams.[14] Four months later, the CODA Building opened as the fourth building at Georgia Tech with this energy-saving technology.

The spread of chilled beam technology around Georgia Tech was not confined to just campus. Around the same time, in 2018, the NCR headquarters opened adjacent to Georgia Tech, also using chilled beam technology. Perkins and Will, a major construction company, also implemented an experimental adoption of chilled beams in 2018 at their biophilic-designed headquarters in Atlanta, just a few blocks from these other projects. Though perhaps due to an interest in saving on costs, they did not install a dedicated outdoor-air system with an ability to dehumidify the incoming air, creating issues with moisture. This issue has plagued a number of approaches to implementing "passive cooling."

A Closer Look: The CODA Building

The CODA Building, located in midtown Atlanta's Technology Square, is a 750,000 square-feet, mixed-use building that contains 645,000 square feet of office space, research labs, retail space that includes a food hall, a 9.6 MW data center, and five floors of underground parking. It contains a high-performance computing center and a sustainable ecosystem that integrates the multi-block Tech Square

---

[11] www.enr.com/articles/11871-enr-southeasts-2013-owner-of-the-year-georgia-tech-builds-greater-expectations

[12] www.enr.com/articles/12245-georgia-tech-research-conjures-platinum-lab-project?page=1

[13] www.hpbmagazine.org/georgia-tech-engineered-biosystems-building/

[14] atlanta.curbed.com/2019/1/16/18184795/georgia-tech-reopens-updated-library

(cont.)

neighborhood development with innovative opportunities in research, business, and sustainability.[15] CODA is designed to enable interactions between university affiliates, researchers, start-ups, Fortune 500 companies, and students. The building integrates novel workplace design with research labs, industry event space, retail, communal spaces, restaurants, and bars.[16]

CODA incorporates several key features of innovative and sustainable design. These include a condenser water infrastructure that provides both heating and heat rejection. Data-center waste heat supplies about 80 percent of the heating needed in the building. The building has an intelligent building system with advanced submetering. It has groundwater and rainwater harvesting to supply 20–30 percent of the data-center cooling-tower makeup water and 100 percent of the office-space cooling-tower makeup water. And it has dedicated outdoor-air units with passive desiccant dehumidification and energy recovery and active-chilled beams as the primary cooling and heating system.[17]

Incorporating green features and particularly a chilled beam air-conditioning system instead of a typical air-conditioning system provided several challenges to the project developers. Operating the chilled beams requires a considerable amount of piping. This generated conflicts with the installation of other equipment like conduits and ductwork. However, almost all conflicts were identified and resolved using extensive Building Information Modeling before any installation was performed.[18] Building Information Modeling uses 3D modeling to help facilitate the architecture, engineering, and construction of a project more efficiently by helping to plan, design, construct, and manage buildings and infrastructure.

In early 2016, Georgia Tech, the primary tenant, selected Portman Holdings and Next Tier HD to develop the CODA project. In April, Georgia Tech and Portman Holdings announced the $375 million project in a gathering of Atlanta's business and civic leaders.[19] John Portman & Associates designed the 21-story facility and construction

---

[15] www.portmanholdings.com/portfolio-posts/coda-tech-square/
[16] https://codatechsquare.com/
[17] www.integralgroup.com/projects/coda-expansion-technology-square/
[18] www.dpr.com/projects/coda-project
[19] www.news.gatech.edu/2016/04/20/georgia-tech-portman-announce-coda-tech-square

(cont.)

began in December.[20] Invest Atlanta, the City's development authority, estimated that the economic impact of CODA could be about $814 million over the next two decades. Vertical construction was completed in September 2018 and CODA opened in May 2019, with Georgia Tech leasing about half of the space in order to house research programs in advanced data analytics and computing.[21,22] The L-shaped building is located on two acres of land owned by the Georgia Tech Foundation between Spring and West Peachtree streets.[23]

According to Portman Holdings' director of leasing, Travis Garland, the inspiration behind the CODA building was how to bring people together. The central idea of CODA's interior design was to give companies different options for workspace collaboration. As part of the design process, Portman Holdings talked to Google, which gave rise to the idea for one of the central design features of the building: the 21-story spiral staircase that became part of the building's collaborative core. According to Google, the highest rate of interaction in their own buildings is found in the staircase.[24,25]

As part of the project, key performance indicators were identified and companies like Integral Consulting Engineering provided electrical, mechanical, fire protection, and plumbing consulting engineering as well as energy-modeling services. CODA seeks to become the first LEED Platinum (Core and Shell) office building and the largest chilled beam installation in the southeastern United States. It is also targeting energy–cost savings of 40 percent compared to ASHRAE 90.1 building standards and an energy-use intensity less than 30 kBtu per square feet per year.[26]

The installation and demonstration of the technology at Georgia Tech, followed by the transfer of the technology to the private sector via Portman Holdings and a number of other major office towers,

---

[20] https://atlanta.curbed.com/2016/12/6/13849574/coda-tech-square-construction-midtown-atlanta

[21] https://news.gatech.edu/features/coda-opening-celebrates-innovation-industry-collaboration

[22] www.dpr.com/projects/coda-project   [23] https://codatechsquare.com/

[24] https://news.gatech.edu/features/coda-opening-celebrates-innovation-industry-collaboration

[25] www.bizjournals.com/atlanta/news/2019/05/03/midtowns-new-nexus-the-game-changing-coda-building.html

[26] www.integralgroup.com/projects/coda-expansion-technology-square/

(cont.)

reflects the potential for the rapid diffusion of new technologies. This is the heart of a demonstration project like this. While the technology failed to catch on in the United States for decades, advancements in temperature control technology, humidity control, and air exchange made the technology more feasible. It was not until chilled beam technology had been piloted and demonstrated in a number of buildings by Georgia Tech that it finally leapt to the private sector in the southeastern United States. The manner in which chilled beam technology was iterated (with some hiccups along the way) allowed it to ultimately gain significant traction. This case highlights many features of the economics of market transformation. We discuss these features next.

Developing a Theory of Market Transformation

Before we explain a theory of market transformation, let us first begin by understanding the economics of information and how it permeates the building and construction industry. In a perfect world, a person considering a home renovation, for instance, would have access to a catalog of all potential technologies, the prices of those technologies, and reliable knowledge of the performance of these technologies. They would know the costs and benefits of different technologies, both today and tomorrow, and be able to quickly calculate the value of the long-term stream of net benefits or *net present value*. In addition to financial values, homeowners might rank options based on other criteria (such as performance or reliability) and create a decision matrix, ranking those factors relative to the financial value. Then, looking at this decision matrix, they would try to select the overall best option. When doing a home renovation or building an addition and when faced with a decision about heating and cooling technology, this sort of decision matrix might be appropriate.

Homebuilders have multiple technologies available for heating and cooling. One could choose an air conditioner and a furnace. The furnace could be natural gas, heating oil, or use electric resistance. Alternatively, instead of a separate air conditioner and furnace, one could choose a heat pump, which itself has multitudes of subcategories (e.g., air source, water source, ground source) and can be paired with other heating and cooling technologies such as radiant floor heating or cooling and zoned heating and cooling.

Now consider the position of the individual who needs to heat and cool their home and is faced with this multitude of technologies. While some ranges for the cost implications of these technologies are available, there are uncertain costs of installing and operating the technologies. Moreover, especially in the case of some of the newer technologies like air-sourced heat pumps, performance characteristics (e.g., noise, reliability, ability to deliver comfort) can be quite uncertain. Some aspects of performance depend on other fluctuating factors outside the home-owner's control, such as energy prices or climatic conditions. Because many of the costs are specific to an individual home, it is difficult or costly to provide estimates of the building and installation costs. A person trying to identify the optimal heating and cooling technologies for their home might reasonably be stumped by these information costs.

Most of these costs and performance characteristics are not unknowable – but they are unknowns. Hypothetically, a person could attempt to calculate costs associated with each option. They could pay the search costs to undertake the time to read reviews and make educated guesses of various performance characteristics. The effort is likely to take valuable time and effort and is, as economists would say, costly. Even after performing research and carrying out the analysis, one is left to make decisions under uncertainty, with gaps of information that are difficult or impossible to bridge. Faced with uncertainty about the costs and benefits associated with a range of competing technologies, a homeowner is likely to turn to a contractor for advice. Now consider that the contractors themselves might not be overly familiar with some of the newer technologies, such as an air-sourced heat pump that uses multiple zones to optimize comfort and reduce energy costs. They might not be able to provide rapid or low-cost estimates, tailored to the homeowner's specific situation. (That is even before we get to the realities that contractors themselves often have preferences over technologies or face incentives to provide advice that might not align with the homeowner. See Chapter 2 for more discussion of these principal-agent problems.)

While the stylized example just discussed pertains to an individual homeowner pricing an individual renovation, the example is illustrative of the decision-making process that occurs for a larger building as well. The same complexities that an individual homeowner faces apply to larger buildings as well, only with more complex technologies, much higher financial stakes, and multitudes of consultants and contractors employed to discern the optimal path forward. For example, highly efficient passive-cooling technologies can be less effective at adapting to dramatic cooling needs. And chilled beam comes with other risks. There are performance risks – the technology could fail to deliver sufficient cooling capacity. There are reliability risks – the chilled beam approach could lead to condensation issues and create indoor "rain." There are cost uncertainties – this new technology could prove to be more expensive than expected, or fail to deliver the promised operating cost-savings. Given the financial and performance risks, decision-makers seek to avoid risk (meaning they are "risk averse"), and typically favor proven technologies that they are familiar with. Risk aversion also applies to contractors in how they assemble a bid for the design or installation work. Due to a procurement process where contractors aim to win a lowest-price bid, they are often hesitant to suggest anything that is expensive up front or has an uncertain performance record. Once a bid is won it is often difficult to revisit major design choices.

Engineers discussing KBISD (see the discussion section in Chapter 6) noted the difficulty of providing detailed estimates before earning a bid on a job. They often "guesstimate" the most appropriate technologies without doing complex calculations. In decision-making theory, we call this the use of *heuristics*, which are rules of thumb or mental shortcuts made to simplify complex decisions.

One of the most well-known heuristics is the "default" heuristic, which means in this case that contractors or individuals might have a favorite technology that they are likely to default to. Perhaps they know how to repair that technology, or they are most familiar with its installation, or it is cheapest and they think they will be more likely to make a sale. There are innumerable reasons that contractors might default to a technology they are familiar with rather than push a new, more uncertain technology. This is also sometimes called the status quo bias. It is likely to require significant new information or significant savings to change that recommendation. In practice this might be even more complicated due to pre-existing relationships with suppliers and contractors that have their own biases or preferences or use heuristics to make decisions. In a network of people and firms making adoption decisions, this kind of heuristic can also help support a sort of "group think" or feedback loops to enshrine a technology as the dominant standard that resists innovation and experimentation. We pick the default technology because that is what everyone else picks. When most people think that way, breaking the status quo becomes very difficult.

Other heuristics can compound this effect. For instance, because we tend to dislike uncertainty or ambiguity, we tend to pick the more well-known options. Picking technologies with more well-known performance characteristics, where the probability that it will work is known with more confidence, reflects an *ambiguity aversion*. Playing it safe often aligns with the status quo bias, especially when the status quo technology has well-known – even if disappointing – performance characteristics. The fear that a decision might lead to regret can also support the playing-it-safe. This *regret aversion* might even lead decision-makers to avoid undertaking more search or analysis of new technologies, which might lead them to regret the decision to go with the status quo. While avoiding information can be a common heuristic to simplify decision-making or avoid unpleasant information, often some information is just more readily available than others. People commonly apply an *availability heuristic* where they use readily available information and examples as the basis for their decisions rather than undertaking a more systematic review of a broader information base. Dominant, status quo technologies can benefit from the availability heuristic as a self-reinforcing mechanism by which the status quo becomes entrenched.

In short, information about new technologies is scarce and costly to obtain. Further, as discussed in earlier chapters, the performance characteristics of new technologies may even be unknowable at the point of purchase. Decision-makers employ various heuristics to handle these information costs and uncertainties. Changing those decisions and spurring innovation depends on addressing these information costs.

How Demonstration Projects Work

Demonstration projects work by supplying valuable information that changes both the supply and the demand for new technologies. When a demonstration project is built, the information and lessons provided by that demonstration are disseminated to the public. With this, we draw a distinction between a demonstration project and a pilot project. A pilot project might be conducted by a private firm in order to test the performance of new technologies. The lessons from that pilot, however, are likely to be used strategically as proprietary information to give one firm a competitive edge. While this may be a sound strategy for an individual firm, if the results of individual experiments remain private, then it dramatically curtails the dissemination of information and technological transitions across society. If a private firm conducts an experiment and keeps the information private, then this information does not meet the demand across the sector. The individual firm that has this advanced technology will charge a significant price premium for this innovative product. While they may be able to find clients who are willing to pay a significant premium for this innovative product, the technology is more likely to remain a niche technology and fail to gain widespread uptake in the market.

It is worth noting that pilot projects likely have a role in developing technology and achieving market transformation as well. Firms that develop advanced energy and environmental technologies can gain a short-term monopoly on an innovative product. This monopoly power can help generate profits that motivates the firm's initial R&D investment – the R&D that allows the monopolist to be greener. This is the conventional economic rationale behind patent protections to spur societally valuable inventions. The carrot of profits from a dominant market position incentivizes the greener innovation in the first place. Then, once the monopolist no longer has a monopoly on the innovative technology, the new technologies that they piloted will disseminate across the industry.

In contrast, if a private firm conducts an experiment and demonstrates the results to a larger set of firms, this information has positive, actionable impacts that accrue outside of the firm that conducted the experiment. Multiple firms benefit from this individual demonstration. That information reduces costs – not just to the firm that conducted the experiment – but to all firms in the industry. Much of the demonstration's value spills over to other firms in the industry. In standard economics theory, this information is likely to be underprovided by the private market because its value accrues outside of the firm that undertook the costly experiment and instead it accrues to the public. This is why research and development funding is often publicly subsidized: because the firm that innovates with R&D investments is unlikely to recoup the full value of their investments. (See Chapter 2 for additional discussion of these spillovers.)

In practice it is likely not quite so simple. There is certainly an advantage to conducting an experiment as opposed to observing an experiment. By conducting an experiment, the firm experimenting with a new technology will get more expertise and experience that can differentiate it from the competition. Similarly, it is impossible for a firm to retain full proprietary advantage over an experiment once that product is built and sold. Once a building is built, for example, it may become visible to all (though the extent to which information is shared varies in practice). Given the broad array of contractors up and down the supply chain that contribute to a building or other demonstration of a new technology, the flow of information from experiments and new products has ripple effects up and down the entire supply chain. For example, the decision to install smart glass on a large project such as CODA or another new building impacts the ease or difficulty of supplying smart glass to nearby buildings – regardless of whether or not the same company serves as the primary contractor. If manufacturing capacity was increased to meet building demand, then a subsequent adopter of smart glass would benefit from that increased capacity. If dozens of laborers had been trained in the installation of smart glass, then those laborers will have that training to work on a subsequent building. This potentially decreases the cost of installing this technology, spurring additional adoption of the product.

Demand-Side Factors

To understand this phenomenon from the demand side, we will dig in a bit further. Perhaps the most obvious way that demonstration projects impact demand is by providing information about the performance of a new technology. Many technologies used in the built environment are known as *experience* goods (see Chapter 2). That is, you do not know how they perform until you experience them. Imagine if someone building a home could go to a model home and observe the new technologies in action, such as multiple heating and cooling technologies in various weather conditions. If you could do this, you would be in much better shape to decide which technologies to integrate into your new home, armed with knowledge about the performance characteristics of the HVAC options. Observing their performance reduces uncertainty about factors like noise and comfort. While there will still be uncertainties about the specifics of the performance of the technology in a particular setting and the long-term operating cost and reliability of the technology, some of the uncertainties about performance and reliability will be reduced.

The second way that demonstration projects work to impact the demand for a new technology is through the spread of this information about the existence and performance of new technological options. The information does not stay private. For example, if one person installs a new technology, such as a high-efficiency variable-speed heat pump in their home, they may tell their friends, neighbors, family, and co-workers about it. They might serve as resources for friends and neighbors thinking about adopting a new technology. These *peer effects* for diffusing information about new technologies are powerful. Peer effects have been observed with many energy technologies, including the purchase of hybrid and electric vehicles, zoned heating and air conditioning, and solar panels. One key reason that peer effects work is that lower communication costs between peers may ease the transmission of information. With costly information, learning through our peers becomes a vital pathway. Further, because friends and neighbors might be trusted sources of information, recipients of information from these sources may give greater weight to its merit and be more likely to adopt new technologies as a result. Peer effects have been demonstrated to occur even when the product itself is not observable. Zoned HVAC systems, for example, are not easily observable from the exterior of a home, yet they are adopted in geographic clusters, indicating that information flows among neighbors may be responsible (Noonan et al. 2015). Demonstration projects can leverage the availability heuristic when peers' adoptions are the most available examples to decision-makers.

Some experts alternatively suggest that peer effects are a form of virtue signaling, where people might drive a Prius or install a solar panel to communicate their environmental values to their friends and neighbors (Kraft-Todd et al. 2018). This phenomenon is also known as conspicuous conservation. (If you know of someone who installed a solar panel where it is shady and produces little electricity, this might be a prime example of pure virtue signaling. The solar panel is clearly not intended to be a cost-effective investment, but instead is intended to make a statement.) This suggests a strategy of virtue signaling – be it signaling environmental values, high-quality, technological savviness or innovation, etc. – in order to build reputation. Building owners and contractors alike might pursue this virtue signaling to inform and influence their peers.

The third way that demonstration projects might impact demand for new technologies is through other networks. Intra-firm networks or corporate ownership might be a powerful way to disseminate new technologies. If a firm installs a new technology in one location and it is successful, they might be more likely to install that technology in another location. Similarly, contractors often make recommendations about technological adoption. This recommendation process might be more aptly described as a supply-side effect, to the extent that contractors make recommendations and the homeowner or developer makes the decision to purchase new technology on that advice. However, because it is the building owner making the decision to adopt the technology, based on information provided by the contractors, we categorize this as a demand-side effect.

Supply-Side Factors

The dissemination of information related to the demonstration can reduce costs and stimulate uptake. This reduction of costs follows from information provided to several stages of the building and construction process. First, as buyers, designers, architects, contractors, and others in the building industry learn about the existence and performance of new technologies, the need to spend valuable resources researching these options declines. The time spent seeking out new technological options or finding contractors willing to work with these new technological options is known as *search costs*. Public dissemination of information about demonstration projects lowers these search costs for the supply side just as it does for demanders. As the information of new technologies disseminates and the technologies become more widespread, the costs of finding someone knowledgeable about those technologies drops. As discussed in the Demand-Side Factors section, a number of innovative building technologies that do not enjoy widespread deployment are subject to high search costs. Chilled beam, smart glass, and mass timber are all nascent technologies in the building and construction sector in the United States. Even if these technologies are prevalent elsewhere in the world, finding a local supplier is costly. As was the case with no-flush toilets in the Genzyme building (see Chapter 1) – procuring these technologies from a foreign supplier entails significant costs. If there are few local suppliers, those suppliers are likely to charge a market premium for access to a new technology or to capitalize on their expense in learning this new technology.

Second, many of the costs associated with new technologies are higher simply because of their novelty. New technologies may require unique designs and specialized skills. These *design costs* and *procurement costs* decrease as the technology becomes more widespread and requires less customization. Chegut et al. (2019), in "The Price of Innovation," estimate that design costs make up more than a third of additional green building costs. In addition, working with innovative technologies requires everyone to put in more effort throughout the process, adding to costs. As these technologies become more ubiquitous, their costs drop. Designs and processes incorporating these technologies becomes standardized. That is, it may be costly for a contractor to install a new technology the first (or several) times, but with each subsequent time a contractor works with a new technology, they become more proficient and the costs drop. Demonstration projects initiate the learning-by-doing process of cost reduction for supplying innovative technologies.

Lastly, there are significant costs to certifying green. These are administrative costs associated with tracking paperwork and documenting credits, as well as the fees paid to Green Business Certification, Inc. or other certifying entity. The documentation requirements associated with certification could add significant costs. For example, to demonstrate energy-efficiency improvements due to green building design, green building labels have historically required multiple building models to be developed to compare a building built to code to the "greener" alternative and to document improved performance. In LEED 4.0, uptake of the new standard was slow. USGBC received feedback that the burden of documenting some of the credits was extraordinary. This led USGBC to streamline the certification process for LEED 4.1. Many of these costs are higher when specialists need to be hired to guide the project. At the beginning of LEED, few people had this expertise. Firms wishing to pursue LEED needed specialized third-party contractors to assist with this process. These barriers increase costs associated with certification. As certification became more common, contractors started to handle LEED documentation and certification in-house. As more firms offer green building services, the additional costs associated with certification dissipate.

Evidence of Market Transformation

There have been many examples of market transformation in energy and environmental technologies over the past decade. As highlighted in Figure 7.2, wind and solar technology, for example, now make up 67 percent of new electricity installations in the United States, with solar alone accounting for 40 percent of new electricity installations in

2019, up 15 percent from 2018.[27] In just six years, the cost of solar PV panels has dropped by 50 percent, and jobs within the solar industry have increased by 160 percent in the last decade.[28] These figures were unthinkable a little more than a decade ago, but market transformation is clearly taking place in the electricity sector. Electric vehicles may be on a precipice of market transformation as well, with California set to ban the sale of new gasoline-powered cars by 2035. In just five years, experts predict there will be 130 electric vehicle models on the market, representing an investment of $225 billion over the next five years by auto makers to electrify their fleets. Clearly, electric vehicles are no longer a fringe market, but rather the direction toward which the auto industry is racing.[29]

The built environment and building technologies represent another area that has experienced market transformation. Beginning with the United Kingdom's BREEAM certification in 1990 and USGBC's LEED label in 1998, green buildings have become increasingly common. By 2019, estimates claimed that 42 percent of office space in major US metropolitan areas was certified, up from less than 5 percent in 2005.[30] In addition, over 300 state and local building codes require some form of LEED standards. In the 2007 Energy Independence and Security Act , the United States made LEED the de facto federal green building policy by requiring federal buildings to be built to LEED standards. LEED had become so ubiquitous in the United States that it was a wonder that people continued to certify, given that most major municipalities and many states essentially required the certification as a standard. (See Table 2.1 for more on this.)

In the green building market, uptake of technologies has followed a traditional S curve for technological adoption, which is well known in the technological adoption literature. This S curve suggests that at first adoptions are slow but, eventually, the pace of adoption speeds up, facilitating market penetration and ultimately market transformation.

---

[27] www.pv-magazine.com/2020/03/18/the-us-added-13-3-gw-of-solar-in-2019-beating-wind-and-gas-in-new-capacity/#:~:text=2020-,The%20US%20added%2013.3%20GW%20of%20solar%20in%202019%2C%20beating,capacity%20now%20tops%2076%20GW

[28] www.energy.gov/eere/solarpoweringamerica/solar-energy-united-states

[29] www.eia.gov/outlooks/aeo/pdf/AEO2020%20Electricity.pdf

[30] www.cbre.us/research-and-reports/US-Green-Building-Adoption-Index-for-Office-Buildings–2019

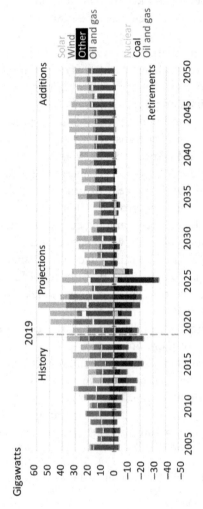

Figure 7.2 Annual electricity generating capacity additions and retirements (EIA).
Source: Energy Information Administration

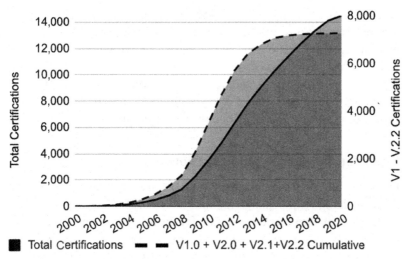

Figure 7.3 S curve derived from cumulative total LEED New Construction certifications (US market)

Indeed – for the first three years of LEED, only 28 projects were built and certified.[31] A similar experience follows the Living Building program where only 24 projects were certified in the label's first 13 years.[32] Even after LEED had built market dominance and popularity, accumulating tens of thousands of certifications, its 2014 version (4.0) only certified 36 new constructions in its first five years. This slow start to technological uptake indicates that high information costs present substantial barriers to the adoption of new technologies.

After an initial period of sparse new adoptions, the experience with LEED highlights the potential for rapid market uptake and market transformation. In the United States, certifications of LEED began to pick up momentum in 2006, and by 2009 over 1,000 new construction certifications were being recorded each year. Figure 7.3 shows the S curve associated with the early versions of LEED and the continued upward trend of the more recent versions of the label. The figure shows that versions 1–2.2 began to tail off in 2014 (at about 7,200 total projects) as LEED 2009 gained market penetration, shown in the steady growth of the solid total certification line. Although LEED version 4.0 was released in 2014, the long-term nature of sustainable

[31] Our calculations from GBIG.   [32] Our calculations from ILFI.

new construction building projects causes a significant lag in new version certifications. Less than 200 projects have been certified under this latest major version to date, compared to roughly 7,000 under LEED 2009. This trend is compounded by many buildings rushing to certify under the old standard, which involves significantly less uncertainty than moving to a new standard. In 2018–2020, new certifications under LEED 2009 have begun to taper off.

Evaluating the Impact of LEED Pilots

How did LEED become so ubiquitous in under 20 years? How did green building really change the industry? Earlier, we suggested that ecolabels provide a market premium for the adoption of new technologies by early movers. Many of these early movers, under the USGBC's LEED system, were recruited to participate in LEED's pilot building program, a demonstration project program that incentivizes early adopters to share data and information with the USGBC and other potential adopters. This technology adoption then spurs the dissemination of information through pilot and demonstration projects as a major catalyst for change. By reducing the costs of new information and demonstrating the performance characteristics of green building technologies, the LEED Pilot program has spurred the uptake of numerous new buildings.

The LEED Pilot program is a collaborative approach where USGBC approached early adopters of a new vintage of a label (e.g., Retail Commercial Interiors) with the opportunity to make their new project a pilot project.[33] The pilot project process is far more collaborative than a typical LEED building certification process. In a typical certification, developers aggregate the documentation necessary for certification and submit this documentation toward the end of the building process. The applications for credits are reviewed and certification is or is not granted. There is little opportunity for technical assistance or

---

[33] It is worth noting that while the LEED Pilot program is called a pilot program, the definition we employ more closely resembles a demonstration project program. The program is structured to facilitate collaboration and sharing of lessons learned, in contrast to our definition of a pilot program, where gained knowledge remains private and proprietary. The "pilot" aspect of the LEED Pilot program lies in how USGBC uses it to pilot new vintages of LEED certification rules.

dialogue with Green Business Certification, Inc. (GBCI), the organization that certifies buildings under the LEED, WELL, and other labels. In contrast, in the pilot project version of green-certified buildings, opportunity exists for significant dialogue, feedback, and assistance along the way. USGBC relies on the feedback from the developers as they try to determine (i) the proper approach for documentation for specific credits, and (ii) the point in the construction process when documentation and verification should happen. The pilot program aims to refine the certification process and launch a new label. In exchange, USGBC gives the developer increased access to advice along the way, and a continuous review process that can help ensure that they achieve certification at the intended level. Discussions from those in the industry suggest that there is more wiggle room and opportunity for negotiation in the process for pilot projects. While LEED is often criticized as following a checklist approach, the LEED pilot project program is thought to be more lenient – especially when it comes to the documentation required to achieve certification.

Blackburn et al. (2020) investigate the impacts of the LEED pilot program. They demonstrate that if a pilot project was adopted in a particular zip code at a particular point in time, the probability of new *non-pilot* LEED projects built in that zip code would double the following year. Figure 7.4 demonstrates the location of pilot projects and nonpilot projects in the United States. A lot of research on the LEED program has shown rapid uptake of LEED buildings in certain cities and has concluded that public policy or other incentives has driven this uptake. There are a number of problems with these existing studies. First, these studies do not typically control for overall growth patterns in cities. Rapidly growing cities are likely to have new construction, and new construction is also more likely to be LEED certified. Second, the USGBC promotes certain vintages of LEED and markets its LEED labels differently in certain locations. Third, technology costs have changed over the past 20 years (partly due to LEED itself) and, as a result, reduced technology costs generally may cause the uptake of LEED in the market. Fourth, changing energy and water costs may drive investments into more efficient technologies. Fifth, cities and states have enacted a vast array of policies and incentives to promote green building (see Chapter 2). In studies that focus on just one of these factors, the other potential drivers of green building uptake are often ignored.

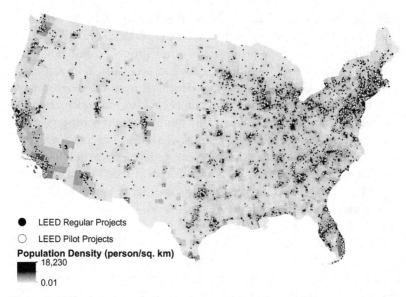

Figure 7.4 The location of pilot projects and nonpilot projects

The Blackburn et al. study uses a unique way of assessing the data that only compares the trajectory of uptake of one vintage of LEED (e.g., New Construction, Core and Shell, Existing Buildings, Retail Interior) with the trajectories of uptake from other vintages of LEED. The approach, called a *difference-in difference-in-differences* model compares differences in space, time, and across LEED vintage to identify the effects of building investments. The strategy isolates the impact of LEED buildings of a particular vintage at a particular point in time. This allows the authors to highlight several key findings.

First, if a LEED pilot project occurs in a certain zip code in a particular year, the authors demonstrate that this building *doubles* the probability that an additional *nonpilot* LEED project will be built in that same zip code. This finding emphasizes the local impact that pilot or demonstration projects can have. While this research is unable to determine whether these impacts are due to building supply chains and reducing costs associated with making it easier to build green or whether the presence of a project stimulates local demand, the authors suggest that a combination of these factors is likely at play.

By building in a particular location, developers create localized demand for similar projects. Developers and construction managers are able to easily observe these new high-performance buildings being built and this increases demand for similar buildings. Further, if there were questions or uncertainties about the performance characteristics of the technology, these can be more easily observed.

This demand-side factor is highlighted in the chilled beam case. Once Georgia Tech had demonstrated the success of chilled beam technology locally, this helped resolve many uncertainties about the performance of the technology in the humid southeast. Further, by encouraging Portman Holdings to use the technology in the CODA building, it helped chilled beams make a leap to the private sector as other buildings like the NCR headquarters adopted similar high-end technologies and attained LEED certifications. Lauren Wallace, a green building consultant with the Epsten Group, notes that "Having a big player in a major urban area like Georgia Tech back chilled beam definitely gave it legitimacy in the marketplace and proved to the industry that the technology was market-ready."[34]

Further, building an innovative green building in a particular city helps build supply chains that lower costs of additional adoption. While this is difficult to observe in the particular case of pilot projects, the impacts of supply chains become more obvious as green building markets mature. While building more green buildings might be expected to reduce the market for additional green buildings (because the market gets crowded and demand becomes satiated), results from Blackburn et al. (2020) also demonstrate that more certified LEED buildings built in a particular zip code beget even more buildings built in the future. That is, there are momentum effects within geographical markets that are likely attributable to the development of supply chains and the subsequent reduction of costs. Today, the US boasts over 200,000 professionals with a LEED credential – LEED AP or LEED Green Associate – all at the ready to advance the Green Building Movement.

Blackburn et al. and others identify additional mechanisms of market transformation. Simcoe and Toffel (2014), for example, highlight the role that public investment plays in creating private investment in green building. Using public entities such as governments, universities, and schools to invest in green building offers a number of opportunities. First, unlike most private developers who sell buildings several years after building them, public institutions are more likely to own and operate their assets. Thus, costly capital investments

---

[34] Interview with author, August 21, 2020.

that pay off over a longer period of time are more likely to make sense. Second, these highly visible, public buildings can also help spur demand and build supply chains. Third, publicly funded buildings may be responsive to a wide set of stakeholders. While privately held buildings might be primarily responsible to stakeholders like investors and employees, publicly owned buildings are responsive to a broader range of taxpayers, citizens, and community members. These stakeholder relationships mean that investments in stormwater management, green roofs, and other technologies that fundamentally provide public services have a vested constituency who benefits from their outcomes. It is not surprising that in Chapter 5 we see government-owned green buildings emphasizing more of these environmental public goods. We further explore the relationship between LEED certification and equity implications for a diverse set of stakeholders in Chapter 9.

Another mechanism that helps drive market transformation is the learning that takes place through multi-locational firms. If Starbucks or another corporation builds a certified building in one location, Blackburn et al. demonstrate that they are also more likely to build green in another location. Thus, firm ownership networks can be important conduits of information about the performance of new technologies and drivers of demand, helping seed technological innovations to new markets. It is also likely that firms are able to embed learning from certification into their procurement process that goes beyond observable outcomes like additional LEED certifications. Some firms' leaders have spoken about learning to build green – even without going through the costly and time-consuming certification process – and the role that early efforts to demonstrate energy efficiency have played in their future investments.

Another manifestation of this may be the role that large networks of consultants and contractors play in large building projects. As highlighted in more detail in Chapter 6, there may be upward of 30 major contractors working on a project, with additional subcontractors. In the green building space, different contractors specialize in certification, building envelope modeling, commissioning and recommissioning, or other specialized green-building services. We think that it is likely that these contractors learn while working on green projects and subsequently play a key role in disseminating knowledge across the industry.

Conclusion

Demonstration projects are an understudied tool that can play a key role in disseminating the lessons of innovative technologies and approaches to managing energy and environmental resources. The LEED Pilot program serves as a prime example where demonstration projects have been seeded in such a way that spurs additional adoptions of innovative technologies. It is worth thinking about some of the lessons of this project that might be applied to other areas – what has made this demonstration project program work, and whether the lessons learned from the LEED Pilot program are generalizable to other contexts.

The LEED program focuses on nascent technologies that are commercially available (yet typically not widespread). In fact, a green building demonstration project is really a combination of nascent or advanced technologies, often put together in a unique way to lower the energy and environmental footprint of a building. It is worth observing that the earliest demonstration projects in LEED did not cause immediate market uptake of LEED. This was also true of the earliest Living Building demonstration projects in the United States, and it has been true, as well, for LEED version 4. It also appears to hold true for earlier adoptions of new technologies like mass timber and chilled beam. Yet this slow growth is a feature of the S curve.

Possible explanations for the slow initial growth of the S curve are that there are too few experiments and that nascent technologies require more refinement before gaining widespread uptake. Demonstration projects can address this. In contrast to nuclear power-plant demonstration projects, clean-coal demonstration projects, and others that are repeated once or twice and then abandoned, the LEED Pilot program appears particularly well-positioned. The dozens of iterations of LEED pilot projects have allowed for the label and technologies to be made market ready. The LEED program has conducted over 1,000 demonstration projects and, ultimately, the LEED Pilot program seems effective at generating significant uptake of the label. In other words, roughly 1 percent of all LEED projects have been demonstrations. This has allowed the iteration of the ecolabel and technologies in such a way that enables the refinement of the product. With LEED, we observe that later iterations of the LEED Pilot program (meaning those buildings built later, rather than earlier) generate more uptake of LEED projects, while earlier iterations of LEED Pilots do not generate additional uptake of LEED. It worked, and the series of experiments with new vintages builds momentum.

The iterations across multiple demonstration projects can help build sufficient capital and knowledge stock in a way that facilitates a tipping point for the adoption of innovative technologies. This emphasizes the value of projects at a small enough scale so that they can be iterated or repeated. Technologies like large nuclear plants and coal gasification with carbon capture and storage may simply be too large to demonstrate effectively because they are too costly to repeat and iterate until the technology works properly. This points to the need to think smaller – something that can be iterated and repeated multiple times until the technology is market ready.

Knowledge and information stock in the supply chain and market must accumulate sufficiently to make adoptions more viable. The LEED Pilot program facilitates significant communication between the builders and contractors working on a demonstration project and the LEED program, again – allowing for USGBC to refine the program and make it market ready. This is not a forgone conclusion. Other projects may demonstrate a new program or new technology but may be rigid rather than flexible, and do not incorporate needed changes to the technology or system. This communication also feeds into a well-developed network of green-building professionals that USGBC has trained. They require continuing education credits to maintain LEED credentials and offer significant opportunities for networking and information exchange, creating a community of professionals who speak the same language and use the same metrics. Despite the construction industry being heavily regional and siloed, USGBC has been effective at transferring information across the United States and even across international borders. It is noteworthy that other international ratings systems also plug into the green building council network and adopt similar practices. This convergence of knowledge likely creates an innovation ecosystem that is conducive to technological progress and change.

Finally, USGBC has been effective at marketing the LEED label. It signifies something of value beyond the energy savings. It commands a market premium for the product. Consumers, employees, and investors demand the certification and the underlying technologies. Part of this market demand is because there is a clear energy-performance benefit to LEED buildings relative to noncertified buildings. Part of this demand is because it may signal quality construction, or it may signal the broader sustainability orientation of the organization. The product sold (office space or buildings) is one that is consumer-facing and is differentiable in the market. Again, this is not a foregone conclusion of energy and environmental technologies. Some innovative technologies likely lack good value propositions. Clean coal and nuclear, for example, need to compete on price with natural gas and solar, that are cheaper. People may not be willing to pay more for a kilowatt of electricity generated from clean coal or nuclear. The take-away lesson, however, is that there may be a limited market for innovative green technologies that is dependent on consumers' willingness to pay extra for them. While consumers are willing to pay more for a green building or sustainably sourced coffee, it is less clear that they are willing to pay more for next-generation nuclear energy or clean-coal electricity. Green markets, ultimately, require green consumers who are willing to pay a premium for green technologies and products.

References

Blackburn, Christopher, Mallory Flowers, Daniel Matisoff, and Juan Moreno-Cruz. 2020. "Do Pilot and Demonstration Projects Work? Evidence from a Green Building Program." *Journal of Policy Analysis and Management* 39: 1100–1132.

Chegut, Andrea, Piet Eichholtz, and Nils Kok. 2019. "The Price of Innovation: An Analysis of the Marginal Cost of Green Buildings." *Journal of Environmental Economics and Management* 98: 102248.

Kraft-Todd, Gordon T., Bryan Bollinger, Kenneth Gillingham, Stefan Lamp, and David G. Rand. 2018. "Credibility-Enhancing Displays Promote the Provision of Non-Normative Public Goods." *Nature* 563, no. 7730: 245–248.

Noonan, Douglas S., Lin-Han Chiang Hsieh, and Daniel Matisoff. 2015. "Economic, Sociological, and Neighbor Dimensions of Energy Efficiency Adoption Behaviors: Evidence from the U.S Residential Heating and Air Conditioning Market." *Energy Research & Social Science* 10, Supplement C: 102–113.

Simcoe, Timothy S. and Michael Toffel. 2014. "Government Green Procurement Spillovers: Evidence from Municipal Building Policies in California." *Harvard Business School Technology & Operations Mgt. Unit*, Working Paper No. 13-030 (May).

8 | Keep Raising the Bar
Green-lighting a Race to the Top!

Introduction

Can building ecolabel programs produce a *race to the top*? Or do these programs at some point become obsolete? In this chapter, we argue participation in voluntary programs can facilitate ongoing quality competition, enabling a race. We advance a theory of self-regulatory competition that may sustain this race. From this perspective, programs can be designed to facilitate a race to the top despite tendencies for label managers to compete for the lowest common denominator or for firms to greenwash and strategically over-represent their environmental performance. Building on the premise underpinning demonstration projects improving supply chains and facilitating uptake of new technologies, we highlight how ecolabel programs can help transform markets. Once a market becomes crowded, new standards can be set, raising the bar for building performance. Data from the LEED program demonstrate that, over time, organizations and especially private firms invest additional resources to attain higher certification tiers, becoming greener as part of a race to the top in a voluntary, green building certification program.

In past chapters, we have demonstrated motivations to certify green to be a first mover and the extent to which early movers facilitate market uptake. In this chapter, we adapt a model of regulatory competition to explore the dynamics of ecolabeling behavior over time. Borrowing from literature that likens regulatory competition to a race (either a race to the bottom or a race to the top), we enumerate the conditions under which regulatory competition results in a race to the top. Such an approach involves more than just the decisions to adopt a building ecolabel (Chapter 5). It also depends on design and implementation decisions by those running the ecolabel system (Chapters 3 and 4) to create the race to the top. We explore the extent to which ecolabels in the building sector have met the criteria for such a race.

Racing to the Bottom or Racing to the Top?

A basic theory of regulatory competition suggests that jurisdictions will adapt laws and policies to attract businesses, investment, employees, or citizens. This phenomenon has received significant attention in terms of taxes, environmental regulation, educational quality, and many other areas. The idea of this competition amongst jurisdictions is appealing because it applies the idea of capitalism and market competition to governments. It argues that governments will compete to provide improved living and working conditions, leading to a *race to the top*. A *race to the bottom*, where governance authorities weaken rules to attract business, will also be addressed later in the chapter. In this model, individuals will move to jurisdictions that provide goods and services that appeal to them. If citizens prefer superior environmental quality, governments will compete to provide improved environmental quality most efficiently. The idea of leveraging a race to the top has been common across a number of policy areas such as education, energy policy, and labor policy.

A race to the top has been the intellectual motivation behind major policy initiatives in the United States such as *No Child Left Behind*. The argument made when pushing this policy initiative was that states and schools would be forced to compete for federal funding. If schools could show improvements toward goals, then they would receive additional funding. If schools failed to show progress, funding would be cut and failing schools would be closed. The initial incarnation of this policy had some problems. Progress metrics were open to being gamed and yanking funds and closing schools in low-performing areas proved politically and ethically perilous. Still, the idea that competition could force improvements was the intellectual motivation behind the Race to the Top education initiative of President Obama, which coerced states to adopt educational reforms to be eligible for increased funding.

State renewable portfolio standards have also been likened to a race to the top (Rabe 2007). State renewable portfolio standards are policies that require electric utilities to source electricity from renewable sources, typically framed as a percentage, by a certain year (e.g., 20 percent by 2020; 50 percent by 2050). In this conception of state renewable energy policy, states compete to attract investment in renewable energy and generate an economy that develops green jobs. A state with aggressive renewable portfolio standards might be able to attract businesses that want to lower their emissions footprint, or citizens who want to live in a state that reflects their environmental values. Over time, more states have adopted these policies as a way to promote renewable energy, and most of them have used successive policy changes to increase the requirements for these policies.

This race-to-the-top pressure can be seen outside of environmental arenas. Inter-regional competition among states and metropolitan areas in the United States has been credited with creating a system where jurisdictions implement policies to enhance amenities, improve regulations and governance, and deploy other efforts to attract a highly skilled, "creative class" to their region (Florida 2014; Moretti 2012). Research has also demonstrated that flows of foreign direct investment have helped improve labor rights in developing countries (Mosley and Uno 2007). In this conception of a race to the top, due to stakeholder pressure at home, firms are more likely to invest capital in countries that have improved protections for labor. Further, firms may transfer improved business practices, including improved rights for workers and improved environmental performance when investing in a country.

Detractors of regulatory competition argue that if jurisdictions compete by weakening environmental laws and reducing taxes (and by consequence, public services), then regulatory competition does not lead to a race to the top, but instead leads to a *race to the bottom*. Ultimately, this concern forms a foundation behind the modern environmental movement in the United States and an impetus for nationalizing environmental regulation. If people prefer lower taxes and lower levels of public services, this can lead government jurisdictions to reduce the provision of these services. Instead of competing to provide the best education and environmental quality, instead, jurisdictions can compete to attract firms and individuals who prefer lower taxes and fewer regulations. The mechanism that allows this race to the bottom can be conceptualized as a "prisoner's dilemma," a single-turn game with two players, where both players have the chance to cooperate or to strike their own selfish deal. Both players maximize their individual utility by "defecting" or cheating the other player. In the prisoner's dilemma, individually rational (self-interested) behavior produces collectively suboptimal outcomes.

In Figure 8.1, we characterize pollution havens as a prisoner's dilemma. For simplicity purposes, this game is played as a

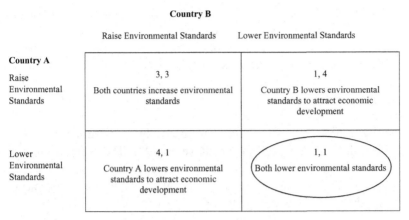

Figure 8.1 Pollution havens and the prisoner's dilemma

simultaneous, one-turn game, without repetition or communication between the countries, even though in reality this game is played repeatedly and communication occurs between countries. In this example, two countries make decisions about increasing or lowering environmental standards. Countries can attract more business by lowering environmental standards. Becoming a "pollution haven" with economic development is seen as the superior alternative to a cleaner environment with little economic opportunity. If both countries opt for higher environmental standards, each country has an incentive to lower their standards and attract the economic development away from the other country. In Figure 8.1, the payoff for Country A is the first number in each cell, and the payoff for Country B is the second number in each cell. Lowering environmental standards and attracting additional business is represented with a payoff of 4, if the other country keeps their environmental standards high. If environmental standards are lowered and additional business is not attracted, the payoff is 1. Further, if environmental standards are high, but business leaves the country, the payoff is 1. If both countries maintain high environmental standards, each country gets a payoff of 3.

Countries are thus incentivized to lower their environmental standards to prevent business flight. Yet both countries face the same incentives. When both countries behave similarly, environmental standards are reduced. But neither country attracts more economic development, with both sharing the available opportunities. This leads to an equilibrium solution (a Nash equilibrium) where environmental standards are lowered across all jurisdictions and economic activity is not increased, represented in Figure 8.1 by the payoff of 1,1 – or a collective payoff of 2. Both countries would have been better off if they raised their environmental standards, each achieving a payoff of 3 and achieving a collective payoff of 6. This collectively suboptimal outcome defines a race to the bottom.

Researchers and policy-makers have also long feared a race to the bottom in environmental policy (Revesz 1992). The pollution haven hypothesis suggests that, in order to attract foreign investment and jobs, countries will weaken environmental regulation or enforcement. Similarly, to develop export driven industry, countries will weaken or fail to enforce environmental laws. This race-to-the-bottom model assumes that weaker environmental regulations reduce compliance costs substantially for businesses. While this is likely true, it is less clear that environmental compliance costs (typically estimated at roughly 2 percent of operational costs) are significant enough to drive firm location decisions. It seems far more likely that other operating costs – such as labor costs – play a greater role in firm location decisions. Mixed evidence regarding the pollution haven hypothesis suggests that, under some circumstances, trade and exports can drive lower environmental regulations in a bid to increase economic activity (Rivera and Oh 2013). However, overall, evidence remains weak for a race to the bottom in environmental regulatory stringency and performance.

One area that has produced a race to the bottom has been corporate and bank charters and other corporate tax and credit card regulations. Researchers have long noted the tendency for small countries to attract investment by lowering tax rates, weakening transparency, and allowing dubious accounting practices (Cousins et al. 2004). Globalization since World War II has resulted in decreasing costs of communication and transportation, which has enabled the mobility of capital, bringing state sovereignty into conflict with globalization (Palan 2002).

In the United States, evidence for this race to the bottom has been apparent in corporate law. Delaware, by enabling a number of regulations that insulate corporate managers (such as making it easy to defeat takeovers), facilitates the ease of anonymously held corporations and provides a number of tax loopholes that allow firms to evade taxes in other states. As a result, Delaware has attracted a startling number of corporate headquarters.[1] Despite having a population that is just one-third of 1 percent of the US total, more than 50 percent of US public companies and 60 percent of Fortune 500 companies are headquartered there. When a 1978 Supreme Court case (*Marquette Nat Bank vs. First of Omaha Service Corp*) declared that credit-card companies could charge interest rates regulated in the state of their incorporation, South Dakota relaxed laws governing interest rates in an effort to attract Citibank. Delaware then followed suit, striking a deal with Chase Manhattan. By 2018, about half of US credit cards came from Delaware (Bruner 2020). In this example, it seems as if the prisoner's dilemma game has concluded through a series of tit-for-tat actions and equilibrium reached, with Delaware and South Dakota winning the credit card race to the bottom.

Other phenomena that lead to suboptimal outcomes can be likened to a race to the bottom. Military (and cyber) arms races represent a race to the bottom by exhibiting a potential for tit-for-tat strategies that can result in uncontrolled escalation. Ultimately, neither side of the arms race finds itself in a demonstrably better position than if the race had never begun. When countries spend scarce tax revenue on arsenals and troops, this diverts spending from other areas to address social concerns. Compounding this problem, arms races promote bribery, kickbacks, and corruption, contributing to governance challenges in developing countries.[2] As evidenced by the Cold War, it can be incredibly difficult to unwind these arms races and achieve détente.

While school choice and educational reforms have attempted to use competition to generate a race to the top in education, there is also significant evidence that school choice can lead to a race to the bottom. Irrespective of good intentions, school choice policies and educational reform might start a race that goes in the wrong direction, at least if increasing diversity, reducing segregation, and getting parents to choose schools based on academic performance are the goals.

---

[1] The sentiment that Delaware represents a race to the bottom is highly contested in the academic literature. Countervailing arguments suggest that this is actually a race to the top due to Delaware's improved ability to return value to shareholders by providing a superior legal framework. From a public perspective, or the perspective of other states, this may most certainly represent a case of race to the bottom by externalizing the cost of business on the citizens of non-Delaware residents.

[2] www.sipri.org/commentary/blog/2013/arms-race-just-race-bottom

Whether ecolabels can green-light a race to the top, or bottom, becomes a critical question for the Green Building Movement.

Can Ecolabels Produce a Race to the Top?

In this chapter, we explore the application of regulatory competition to ecolabels. In this conception of regulatory competition, ecolabels are governing bodies that have a set of rules and policies aimed at attracting participants to certify firms or organizations. There may be multiple ecolabels competing for participants. In the coffee market, does a producer get fair trade or SANRA or UTZ certified? Or, if you are Starbucks, do you create your own sustainable coffee certification, or utilize an existing certification? If you are purchasing coffee at the grocery store, which label will you pay more for? Do you even know the difference? In the building market, does one get BREEAM, Green Globes, Living Building, or LEED certified? Or some combination of these? Or do something else entirely? In our analogy that likens the eco-certification market to regulatory competition, we suggest that conceptualizing the relationships between certification bodies and participants in the ecolabels can help us understand the temporal dynamics that lead ecolabels to facilitate a race to the top or a race to the bottom.

In a race to the top facilitated by ecolabels, organizations compete for top talent and sales premiums by focusing energy on their sustainability performance. If being greener leads to increased productivity and profitability, this attracts the attention of competitors, who will quickly seek to implement similar changes. When peer and competitor organizations compete for these returns, we observe competition driven by sustainability practices, or a race to the top. While these efforts may largely be for marketing purposes or to take advantage of a wide range of economic benefits from improving environmental behavior (see Chapter 2), firms may also improve their environmental performance in order to achieve this marketing signal or recognition (see Chapter 5). Consider an example where firms (or universities) are competing to have the "greenest building," "greenest stadium," or the "greenest campus." The marketing value for being noted as the "greenest" might be quite large. At a business, these sorts of accolades can help build employee morale, attract and retain quality employees, and help generate a culture of innovation and strategy around sustainability. At a university, this might help build campus spirit, attract students, facilitate learning opportunities, attract donations from alumni, and improve relations with the community and external constituents. Similar factors might influence an NGO seeking to curry favor with employees, donors, and the broader community. The competition to be greenest might be pervasive across industries. In professional sports, it is obvious that teams compete for a league championship. But professional sports teams also appear to compete to have sustainable stadiums or arenas! The dynamic relationship between competition and prestige in professional sports provides a useful analogy. The halo from a league championship might be fleeting – and after winning, few teams are willing to rest on their laurels. Similarly, competing organizations may seek to build a greener or more sustainable project, capturing the value from having the top position in the market.

In a race to the bottom, weak ecolabels allow firms to greenwash or market themselves as green and sustainable without taking substantive action to improve their environmental performance. The flexible nature of ecolabels opens the very real possibility that some ecolabels can lead to greenwashing – or the over-representation of environmental performance. In the context of ecolabels, this can happen through several mechanisms. First, if ecolabels do not force improved environmental behavior by participants and award labels to poorly performing entities, these weak ecolabels can lead to confusion in the market. Firms may seek to cheaply purchase legitimacy by seeking out weak ecolabels, taking advantage of confusion in the marketplace to over-represent their environmental performance to consumers. Second, because even strong ecolabels offer flexibility within certification pathways, it is possible that firms can seek out particular credits that allow them to achieve certification without meaningfully changing behavior. These approaches to certification might be called "symbolic certification," where firms learn to game the system and purchase legitimacy by participating in voluntary initiatives but fail to improve the operational quality of the firm.

In this race to the bottom, it is difficult for consumers to accurately evaluate the environmental performance of organizations, and these organizations can mislead customers by joining green certifications with weak standards. Without means to differentiate high-performing organizations from low-performing organizations, there is little incentive for firms to improve performance. Organizations might choose to certify with the least costly and least environmentally effective ecolabels, and consumers would not know the difference. Thus, they might "buy green" without it actually being effective. Alternatively, multitudes of ecolabels with weak standards would muddle the market for environmental goods, and consumers – unable to discern environmental quality – might tune out environmental labels entirely. The saturation of the market with many labels can render them meaningless, eliminating the effectiveness of any of the labels, even the strong ones!

To better understand the dynamics of a race, it is important to understand the range of dynamic pressures faced by organizations that sponsor ecolabels and the motivations of participants in that market. Participants join to get marketing benefits associated with being a member. By agreeing to adhere to standards set forth by the ecolabel, participating organizations get to advertise that they are part of an exclusive, elite group. These are known as *green clubs*. For firms or organizations that become members of a green club, they may have access to more expansive markets, find it easier to hire and retain the best employees, or be able to command a price premium for their product.

Certifying organizations offering labels need to attract participants. They set rules and policies for participants and in exchange offer a marketing benefit associated with joining. Nonprofit organizations launching labels are likely motivated by the desire to provide a product label for higher quality standards and as a way for participant organizations to advertise higher quality associated with improved environmental practices. Other organizations may have less beneficent motives: If an environmental NGO is offering an ecolabel, an industry association may choose to launch or support a weaker competing ecolabel to sow confusion in the market and to reduce pressure for costly improved environmental performance. Though we see it differently for agricultural ecolabels in Chapter 3, research suggests that environmental benefits may be smaller with two labels than with the NGO label alone (Fischer and Lyon 2014, 2019). The Sustainable Forestry Initiative (SFI) is an example of this. Launched by the paper and timber industries, it has been called an "Industry Sponsored Scam" by Forest Ethics, an NGO that filed a complaint with the Federal Trade

Commission (FTC) alleging that SFI violated the FTC's "green guide" aimed at preventing greenwashing behavior.[3,4]

Given the potential for multiple organizations to offer labels, potential confusion resulting from competing labels (as well as some offered by industry or government) may create incentives for the certification body offering an ecolabel to lower standards to attract members (since nearly all of these are supported by dues or fees). The situation is ripe for a prisoner's dilemma game like in Figure 8.1. For example, Green Globes advertises itself as a cheaper and more flexible alternative to LEED. LEED itself, after receiving less interest than expected for LEED 4.0 (a major enhancement and tightening of environmental performance criteria), offered revisions in LEED 4.1 as an effort to streamline the certification process and make certification easier.

The environmental implications for competing labels are unclear. It is possible that getting broad-based participation for a weaker standard may be a more effective strategy than having rigorous standards but no participants. That is, if there are no participants in the label, then the label generates no environmental benefit! Among scholars who study voluntary programs and international treaties, this is known as the "deep but narrow" versus "shallow but wide" tradeoff. Including Georgia Tech's KBISD building (see Chapter 6), the International Living Future Institute's Living Building label has just 30 buildings achieving full "Living" certification. While the LEED label is far less stringent than the Living Building Challenge and associated Living Building label, it has orders of magnitude more participation, with upward of 60,000 certifications in the United States, as well as tens of thousands abroad.

Participation results in increased costs, many of which are simply the cost of handling the paperwork associated with certification. Other increased costs include those associated with producing a higher quality product. Participants are hoping to receive a market premium from "green" consumers by joining the label (otherwise they could simply adopt improved practices without certifying) and signaling their high quality. This market signaling benefit is a function of the competitive landscape. A premium may exist for being the first mover into the

---

[3] www.fastcompany.com/1704891/sustainable-forestry-industry-sponsored-scam
[4] www.greenbuildingadvisor.com/article/sustainable-forestry-initiative-accused-of-greenwashing

market. A crowded market of adopters may reduce the value of a premium eco-certification label. That is, being the 52nd office building to certify LEED Silver in a metropolitan area is unlikely to generate the same financial premium as being the first LEED Platinum office building.

The key in determining whether a race to the top or race to the bottom exists is understanding how these dynamics play out over time. Does performance increase over time? Are these increases persistent and iterative? Or do these improvements dissipate over time? Do firms continue to certify even as the market becomes increasingly crowded? If so, a race to the top may exist in the market. Below, we outline conditions that must be observed in order to classify as a race to the top.

Conditions for a Race to the Top

Participants Need to be Getting Greener

A core requirement of a race to the top is that the participants (in this case – buildings) need to be getting greener over time. This may seem obvious or tautological, but there has been ample criticism (summarized in Chapter 5) that LEED-certified buildings might be more energy intensive than noncertified buildings. In fact, as LEED was gaining popularity, there was much skepticism within academia that LEED was any more than a marketing ploy. While some early findings that suggested LEED buildings may consume more energy than non-LEED buildings, this may be due to the higher performance characteristics of green buildings. It is important to establish that certified green buildings are, in fact, more environmentally friendly than noncertified buildings, and – for there to be a race to the top – that this performance is improving over time. Since the criticism of LEED began, three things have happened. First, academic research has been able to conclusively demonstrate the performance benefits of LEED certification. While there may be some remaining questions about the performance of LEED buildings relative to older buildings, when comparing similar buildings (e.g., Class A office buildings of a similar vintage), LEED-certified buildings have superior performance on average (Asensio and Delmas 2017). Second, as discussed later in this chapter, the LEED certification itself has shifted toward ensuring performance improvements in new certification vintages by implementing a number of prerequisites for energy and water efficiency and requiring monitoring of energy and water performance. Third, throughout the United States, energy and building codes have been updated to align with LEED Silver requirements. A large number of states and municipalities have requirements or incentives for public or even private buildings to be built in accordance with LEED standards. LEED's impact on increasing environmental requirements even for nonparticipating organizations indicates a larger-scale greening of the built environment as a result of market forces.

The greening of the sector alone, however, is insufficient to establish a race. After all, increasing availability and lowering prices of newer technologies or implementing policies requiring green building could generate similar outcomes. Further, as we discussed in Chapter 7, a key role of early adopters is to help lower the price of nascent technologies, making it difficult to distinguish the impacts of competition for green marketing from the changes in prices of the associated technologies due to pilot and demonstration projects. If the lower prices available are a result of early adoption for demonstration purposes, this then further increases market uptake, producing a virtuous cycle of lower prices and higher uptake. This is indicative of a race to the top. Policies may also play a role by causing increased uptake that can, in turn, lower prices or help build the supply chains necessary to facilitate market uptake. This complex relationship between prices, policies, and uptake means that evidence of greening is necessary but insufficient to demonstrate a race to the top.

In Figures 8.2 and 8.3, we establish the increasing number of green buildings. The S curve shown in Figure 8.2 demonstrates the increasing number of New Construction-certified buildings accumulating in the United States. In Figure 8.3, we show the increasing percentage of projects at higher tiers relative to lower tiers for the early versions of LEED. In particular, from 2004 to 2009, the share of Gold-certified projects increases, while the share of Certified projects decreases. This happens during a rapid increase in the total amount of buildings being certified, highlighting the increase in the "green-ness" of buildings. In 2009, USGBC introduced the LEED 2009 (v3) certification label, which appears to interrupt this process, though the buildings are likely getting greener beyond 2009, a process demonstrated by the increasing requirements for newer vintages. Separate analyses might demonstrate greener buildings by showing lower energy-use intensities over time, a higher number of LEED points achieved, or other indicators that buildings are becoming greener. As discussed next, the increased focus on prerequisites and requirements for LEED certification seems to indicate a shift in the baseline. Energy specifications required as part of LEED were

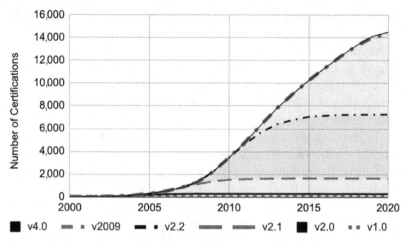

Figure 8.2 Increasing certifications over time (new construction)

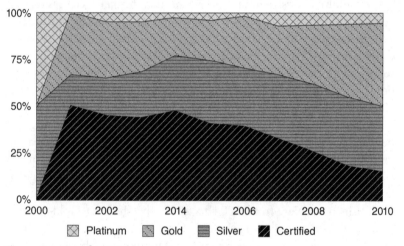

Figure 8.3 Certifications by tier (new construction)

making their way into building codes and municipal and state policies. LEED responded by increasing the requirements for certification.

The Criteria for Certification Need to be Increasingly Rigorous over Time

As discussed earlier in this chapter, there is ample reason to believe that there are incentives for ecolabels – and organizations sponsoring ecolabels – to weaken standards to attract membership. Indeed, there have been numerous efforts by industry to weaken label requirements or by compelling organizations or industry associations to offer competing labels that provide easier paths to certification. Green Globes, the International WELL Building Institute, and others attempting to challenge the market dominance of LEED have introduced labels aimed at providing easier paths to certification. If USGBC responds by weakening their label to retain market share, they risk undermining the label and promoting greenwash. If, instead, they maintain or increase the stringency of the labels, they risk ceding market share to alternative labels. Indeed, with the slow start of LEED 4.0 and the entrance of competing and weaker labels, there is reason to be concerned that crowding in the green building label space may undermine progress. If a *race to the top* exists, then the standards for certification need to be getting increasingly rigorous over time. Several characteristics of the LEED label appear to meet these criteria and are discussed in depth in the included case study. While the label has made some minor concessions to the timber industry, overall, our case details numerous ways that USGBC has ratcheted up the requirements over time, making the LEED label increasingly rigorous. Further, over time, as demonstrated in Figure 8.4, we observe individual trends for certification vintages. This figure shows the phasing in of new, stricter certifications and the phasing out of older, obsolete certifications. In the next section, we describe in detail how the LEED program has increased stringency over time.

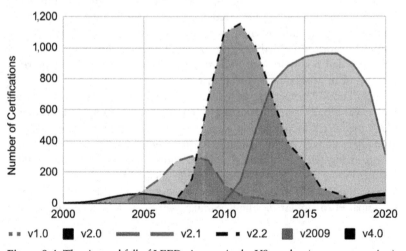

Figure 8.4 The rise and fall of LEED vintages in the US market (new construction)

A Closer Look: LEED Increases Requirements over Time

Since its start in 1998, the LEED ecolabel program has evolved along with the real estate market and the pace of green innovation. Despite the inherent flexibility of the rating system, many requirements of LEED certification for new construction projects have grown more stringent over time, particularly in the move from LEED 2009 to LEED v4 in 2013. This section details the evolution of LEED criteria over time and highlight evidence of "ratcheting up" in environmental stringency, supporting a race to the top dynamic in green building certification.

LEED v2 was released in 2000 with five major credit categories. Sustainable sites included credits such as rehabilitating a contaminated site, being located within a half-mile of a rail station, and implementing a stormwater management plan. Water efficiency credits focused on reducing landscaping water use by 50 percent, reducing wastewater use by 50 percent, and maximizing indoor water efficiency. Energy and Atmosphere included prerequisites for fundamental building systems commissioning, meeting local minimum energy-efficiency standards, and avoiding use of chlorofluorocarbons. Credits were offered in this category for achieving additional energy efficiency, generating onsite renewable energy, and purchasing renewable power. For Materials and Resources, project teams had a prerequisite requirement to store and collect building occupants' recyclables, and offered credits including building and materials reuse and recycling 50 percent of construction waste. Prerequisites for the Indoor Environmental Quality were establishing minimum indoor air-quality performance and prohibiting smoking in the building, and credits included CO_2 monitoring, increasing ventilation, and low emitting materials. Innovation and Design, the final category, provided design teams and projects the opportunity to be awarded points for exceptional performance above LEED requirements or in areas outside LEED criteria.

LEED 2009, sometimes known as LEED v3, was released nine years after v2. It had three enhancements in mind: Harmonizing prerequisites and credits for increased consistency, adjusting credit weightings based on their impact on human and environmental health concerns, and prioritizing select credit weightings to address regional environmental issues. Some updates to the scorecard included adding a new prerequisite to the Water Efficiency category to reduce water use by 20 percent compared to similar buildings. Similarly, the Energy and Atmosphere

(cont.)

category revised a prerequisite to include minimum energy performance improvement, which had previously been only a credit. In Indoor Environmental Quality, the allowable threshold of formaldehyde levels was revised down for the construction Indoor Air Quality management plan credit, and flooring systems requirements under the low-emitting materials credit were increased and broadened. The weights of several credits were changed to reflect how much influence each has upon human and environmental health. Greater influence was placed on a building's carbon footprint in areas like energy efficiency and alternative transportation. A new category, Regional Priority, allows projects to earn bonus points for specific regional issues based on zip codes and regional councils.

LEED v4.0 was launched in 2013 with the certification system's biggest changes yet. Under a call to "demand more from our buildings," LEED's previously implied goals were stated explicitly:

- Reverse contribution to global climate change;
- Enhance individual human health and wellbeing;
- Protect and restore water resources;
- Protect, enhance, and restore biodiversity and ecosystem services;
- Promote sustainable and regenerative material resources cycles;
- Build a greener economy; and
- Enhance social equity, environmental justice, and community quality of life.

The update placed a great focus on increasing technical stringency, expanding requirements for new project types and challenging teams to pursue excellence. A user guide detailing each change from the previous version was released. Some notable developments included the creation of a new category, Location and Transportation, intended to emphasize the transportation credits previously housed under Sustainable Sites that have large impacts on a building's carbon footprint. In terms of credit requirements, Location and Transportation's green vehicles credit was ramped up to require 5 percent of parking be reserved for green cars, and an additional 2 percent to have charging stations. Also, in this category, distance to transit access was changed to the walkable distance instead of a radius to ensure routes to the transit are walkable. A new Energy and Atmosphere credit offered points for making the building demand–response capable, and the energy efficiency prerequisite and credit were updated to more stringent standards. Additionally, the energy metering prerequisite was updated to require

(cont.)

all buildings to be capable of measuring whole building energy use. Similarly, Water Efficiency required whole building water use measurement and EPA WaterSense labeling in the United States as prerequisites. A similar information approach was seen in the Materials and Resources credits for environmental product declaration and reported material ingredients, encouraging transparency and sustainable material sourcing. Indoor Environmental Quality prerequisite air quality standards were ramped up, and specific requirements for residential projects were added, while the low-emitting materials credit was expanded to include ceilings and insulation.

LEED v4 was certainly the most environmentally stringent vintage of LEED to date. While it represented a large step toward the highest standards of green building, the USGBC admitted that many of the new requirements proved too challenging for project teams to achieve, necessitating a pivot to a broader market with the release of LEED v4.1. The goals of the latest update were to:

- Address market barriers and lessons learned from LEED v4 project teams.
- Update performance thresholds and reference standards to ensure LEED remains the global leadership standard for green buildings.
- Expand the marketplace for LEED.
- Improve performance throughout the life of buildings, reward leaders based on their performance, and incorporate performance reporting to enable building owners to track progress toward environmental, social, and governance goals.

While not an entirely new LEED version, LEED v4.1 was intended to streamline the certification process in response to lower than anticipated certification figures under v4. The mix of credits and their point values on the scorecard were almost entirely unaltered in v4.1, but certain accreditation processes were streamlined, including those for heat island reduction, low-emitting materials, and rainwater management. Some performance thresholds were also updated to new standards. While the stringency of requirements seems largely unchanged, this version of LEED offers more inclusivity to a broader market by prioritizing public comments and feedback to hear from project teams about what does and does not work.

LEED v4's clear increase in stringency for new construction credits provides the strongest case for an environmental quality "ratcheting up" effect in the certification program. Furthermore, from 2000 to

(cont.)

2019, the LEED rating system has increased its number of prerequisites from 7 to 15. Every update has raised standards to remain on the cutting edge of technological innovation. These additional metrics show a general trend of increasing stringency from the program's inception. LEED is clearly continuing to raise the bar for the health and environmental effects of the built environment.

Figure 8.4 shows the trajectory of LEED vintages – each rising and falling as it is replaced by an upgraded, more stringent certification. LEED v4, however, appears to be taking much longer to gain momentum and transform the market than previous versions. USGBC attempted to address this worrisome lag by streamlining the certification process and prioritizing public feedback with the release of LEED v4.1 in 2018. It remains unclear whether LEED v4.1 or other innovative labels like the Living Building certification will ultimately gain market traction and rapid uptake, whether these might cede ground to other competing certification schemes, or whether the trend of ecolabels and market greening is simply a temporary fad that has run its course by being incorporated into building standards and other standard operating practices. Industry experts tell us that LEED standards have evolved from being "ahead of the curve" with green buildings, to being a scheme "at the frontier" – not ahead of where everyone is, but in line with where at least someone is. USGBC must balance the pressures to push and drive the market with being accessible enough to attract ever-more participants. While the success of individual ecolabeling programs does not seem certain, throughout this book we detail a number of market trends that suggest that greening the built environment does *not* appear to be a short-lived fad with a prompt expiration date. Trends in the market point to a repeated and iterated transition to advanced energy and environmental technologies and a broader market transformation.

Participation in the Ecolabel Needs to be Increasingly Substantive

Learning and engagement needs to happen. The race to the top is not just about accounting. An ecolabel that has a goal of promoting advanced energy and environmental technologies and practices should observe improved knowledge, understanding, and deployment of these approaches. This improvement in operational quality of the firm is linked with substantive participation, where firms engage in purposeful adoption of improved operations aligned with achieving certification. Substantive participation requires iterative evolution and thus produces *learning* related to the underlying performance of technologies and practices associated with the ecolabel. This process of iteration – or successive improvements and learning – is what indicates a race to the top. Observing this iterative process of successive improvements and learning, and then separating it from herding behavior, price changes, or other processes that might generate similar empirical outcomes, is difficult. The presence of three conditions (greener buildings, ratcheting up label standards, substantive participation) strongly indicates a race to the top.

As noted and discussed in more detail in Chapters 3–5, ecolabels typically provide considerable flexibility to allow certification via various paths. This flexibility opens up the opportunity for participants to achieve certification by cheaply purchasing legitimacy by investing in upgrades that they would have done without the benefit of the ecolabel. This behavior may be defined as freeriding, shirking, or greenwash behavior. In the context of ecolabels for buildings, as discussed in Chapter 5, this may mean investing only in building upgrades that provide private returns and avoiding investments that provide public benefit. Further, given the investment thresholds necessary to achieve higher tiers of certification, *symbolic* certification might be identified in firms that earn just enough points to qualify for their tier, and no more. Points earned beyond the tier threshold convey no marketing benefits to the firm, but they do improve environmental quality. This upgrading behavior highlights that the certifier was likely more interested in maximizing the marketing benefits of certification than in providing improved environmental performance.

The logic for this is relatively simple. Consider a developer making a decision to invest in energy efficiency. Presumably that developer would consider a number of options and choose the amount of energy efficiency that provides a balance between low energy bills and upfront capital costs. Let us imagine this optimal amount of energy-efficiency investment. We might not know exactly what the optimal amount of energy efficiency investment is for a particular owner, but across owners there are different amounts of optimal investments, and the distribution across those investments should be smooth. Now, imagine that there is an ecolabel available that provides some marketing benefit if the developer invests a bit more than that "optimal" amount into energy efficiency. In a world where the developers see this marketing benefit, some will choose to invest additional resources into energy efficiency to take advantage of the marketing benefit available to them at the higher investment level. What is interesting about this simple example is that if the ecolabel level is lower than the "optimal" investment level, it will not impact the investment level. That is, a developer would never invest *less* in energy efficiency if their optimal level exceeds the certification level. In contrast, if their optimal level is less than the certification level, because the certification carries additional marketing benefits, the developer (or some percentage of developers) may decide that it makes financial sense to spend additional resources to achieve the ecolabel.

In LEED, as with many other multi-tiered ecolabels, this process produces an unusual sawtooth histogram where some participants (though not all) appear to invest extra resources to achieve the marketing signal. These participants who are motivated by this marketing signal are more likely to be symbolic certifiers because they are doing the minimal amount possible to gain the certification and marketing benefit. This phenomenon can be seen in LEED New Construction certifications in Figures 8.5–8.7.

Consider a project built just at a certification level versus a project built just below that level. The environmental performance levels of those projects are nearly identical, yet the project that meets the certification requirements gets a big shiny sticker, while the one just below the threshold does not (or alternatively gets a less shiny sticker). In a system of flexible ecolabels, where the participants can choose from a menu of potential investments, there may be several easy investments that can be purchased to achieve certification if one is a little short of credits to achieve certification at a higher tier.

Conversations with professionals in the industry suggest that the purchase of renewable energy credits (RECs) is an easy way to gain a few points near the end of the project to try to achieve the next level of certification. Now consider the decision to invest in an advanced HVAC system versus the decision to purchase renewable energy certificates from a broker. The decision to invest in an advanced HVAC system requires significant analysis and engineering expertise. In contrast, purchasing renewable energy credits (which many consider to be greenwashing behavior) requires little deviation from business as usual

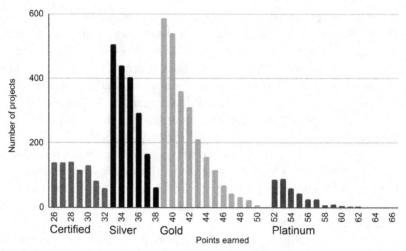

Figure 8.5 Upgrading behavior in LEED NC v2.0–2.2 projects

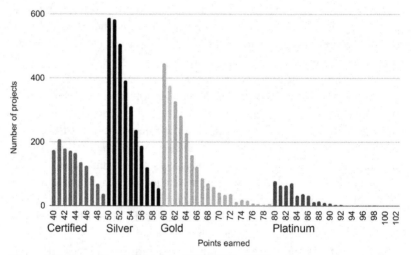

Figure 8.6 Upgrading behavior in LEED NC v2009 projects

behavior, very little analysis, and no engineering expertise. The building that has the RECs is no different than the building without the RECs. The REC-purchasing firm demonstrated no learning and simply attempted to purchase environmental credibility. The investment in an advanced HVAC system produces learning and is substantive. The

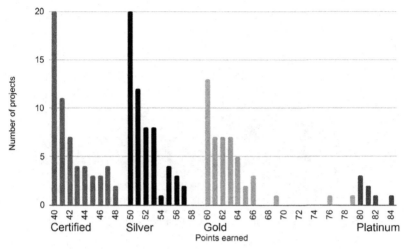

Figure 8.7 Upgrading behavior in LEED NC v4 projects

REC building and the HVAC building, however, will be viewed equivalently by the market because they achieved the same certification level. The purchase of renewable energy credits may be likened to the attempted purchase of credibility and might be considered symbolic certification, or greenwash. In practice, this is further compounded with multitudes of choices of credits to achieve, such that there is no optimal mix of credits for any set of buildings.

Now, presumably even in the absence of the marketing signal, a proportion of builders would invest the amount required by the eco-label because that investment level also happens to be the "optimal" amount of investment for that individual. Thus, we cannot observe any one particular building and declare whether it is substantive or symbolic. But we know that buildings that are built at the thresholds are more likely to have made an effort to purchase upgrades at the tiers; and we know that buildings built in between the tiers chose not to spend additional resources to achieve a marketing benefit. We can say that, at the thresholds, buildings are more likely to be symbolic and, between thresholds, we might think that buildings are more substantive – or focused on the qualities of the underlying technologies.

In Figure 8.8, we examine the percentage of buildings built just at the certification thresholds over time. We show that, despite builders presumably improving in their ability to build green buildings at a

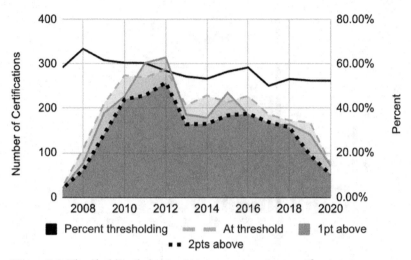

Figure 8.8 Thresholding behavior in new construction certifications

particular tier, we see evidence that, over time, fewer buildings are being built just at the tier. To us, this means that, over time, the value of the underlying technologies for certification are gaining value relative to the marketing benefit. Increasingly, firms pursue certification for the performance benefits of the underlying technologies, rather than simply build to the threshold.

Conclusion

This chapter introduces a process where competition, initiated by an ecolabel, drives increasing investments in green behavior that we call a race to the top. The analogy to a race to the top (or bottom) is driven by a wide range of studies that observe a dynamic relationship between regulation and the behavior of regulated targets.

We identify three criteria that are necessary to demonstrate a race to the top in green building. First, buildings need to become greener over time. We demonstrate evidence that shows that more buildings are certifying green and more buildings are certifying green at higher levels. Second, the criteria to certify green need to become more stringent. As the market has crowded, USGBC has made the criteria to certify more stringent, and we detail a long-term shift of USGBC toward performance-based metrics. More new buildings are getting certified, and those buildings are greener than prior generations. Third, and finally, we need to be sure that firms are not gaming the system and instead are iterating, learning, and are substantively improving their performance over time. One might expect that, over time, firms get better at building green in such a way that allows them to maximize the marketing benefits while minimizing the environmental contribution of the building, allowing firms to greenwash. Instead, our evidence shows that achieving the highest possible marketing benefit relative to technology investment becomes *less* important over time, even when the overall levels of certification and total points achieved are increasing over time. This suggests that the LEED label has helped buildings to realize the value of the underlying technological investments.

In this particular case, ecolabels incentivize participants (builders) to invest in energy and environmental technologies that are part of the LEED label. By being an early adopter of LEED, buildings gain a marketing premium that gives them access to higher rental prices, lower vacancy, a recruiting and retention advantage, and all of the other benefits provided by being distinguished as a green building. As the market becomes more crowded for green buildings these premiums are likely to diminish. Builders respond by building at higher tiers. When these higher tiers become more crowded, the USGBC program has responded by tightening regulations and making it more difficult to certify green. As firms invest in higher levels of energy and environmental technologies over time, it appears to drive a race to the top through green competition.

References

Asensio, Omar Isaac and Magali A. Delmas. 2017. "The Effectiveness of US Energy Efficiency Building Labels." *Nature Energy* 2: 17033.

Bruner, Christopher M. 2020. "Leveraging Corporate Law: A Broader Account of Delaware's Competition." (February). Available at SSRN: https://ssrn.com/abstract=3530397.

Cousins, Jim, Austin Vernon Mitchell, and Prem Sikka. 2004. *Race to the Bottom: The Case of the Accountancy Firms*. Basildon, UK: Association for Accountancy & Business Affairs.

Fischer, C. and T. P. Lyon. 2014. "Competing Environmental Labels." *Journal of Economics & Management Strategy* 23, no. 3, 692–716.

Fischer, Carolyn, and Thomas P. Lyon. 2019. "A Theory of Multitier Ecolabel Competition." *Journal of the Association of Environmental and Resource Economists* 6, no. 3: 461–501.

Florida, Richard. 2014. *The Rise of the Creative Class – Revisited: Revised and Expanded*. New York: Basic Books.

Moretti, Enrico. 2012. *The New Geography of Jobs*. New York: Houghton Mifflin Harcourt.

Mosley, Layna and Saika Uno. 2007. "Racing to the Bottom or Climbing to the Top? Economic Globalization and Collective Labor Rights." *Comparative Political Studies* 40, no. 8: 923–948.

Palan, Ronen. 2002. "Tax Havens and the Commercialization of State Sovereignty." *International Organization* 56, no. 1: 151–176.

Rabe, Barry. 2007. "Race to the Top: The Expanding Role of US State Renewable Portfolio Standards." *Sustainable Development Law & Policy* 7, no. 3: 10–16.

Revesz, Richard L. 1992. "Rehabilitating Interstate Competition: Rethinking the Race-to-the-Bottom Rationale for Federal Environmental Regulation." *New York University Law Review* 67, no. 6: 1210–1255.

Rivera, J. and C. Oh. 2013. "Environmental Regulations and MNC Foreign Market Entry." *Policy Studies Journal* 41, no. 2: 243–272.

9 | *It's Not Easy Being Green*

Environmental and Equity Impacts of Green Building

Introduction

As Kermit The Frog tells us, it's not easy being green. We must pay attention to serious challenges and complicated considerations for the otherwise positive story of green market transformation. For all of the gains that have been made in the green-building sector, for example, there are major concerns. These concerns typically revolve around the ultimate environmental impacts of green buildings and the equity implications of how we transition to a greener built environment. Green buildings may not be as green as we expect or want, and price premiums for green buildings work against affordability. Our green market transformation story is not a naïve, romantic, idealized story of perfectly sustainable practices overtaking our foolish old ways. This transformation story is messy, fraught with imperfections, and leaves ample room for improvement. In fact, that is part of the essence of this story: Iterative, ongoing improvements, building momentum toward a more sustainable system. Sometimes it feels like two steps forward, and one step back. But openly drawing our attention to these concerns and shortcomings can help us turn them into opportunities for continued gain and building on that momentum. Market transformation does not happen overnight, and it does not stop after a singular change. It is an ongoing evolution. This chapter reviews some of the shortcomings and concerns about this otherwise positive evolutionary path for green buildings.

A Closer Look: What Does It Mean to Build Green?

The Green Building Movement evokes a reformation of the urban jungle, eschewing brutalist concrete facades for organic curves layered in renewable bamboo paneling, wide windows letting daylight stream

---

(cont.)

through to interior garden spaces, and foliage atop tree trunks arching skywards from their rooftop roots. Any image search for "green building" will reinforce these romantic impressions with illustrations of buildings – real and imagined – that integrate nature and manmade features with seemingly impossible engineering. The architectural feats undertaken to create these buildings are nothing less than extraordinary: for example, Singapore's modern Jewel Changi airport has been heralded worldwide as a "crown jewel" of architecture. The award-winning design boasts the world's largest indoor waterfall, circulating up to 10,000 gallons of water every minute. This "rain vortex" is framed on all sides by an impressive multi-story tropical forest, a terraced home for thousands of trees and plants from across the globe. Visitors can explore the forest through a network of trails linking gardens, waterfalls, shops, and restaurants all nested inside the building. The airport's various commitments to sustainability are plainly highlighted on its website, alongside attractions advertised to Singapore's tourists – and layover travelers.

Unfortunately, Jewel Changi is not a green building – or at least not a certified one.

The tension between the aesthetic of green building and the substantive impact of a building on the environment is the subject of much critique. Critics call to question whether developers are focused more on whether a building looks green rather than it being sustainable. After all, a green building design can be accomplished with little fanfare. The North Atlanta High School is a modern if functional space serving thousands of students. The office-tower-turned-public-high-school was certified to LEED Silver by renovating an existing building with designs that are highly energy efficient and which protect student health by minimizing indoor air pollutants. Among dozens of sustainable features, the design prioritizes local environmental concerns related to transit accessibility, stormwater runoff, and locally sourced materials. In its advertising materials, the design company reserves the spotlight for the functional use of the space as a learning environment, rather than the building's sustainable features. This building is green in terms of its environmental impact, but refrains from the extravagant aesthetic.

More than a battle of beauty versus substance, a debate faces off within the Green Building Movement over which of the multifaceted environmental impacts should be accounted for. Green building programs like LEED and the Living Building Challenge seek to address the

(cont.)

entire building's environmental footprint – a task easier imagined than accomplished. The environmental impact of a building is interdependent with the raw materials sourced, the location selected, the integration of materials into (in)efficient designs, the ways people manage or use the space, and eventually the disassembly or destruction of the building. Whereas some standards (like the Living Building Challenge, or even LEED Platinum) expect excellence in all areas, this is not feasible for all buildings. Other programs offer greater flexibility (like lower tiers of LEED) or limit assessment to fewer criteria (like Energy Star), but this produces trade-offs and gaps in the overall environmental impact. Should all green buildings be highly energy efficient? Should efficiency be prioritized over other environmental concerns, like transit accessibility, or habitat protection? Should environmental impacts be prioritized over community concerns, like gentrification and public art? The struggle to answer these questions – and to define what it means to build green – are highlighted by push-back against green buildings worldwide.

A Schematic of Possible Dark Sides

In our review of the possible downsides of the green transformation in the building sector, we focus on a few broad categories of concerns. First, our greener buildings may not be quite as green as we want to believe, and the greener market might not be quite as fair and equitable as we might hope. As we will review shortly, the evidence about the environmental impacts of greener buildings may not be as rosy as proponents would like. It is not that the evidence of environmental impacts is very mixed, but rather that the evidence base itself is quite small. Much of the environmental benefits of green buildings is derived from simulations based on engineering models. Unfortunately, evidence based on actual performance or actual behavior is far more difficult to obtain and thus much scarcer. Like the evidence for energy-efficiency gains from greener technology more generally, we would expect to see a sizable gap between the engineering models of greener performance and the actual greener performance of these buildings. This focus on environmental performance, and its lack of evidence, should not distract us from another central sustainability priority: Equity considerations. Who bears the burden of transitioning to greener buildings? Who has access to them and who gains the benefits from their higher quality and greener performance? There are key social equity concerns that warrant our ongoing attention during this market transformation, especially if the transition is to be sustainable and equitable.

Second, there are potential downsides in terms of the economics of the green building transformation, including limits to the scope or extent of such a transformation. Our review of the evidence of green buildings also draws our attention to possible problems and limitations of green market transformation. For all of the theoretical gains, the triple-bottom-line arguments, and other promises that green buildings might deliver, there is reason to believe that not all of the promises are perfectly delivered. Moreover, there may be important limitations to this market transformation involving issues of public policy, market context, environmental sentiment, and other decision-making priorities and processes that can limit this success story. The evidence on some of these concerns is largely speculative at this point, as we shall see, but paying attention to these challenges can help those pursuing sustainability to manage or avoid them.

Environmental Impacts

Expected Impacts

Green buildings are supposed to have positive environmental impacts. After all, that is the point. Yet the law of unintended consequences is blind to environmental priorities. Just intending to save the planet does not guarantee that some environmental harms will not occur. Generally speaking, a green building should reduce energy and water consumption, reduce airborne pollutants, use more sustainably sourced materials, be located in places that reduce wasteful commutes and sprawl, and much more. In practice, however, the menu-based approach of holistic green building approaches implies or allows for tradeoffs across these many dimensions. Building designers may, for instance, reduce water and energy use by picking a more remote location or larger acreage footprint that affords greater opportunities for energy production, or more flexibility to pursue on-site water treatment. These choices might entail longer commutes and increased greenfield development. A certifying scheme might give credits for the greener decisions, but not penalize for the "browner" decisions. Beyond the tradeoffs that might occur within a menu-based approach, concerns remain about other environmental impacts of green buildings even outside of the standards themselves. More buildings of any sort, green or otherwise, entail greater material, energy, and water consumption. Further, greater efficiency is associated with the oft-referenced "rebound effect" (Figge and Thorpe 2019). Improve the energy efficiency of a building, and users might respond to the lower effective cost of energy by increasing their usage of energy. The environmental gains from building greener should be substantial, but they are by no means universal or guaranteed.

A Closer Look: Habitat for All

The question of who should be able to live in an area persists in urban development. As green building becomes more popular within upcoming urban neighborhoods, it has also been associated with gentrification effects that make the areas less accessible to long-standing communities. Logan Square in Chicago is one neighborhood that faced a development boom around 2015, bringing hundreds of new and green certified dwellings to the neighborhood, but all at above-average rents. The development of L, a six-story LEED-certified apartment building in the area, was met with grassroots community protests voicing equity concerns over housing affordability. The developers highlighted both sustainability and provision of space for public art in their designs, but this was not enough for residents facing steep increases in housing prices due to the high rents of the luxury apartments and its peers being developed throughout the neighborhood.

Environmental sustainability is just one aspect of a building's impact: The built environment intersects with society at every level – for better or worse. A building's interior technology and design can give us new ways of connecting to work and learn efficiently. Its location can change our commutes and the migration patterns of wildlife. And its exterior can bring new aesthetics to a neighborhood. The latter was the case for Museum Tower in the heart of Dallas' arts district. The sleek, LEED-Gold luxury condo building boasts remarkably green interiors, to the comfort and health of its renters. But the curved, 42-story glass frame stoked controversy as sunlight reflected off its sides and into the

(cont.)

surrounding neighborhood. Residents complained of the blinding glare, and the nearby Nasher Sculpture Center was forced to remove and relocate artwork to protect it. The interior of the museum was designed by Renzo Piano to provide natural lighting while protecting the artwork, but the tower's intense glare now threatens any paper or canvas work displayed inside. The museum was forced to remove Pablo Picasso's Nude Man and Woman, and Skyspace artist James Turrell considers his installation there, Tending (Blue), permanently destroyed. Years of conflict and failed mediation between the arts community and developers produced no solution to the glaring problem.

The bigger picture of a building's impact includes the nuances of the natural environment alongside the social and built environment in which it is located. As a result, there is not yet a defining image of what a green building should be, what it should look like, or what impacts it should prioritize. The reality is that trade-offs exist between many design choices, with improvements to one feature exacerbating impacts in some other area. Should we build a new building from scratch, in a new or distant location, or should we modestly renovate a building in an existing location? Should we keep the space affordable, or spare no expense for environmental design? Should we prioritize the health of tenants inside, or the comfort of surrounding communities? These open questions lack easy answers and leave us with many shades of what it means to build green.

Observed Impacts

The evidence of green buildings' positive environmental impacts offers a somewhat mixed bag. The Green Building Movement and innovative technologies risks getting our hopes up too high. Perhaps the strongest piece of evidence supporting the promise of advanced building technologies comes from Asensio and Delmas (2017). Their study employs rigorous evaluation techniques to measure the real-world impacts of green buildings versus otherwise comparable buildings. Firstly, they find substantial energy savings – from 18 percent to 30 percent, depending on the particular green building program. This looks promising for the commercial building sector, but they note that large buildings are driving those results. Small- and medium-sized buildings, which account for two-thirds of commercial-building emissions, experienced little emissions reduction. At least the bigger buildings showed large gains! The 30 percent average energy savings for LEED buildings may also overstate the likely energy savings for the "next" building to get certified. After all, as a voluntary label, we expect that the buildings with the most to gain are those that volunteer first. Moreover, Fuerst et al. (2014) find that cities with the greatest market penetration of LEED buildings are those with higher electricity prices and lower carbon emissions. This suggests that the "cleaner" places are those that are reducing their carbon footprint even more. What drives adoption more than carbon emissions, apparently, is public sentiment for environmental protection (Braun et al. 2017).

The gap between *expected* building performance and *actual* building performance remains a puzzle. This is a common challenge for energy efficiency upgrades for a whole host of energy-using technologies like appliances, vehicles, etc. There is often a gap between the expected and actual adoption rate or between the expected and actual gains (Gerarden et al. 2017). Liang et al. (2019) survey facility managers in the United States to learn about this gap for green buildings. They find occupants were using more energy than was expected, partly because there were more occupants in the buildings than originally designed for and partly because the technologies had some failures. Further, LEED buildings tended to lack submetering for air conditioning and had longer operating hours, both of this can help account for the performance gap.

Social Impacts

From an environmental justice perspective, green buildings pose a thorny problem. On the one hand, they represent progress toward a reduced environmental footprint and greener economic activity. On the other hand, they might pose disproportionate burdens and involve unequal access for certain segments of the population. The green-building price premium, which gets lauded in previous chapters and elsewhere in the green building community, is also directly connected to issues of affordability and gentrification. This raises concerns about equitable implications of green buildings. Moreover, who gets access to these buildings, as users or owners, is an open question that should raise concerns from an equity standpoint as well. Even if affordability and gentrification were not a concern, there is hardly any guarantee that new green buildings will be distributed evenly, that tenants or occupants will resemble the broader population, or that disadvantaged communities will have fair or equal access to such innovations. We consider these two questions, equity aspects of green buildings costs and equity access to their benefits, separately and next.

A Closer Look: Accounting for a Bigger Picture

Energy efficiency is an accepted norm under most green building standards, but a true account of a building's energy efficiency may not be straightforward. Some evaluate energy use intensity in terms of actual electricity consumed per unit of floor space, though most often efficiency is estimated based on simulations of the building's design. The assumptions required to conduct such simulations are prone to error, with major consequences for energy use. For example, the Bank of America Tower in New York City became the first skyscraper to achieve LEED Platinum certification after demonstrating that its design met at least 80 percent of LEED's criteria. The building's advanced heating and cooling system prioritizes comfort for workers alongside an emphasis on natural daylighting and on-site clean energy plant and water recycling. But analysts soon realized the city's greenest tower was also among the biggest consumers of electricity: The tower uses more than double the energy (per square foot) as the much older Empire State Building. The advanced indoor air quality and comfort system which hogs much of the power is produced with clean energy on-site, and a more energy efficient design could have allowed that clean energy to stretch farther, potentially at lower cost.

By comparison, the Chesapeake Bay Foundation's Brock Environmental Center was designed to maximize energy efficiency. The Center achieved both LEED Platinum certification and Living Building status after maxing out its sustainability in nearly every aspect of its design. The building boasts both energy and water independence and is used to educate the public about green building and broader conservation concerns. The catch? The remote suburban location on Maryland's coastline requires tenants and visitors to commute – by car – on a daily basis, driving up the energy use intensity through transportation. Though as much as 30 percent of a building's typical energy use occurs through commutes, energy used for transit is not accounted for in the certification standards. Thus, the Brock

(cont.)

Environmental Center's accolades do not reflect the energy burden of transportation that the location imposes. A more thorough accounting of energy efficiency might acknowledge the interdependence of location and energy use, but green building standards do not currently require such a broad scope of energy impact assessment.

The choice of location has bearing on the energy demands of a building, but energy is just one component of a building's overall environmental impact. As cities expand worldwide, they encroach on the boundaries of natural habitat. Though green building programs encourage redevelopment rather than new builds on wild lands, most green real estate is newly constructed. For example, Songdo International Business District is a recently developed area of Incheon, just outside of Seoul. Roughly a dozen buildings (some 20 million square feet) within the development reached LEED certification as part of a smart city development plan. The district represents a milestone achievement for sustainable city planning – but sits entirely atop a filled tidal flat. The rocky outcrop used to provide critical breeding grounds and habitat to migratory birds like the iconic black-faced spoonbill and the eastern oystercatcher. In this case, developing new and sophisticated human habitat took precedent over conserving natural habitat.

Observed Impacts

The evidence concerning the costs of green buildings points to big concerns about the affordability of owning or leasing green buildings. The higher cost of construction, which is generally observed, and the significantly higher rental and sale prices, which are almost always observed, indicate that affordability is an inescapable issue here. There is good reason to believe, as the green building practice continues to diffuse and becomes the standard practice for building (Holtermans and Kok 2019), that this additional cost and price premium will largely vanish. And while that might mask the possibility that all buildings are now just that much more expensive and unaffordable, the significant benefits that come from these green buildings should more than offset those greater costs. Nonetheless, as part of the transition, the higher costs should raise concern about affordability and also implications for gentrifying neighborhoods. Changing building codes to achieve energy savings tends to impose disproportionately greater costs on lower-income households (Bruegge et al. 2019). Price premiums for greater energy efficiency can mask inequities in impacts – wealthy home-owners see their home values rise, while poorer households see falling home values as their square footage shrinks to achieve the energy savings. Combining affordable housing with green building approaches holds some promise, as the market still recognizes the higher-quality, greener construction with a market premium even at the lower-end of the price range (Yeganeh et al. 2019).

The accessibility concern is particularly important, as it goes beyond the owners and investors who may be benefiting from their costly investment and green buildings. The accessibility issue refers to the tenants, residents, occupants, and users of green buildings. If larger projects are more likely to become green buildings, then we might wonder whether the workforce or tenants in those larger buildings tends to be a minority or otherwise disadvantaged group. If buildings full of white-collar, highly educated office workers are most likely to become green buildings, then access to this green revolution is hardly fair. On the other hand, if large urban centers with apartment buildings tend to be more likely to go green, and residents in those areas tend to be a minority or poorer than their suburban counterparts, then the equity of access story might flip in the other direction. Overall, the evidence in support of one side or the other is lacking to date. We expect that the equity of access story will be a rather mixed tale, where certain sectors tend to favor certain subgroups in terms of access to green buildings, while other sectors and regions favor another. For LEED-certified commercial space, Fuerst et al. (2014) show that LEED buildings tend to follow market size, education levels, and economic growth. The Green Building Movement has not made it to smaller, lagging, and less educated cities yet. We might expect that the injustice of access to greener buildings is largely a coincidental or unintended consequence of how we are transitioning to greener buildings. But even coincidental inequities merit attention and remedy.

If inequity in owning or using green buildings represents the symp-toms of possible injustice, then it bears genuine consideration of the root causes. This points to core conceptions of *inclusion* and *process* in the Green Building Movement in addition to merely reflecting on inequitable distribution of opportunities. Arguably, much of the Green Building Movement has developed with an eye toward sustain-able design as defined by those in powerful positions in the industry, those who could afford priorities that might not line up with the most vulnerable in society. Recently, the Green Building Movement and certifiers have engaged in serious conversations about improving the inclusivity of their governance processes, about better appreciating the benefits that matter most to communities, and embedding equity concerns in the ecolabel standards (USGBC 2020). As it stands now, social equity is rarely (or never) a major component of green building rating systems. Improving the affordability of green buildings stands as the top priority in addressing equity in this context, which brings us back to some raw economic concerns. More work remains to improve the inclusivity of governance processes and in bringing social equity into certification systems.

A Closer Look: Environmental Justice of Green Schools

Tens of millions of children attend over tens of thousands of schools in the United States every school day, yet the great majority of schools were constructed before 1970. Shifting this massive inventory of schools to greener buildings stands to noticeably move the needle in reducing water usage, energy consumption, and greenhouse gas emissions. Even more, the holistic approach to greener buildings holds great potential for improving the indoor environmental quality for the benefit of teachers, staff, and students alike. Evidence continues to accumulate to support the incredible value of improved environmental quality – better air, better daylight, etc. – in promoting student learning and achievements. Plus, exposing these young minds to innovative, greener building technology can help educate the next generation on the positive value of green buildings more generally. This vulnerable population of young people, combining often sensitive physiology with limited discretion over when and where to attend school, represents a critical subpopulation of concern for environmental justice. Greening our schools has enormous potential for reducing environmental harms while also advancing justice goals.

Thankfully, many new schools being constructed now qualify as green buildings. These new, green schools may also help with financing their operations and maintenance if these buildings entail reduced energy and water expenditures. These schools can also be community resources, hosting public events like town hall meetings, serving as polling locations, and providing other community benefits. Neighbors

(cont.)

can enjoy many of the advantages of green schools even if they are not students.

Yet, who does have access to these new, green schools? Are they merely the playgrounds and classrooms of the rich, white, suburbanites? Or are they only to be found in those high-density, urban environments? And are private schools much more likely to be built to green standards? To answer these questions, we examined a sample of all the new schools built in the United States between 2000 and 2014 (see Zhao et al. 2019 for more details). We looked at all these new schools – 31,507 in total – and tracked which ones were registered with the USGBC as green schools (whether or not they were yet "certified"). While only 6 percent of these schools were built "green," over 30 percent were private schools and most were in urbanized areas. In mapping all of these schools, we also collected data on their student enrollment and the demographic composition of their surrounding neighborhood. Thus, we were able to see the racial and ethnic composition of their student enrollment, how many students were eligible for free- or reduced-school lunches (for public schools), and its neighborhood's average income, educational attainment, and racial and ethnic composition.

Our analysis turns the typical environmental justice analysis on its head, testing whether there is disproportionate "exposure" to the environmental *amenities* of green schools rather than to environmental disamenities like toxic waste. We sought to determine if schools with more minority students or those in wealthier or more educated neighborhoods tended to have their new schools built as green or not. Crucially, we also wanted to see if this tendency depended on whether the school was a public school or a private school, or whether it was in an urbanized or a rural area. We controlled for the overall size of the school, thinking that bigger school projects may be more likely to be green because of the scale economies and benefits of the fixed cost of building green. We also wanted to control for the grade levels served by the school, making sure that our results were not driven by, say, only kindergartens or high schools.

Our results were striking in the consistently surprising results. Some findings were not so surprising, such as noting that bigger new schools (in terms of enrollment) were much more likely to be green. The grade levels served by the new schools did not correlate much with the likelihood of being green, except for preschools. New schools with pre-kindergarten ages were more likely to be built green than other

(cont.)

new schools. The most interesting results, however, regard the equity in representation, by income and by race, for the new schools' enrollment and neighborhoods for new green and nongreen schools. For this, we turn to a summary in Table 9.1.

Table 9.1 shows whether each of the demographic factors (percent African American, percent Hispanic, income, or percent with a college degree) makes the likelihood of a new school being green more (+) or less (−) likely. A "0" indicates that the relationship is not statistically significant. The income measure is based on the share of students eligible for free or reduced (public) school lunches at the enrollment level and on median household income at the neighborhood level. The share of college graduates is available for the neighborhoods of schools but, naturally, is not available to describe student enrollment. The results in Table 9.1 show the patterns across different subgroups based on public versus private schools and based on urban versus rural locations. Overall, new schools tend to be green as their enrollments include *more minorities*. In addition, even after controlling for the student body of each school, the greener schools tend to be surrounded by more minority neighborhoods. New schools are also more likely to be green schools when they are located in lower-income neighborhoods and in more educated neighborhoods. The neighborhood income and

Table 9.1. *Summary results for EJ analysis of new green schools*

		Urban		Rural		
		Public	Private	Public	Private	All
Enrollment	% African American	+	0	0	0	+
	% Hispanic	0	0	+	0	+
	Income	−		0		0
	% College*					
Neighborhood	% African American	0	0	+	+	+
	% Hispanic	0	0	0	+	+
	Income	−	−	−	−	−
	% College	+	+	+	+	+

* % College is not applicable for the student population enrolled in primary and secondary schools, so has no data.

(cont.)

education tendencies persist across each of the four subgroups based on urban/rural and public/private groupings. For new, urban public schools, they are more likely to be green when they have more African American students and lower-income students. New urban private schools do not show that same racial tendency with respect to their enrollment. New rural schools also do not exhibit as much correlation between student enrollment and green status. The one exception, however, is that new rural public schools are more likely to be built green when their enrollment is more Hispanic. Taken altogether, except for the tendency of more educated neighborhoods to build their new schools greener, these results point to a strong tendency to build new, green schools for more minority students and in more minority neighborhoods. These tendencies are particularly strong for urban public schools, but the neighborhood effects for income and education are consistent across all four types of schools.

These results tell us a few important lessons. First, simply, these results point to a success story for green buildings in terms of providing one of the most vulnerable subpopulations (children, especially those in public schools) with extra access to environmental amenities. New green schools are more likely to be used by minority and vulnerable students, and they tend to go to more minority neighborhoods. This is especially true for public schools. Second, more educated neighborhoods tend to get their new schools built to green standards, which suggests a key role for local education levels. Third, these strong results are consistent, and they point to some important differences between public and private schools and between rural and urban contexts. We should be paying attention to these distinctions going forward, encouraging more private-school green construction and continuing to support equitable access in rural settings. (After all, all else equal, new schools in rural locations are more likely to be built green than new urban schools.) Lastly, it is worth emphasizing that this analysis is all conditional on a new school being built in the first place. That new schools are more likely to be green in, say, more minority neighborhoods (versus whiter and wealthier neighborhoods) may be heartening, but it does not mean that those minority neighborhoods get more new schools in the first place. A key area for concern should be the equitable provision of new buildings to vulnerable members of our society. If vulnerable groups rarely get new buildings like schools, then the fact that the new ones tend to be greener for them is little consolation.

Economic and Policy Impacts

This greener market transformation for the building sector holds big implications in terms of economics and policy. The economics have initially straightforward implications – higher-quality construction brings high upfront costs and lower ongoing operating expenses – but the power of markets to adapt and evolve ought not be under-appreciated. Over time, as markets adapt to greener buildings, the price and cost premium of green buildings fades. This results from a confluence of forces, including the cost reductions from ever-growing adoption and learning about these new technologies and building practices as the Green Building Movement becomes standard. Also, nongreen options become more expensive if the green premium shifts demand in that direction, leading to an equilibration process in the market (Brusselaers et al. 2017). The dual trend of lowering and converging prices pushes the market transformation forward – deeper and wider – and market pressure from buyers and other stakeholders (investors, public relations, regulators) continues to make the economic case for adoption more compelling. This trend also supports an upward pressure on regulation and green building policies. As green buildings become more affordable and more common, the (political) resistance to regulations and mandates erodes. The ever-expanding frontier of green buildings leads to an expansion of public policies to support green building adoption. We also expect increasing demand and benefits from green building, as more development activities urbanize, as income and environmental preferences grow, and as risks associated with dependency on energy and water inputs continue to grow. The fundamentals behind green building are strong. Demand should continue to grow, supply costs should continue to decline, and strong peer-effects from learning from (and competing with) one another should make for a burgeoning market.

But not all is rosy in terms of economics and policy. We expect that free-rider problems for providing public goods can remain. We expect that, while corporate social responsibility is the real deal, it is not universally dominant and has its limits. We expect that merely solving information asymmetries just allows for a differentiated market, efficient in providing for green and nongreen buildings alike, and not fostering universally greener construction. We expect that shifting toward regulatory (compliance) pressure instead of voluntary (market-based) rewards may reduce incentives for innovation in the sector. We also expect that reducing the green building premium as it becomes more commonplace risks reducing incentives to build, and brag about, green – unless we keep raising the bar for greener and greener buildings. We expect that rising (upfront) costs for greener construction will apply downward pressure on adoption rates, especially for those with particularly high discount rates, such as policymakers and other elected officials.

Observed Impacts

The scientific evidence on the effectiveness and economic impacts of green buildings and their certifications shows considerable promise. As reviewed in Chapter 2, there is substantial and consistent evidence of a price premium for these buildings that can signal their higher quality. Aydin et al.'s (2020) analysis of Ireland's energy-performance certificates confirms this while going further. They note that the premium for energy efficiency is commensurate with expected cost-savings from the better building performance. This sign of a very well-functioning signal of higher quality building design highlights the power of private market solutions to induce and reward greener building technology. The green building premium also leads to lower default risk on mortgage-backed securities, giving owners of green buildings more favorable loan terms (An and Pivo 2020). Even building appraisers are now starting to recognize this market price premium as assessed values reflect energy-efficiency benefits (Chegut et al. 2020). These consistently observed price premiums stand out even more in light of the lack of consistent evidence that green buildings cost appreciably more to construct in the first place. To the extent that extra construction costs are observed, they appear more than offset by the returns in the form of higher sales prices (Yeganeh et al. 2019).

Yet just because there is value to adopting green buildings and ecolabels help enable those markets does not imply widespread adoption. Fuerst et al. (2014) offer some sobering, yet a bit dated, statistics about the market penetration for LEED-certified buildings in the United States. The average metro area's share of commercial floor space that is LEED-certified was only 0.87 percent and only rarely greater than 3 percent. Obviously, market penetration remains a work in progress.

It merits mentioning that much of the evidence of the green buildings should skew toward early success stories. Early adopters may experience some "growing pains" associated with newer technologies, but also the areas to go greenest first ought to be those with the biggest net benefits from doing so. Bigger buildings, those where water prices are greater (Simons et al. 2009), and those facing more extreme climates (Holtermans and Kok 2019) are more likely to adopt ecolabels and to enjoy bigger price premiums. Similarly, the public sector and some private sectors of the building industry have more aggressively adopted green building practices, suggesting that some of the laggard sectors might not enjoy the same gains. Fortunately, the diffusion S curve catches up to them as costs of adoption continue to decline. Yet the strong presence of ecolabels, especially mandatory ecolabels, can restrict entry of new firms into the market and impose greater costs on entrants with fewer resources (Tian 2003).

The importance of ecolabel mandates for market penetration can be seen in several studies (e.g., Adekanye et al. 2020; Choi 2010; Fuerst et al. 2014). That mandates improve adoption rates is hardly surprising, although the limited effect of more incentive-based policies in these studies is perhaps more surprising. A softer approach to supporting the green market transformation through public policy involves the use of public procurement to kickstart or bolster the green building industry. Public procurement policies for greener products can boost supply, as has been seen for organic agriculture (Lindström et al. 2020), certified wood (Brusselaers et al. 2017), and green buildings (Simcoe and Toffel 2014).

Caution: Construction Zone

Enthusiasm for green building ecolabels should be tempered with caution for several reasons. The evidence reported here points to performance that falls short of expectations set by engineering models. Green performance may yet improve as ecolabeling schemes shift their attention to performance monitoring and standards. But the ecolabel focus on construction and conditions at a single point in time raises more general concerns about auditing quality, ongoing monitoring, and long-term or lifecycle performance of these new, green buildings. (These sorts of concerns about ensuring ongoing performance standards apply to conventional command-and-control regulatory approaches as well.) Entry of new ecolabels into the market can also induce a race to the bottom or lead to confusion in the market that dilutes the efficacy of all ecolabels. While this does not appear to be a major concern in the US green building context, the lack of competition among ecolabels might instead raise concerns in its own right. A lack of transparency, responsiveness to stakeholders, or other issues may weaken ecolabels' effectiveness.

While performance of green buildings might disappoint some, we find a bigger concern to be adoption rates. Researchers rightly face difficulties in credibly establishing a counterfactual environmental performance (i.e., how the building would have performed if it were not green) when participation is voluntary. The volunteer buildings might have been greener even without the label. Self-selection into the Green Building Movement suggests (a) we may be undercounting the greenness of buildings by only looking at new construction that gets certified (Aydin et al. 2020), and (b) ultimately the scope of impact for these ecolabels is largely confined to just the volunteers. Major market transformation thus requires either widespread take-up of the ecolabel or spillovers from market segments that do participate to those who do not. Despite impressive growth rates in adoption of building ecolabels, participation is hardly universal. Large segments of the building sector and some markets around the world have eluded this movement. This brings us back to the spillovers from participants to nonparticipants – a major aspect of truly transforming a market. As knowledge and practices diffuse, and as greener products and expertise becomes more available in markets, even those not pursuing an ecolabel can find themselves making greener choices with their buildings. Evidence for this spillover, where ecolabels like LEED also help make non-LEED buildings greener, remains limited at this point. But the cases and research described here, especially in Chapter 7, suggest that spillovers from green buildings do function in important ways to help green subsequent buildings.

Another risk present for ecolabels generally regards stringency: How strict are the standards and how do they evolve? Competitive forces may push an ecolabel to water down its standards, or relax its monitoring or auditing, to gain traction in the marketplace. Greenwashing ensues. Such a risk remains in the case of building ecolabels. Pressures to weaken standards to attract more participants may arise even when an ecolabel dominates its regional market. This might arise in attempts to keep ecolabels simple enough for nonexperts, or to relax standards to fit the "lowest common denominator" in order to appeal to those looking to build in different markets. And no matter an ecolabel's current stringency, the builders may be pursuing greenwashing strategies of minimal compliance with standards. Though the evidence (see Chapter 5) suggests that this is not prevalent in the LEED context – where arguably the LEED system design prevents most greenwashing – there is no guarantee that this continues. Ecolabels that certify attributes or behavior with more private benefits rather than environmental gains or that certify superficial improvements can undermine the impact of these voluntary mechanisms. Chapter 3 discusses some of these issues in designing ecolabels. With so much flexibility in designing ecolabels, it proves difficult to identify exactly which design features lead to which outcomes. Similarly, the holistic and multidimensional nature of green buildings eschews a one-size-fits-all approach but can also obscure what ultimately qualifies as a green building. Certainly, not all ecolabels are created equal, and their impacts should also vary.

Finally, we conclude by reiterating the concerns about equity, diffusion, and stringency in ecolabels generally and with building ecolabels specifically. If higher prices evidence well-functioning ecolabels, then equitable access to green buildings may be lost. Expanding access to green buildings, and doing so equitably, entails more meaningful engagement with broader groups of stakeholders. Yet including more stakeholders in the governance of ecolabel schemes risks weakening standards or reprioritizing the attributes being certified. Some of these shifts may be needed improvements, while others might dilute the ecolabel's signal or allow for lesser performance. Holistic ecolabels like LEED always face problems with a unidimensional signal reflecting multidimensional quality, where some dimensions might be discounted (as in the "A Closer Look: Accounting for a Bigger Picture" examples above) (Darnall and Aragón-Correa 2014). Striking a balance between greater participation and greater stringency remains a core challenge for ecolabels and using other design features (e.g., multiple tiers) to mitigate the tradeoffs can help. Time will tell how building ecolabels will evolve to expand participation while improving environmental performance.

References

Adekanye, Oluwatobi G., Alex Davis, and Inês L. Azevedo. 2020. "Federal Policy, Local Policy, and Green Building Certifications in the US." *Energy and Buildings* 209: 109700.

An, Xudong and Gary Pivo. 2020. "Green Buildings in Commercial Mortgage-backed Securities: The Effects of LEED and Energy Star Certification on Default Risk and Loan Terms." *Real Estate Economics* 48, no. 1: 7–42.

Asensio, Omar I. and Magali A. Delmas. 2017. "The Effectiveness of US Energy Efficiency Building Labels." *Nature Energy* 2, no. 4: 1–9.

Aydin, Erdal, Dirk Brounen, and Nils Kok. 2020. "The Capitalization of Energy Efficiency: Evidence from the Housing Market." *Journal of Urban Economics* 117: 103243.

Braun, Thomas, Marcelo Cajias, and Ralf Hohenstatt. 2017. "Societal Influence on Diffusion of Green Buildings: A Count Regression Approach." *Journal of Real Estate Research* 39, no. 1: 1–38.

Bruegge, Chris, Tatyana Deryugina, and Erica Myers. 2019. "The Distributional Effects of Building Energy Codes." *Journal of the Association of Environmental and Resource Economists* 6, no. S1: S95–S127.

Brusselaers, Jan, Guido Van Huylenbroeck, and Jeroen Buysse. 2017. "Green Public Procurement of Certified Wood: Spatial Leverage Effect and Welfare Implications." *Ecological Economics* 135: 91–102.

Chegut, Andrea, Piet Eichholtz, Rogier Holtermans, and Juan Palacios. 2020. "Energy Efficiency Information and Valuation Practices in Rental Housing." *The Journal of Real Estate Finance and Economics* 60, no. 1: 181–204.

Choi, Eugene. 2010. "Green on Buildings: The Effects of Municipal Policy on Green Building Designations in America's Central Cities." *Journal of Sustainable Real Estate* 2, no. 1: 1–21.

Darnall, Nicole and J. Alberto Aragón-Correa. 2014. "Can Ecolabels Influence Firms' Sustainability Strategy and Stakeholder Behavior?" *Organization & Environment* 27, no. 4: 319–327.

Figge, Frank and Andrea Stevenson Thorpe. 2019. "The Symbiotic Rebound Effect in the Circular Economy." *Ecological Economics* 163: 61–69.

Fuerst, Franz, Constantine Kontokosta, and Patrick McAllister. 2014. "Determinants of Green Building Adoption." *Environment and Planning B: Planning and Design* 41, no. 3: 551–570.

Gerarden, Todd D., Richard G. Newell, and Robert N. Stavins. 2017. "Assessing the Energy-Efficiency Gap." *Journal of Economic Literature* 55, no. 4: 1486–1525.

Holtermans, Rogier & Nils Kok. 2019. "On the Value of Environmental Certification in the Commercial Real Estate Market." *Real Estate Economics* 47, no. 3: 685–722.

Liang, Jing, Yueming Qiu, and Ming Hu. 2019. "Mind the Energy Performance Gap: Evidence from Green Commercial Buildings." *Resources, Conservation and Recycling* 141: 364–377.

Lindström, Hanna, Sofia Lundberg, and Per-Olov Marklund. 2020. "How Green Public Procurement Can Drive Conversion of Farmland: An Empirical Analysis of an Organic Food Policy." *Ecological Economics* 172: 106622.

Simcoe, Timothy and Michael W. Toffel. 2014. "Government Green Procurement Spillovers: Evidence from Municipal Building Policies in California." *Journal of Environmental Economics and Management* 68, no. 3: 411–434.

Simons, Robert, Eugene Choi, and Donna Simons. 2009. "The Effect of State and City Green Policies on the Market Penetration of Green Commercial Buildings." *Journal of Sustainable Real Estate* 1, no. 1: 139–166.

Tian, Huilan. 2003. "Eco-labelling Scheme, Environmental Protection, and Protectionism." *Canadian Journal of Economics/Revue canadienne d'économique* 36, no. 3: 608–633.

USGBC. 2020. *Equity Summit Report – June 2020*. Available at: www.usgbc .org/resources/usgbc-equity-summit-report-june-2020

Yeganeh, Armin Jeddi, Andrew Patton McCoy, and Steve Hankey. 2019. "Green Affordable Housing: Cost-Benefit Analysis for Zoning Incentives." *Sustainability* 11, no. 22: 1–24.

Zhao, Shuang, Shan Zhou, and Douglas S. Noonan. 2019. "Environmental Justice and Green Schools: Assessing Students and Communities' Access to Green Schools." *Social Science Quarterly* 100, no. 6: 2223–2239.

10 | *A Blueprint for Green Market Transformation*

Summarizing a Theory of Market Transformation

We have laid out a theory of green market transformation through voluntary market mechanisms throughout this book and use this chapter to provide a more formal presentation of our assumptions, theory itself, testable hypotheses, and boundary conditions and limitations of our theory. To summarize our theory, introduced in Chapter 1, we begin with a perspective that getting the prices right is likely an insufficient condition to achieve the types of market transformation necessary to combat climate change and achieve the kind of deep decarbonization that climate scientists say is necessary to avoid the worst impacts of climate change. The built environment is responsible for more than a third of global greenhouse gas emissions, and has, historically, been a challenging sector to address. Further, the long lifespan of buildings (usually far greater than 30 years) means that even the most immediate changes are slow to permeate the sector.

We begin with a conceptualization of a marketplace with lots of actors – producers, consumers, and regulators who make conventional (nongreen) goods. We define Green Market Transformation as the condition in which a substantial portion of this marketplace changes to consist of producers and consumers actively pursuing greener products and practices. This story assumes a vibrant, competitive marketplace, with lots of actors, goods with significant negative environmental production or consumption externalities, serious information asymmetries for the goods in the market, and a number of other market barriers that inhibit this transformation. The transformation here is not one of a single entity or a few actors "seeing the light" and "going green," but rather the predominant mode of production or consumption shifting to embrace greener features across the market as a whole, a transformation likely to take many years to make meaningful progress.

Key to the assumptions underlying our theory, we observe that there are a number of barriers to moving nascent technologies to widespread adoption in the marketplace. In Chapter 2, we identified the key challenges, especially information problems – both the under-provision of learning and R&D in innovative green building technologies and the "market for lemons" inhibiting the diffusion of greener building approaches. In addition, other "information problems" include high search and transaction costs associated with the adoption of innovative technologies. These costs impact both buyers and sellers of green technologies. Identifying the foundational problems also points to the elements that need to be in place to catalyze market transformation for a more sustainable built environment.

The barriers are related to the availability and cost of information. We hypothesize that uncertainty associated with the cost and performance of new technologies dissuades potential uptake of these technologies in the marketplace. These technologies remain expensive because there remain few suppliers and little experience with these technologies. The cost of acquiring new information is high, and sellers pass those costs onto prospective buyers. For buyers, the high costs and little experience with nascent technology become self-reinforcing barriers to green market transformation, producing a potential Valley of Death, where promising technologies fail to gain widespread traction in the marketplace.

This chapter outlines our theory of Green Market Transformation for the building sector by first describing the *conditions* associated with this transformation. These are factors that support the transformation occurring. To transform markets through voluntary mechanisms requires the strong rule of law, institutions to curtail fraud and to support property rights to encourage long-term investments. These boundary conditions become assumptions about the context that can help enable Green Market Transformation.

Next, we review the *catalysts* – those causal mechanisms that actually bring about the deep greening of the building sector markets – that previous chapters detail. Our theory of Green Market Transformation argues that the dissemination of information through voluntary mechanisms can help address the barriers and market failures that produce the Valley of Death. We hypothesize that these mechanisms include, though are not limited to, well-designed ecolabels and iterative demonstration projects that overcome market barriers by disseminating information about the cost and performance of nascent technologies to the marketplace, lowering costs and risks associated with the adoption of greener technologies.

This chapter organizes the review of our perspectives on Green Market Transformation into factors that predict and that explain Green Market Transformation. These predictive conditions and causal mechanisms form the blueprint for those seeking to engineer green market transformation.

The Conditions: Factors that Predict Market Transformation

The story we have laid out over the preceding chapters tells a tale of rapid and substantial transformation of an industry and green building practices across many dimensions. In large part, the building sector is transforming, the investment side of the picture is transforming, and tenants and buyers have changed their expectations and clearly express substantial demand for greener buildings. We have demonstrated the importance of information problems and how green certification and ecolabel systems play crucial roles in catalyzing this transformation. In theory, the combination of growing demand, fueled by cost advantages and many other co-benefits, will set the stage for market transform-ation even if the market struggles to "go green" because of major information problems. These conditions can set the stage, but infor-mation problems can keep the lights down. Enter from stage left: Voluntary market-based solutions. We can see opportunity for volun-tary and market-oriented actors' solutions to come in, turn the lights on, and let the show begin!

Yet this sort of transformation is hardly inevitable. In theory, these conditions help make it more likely that transformation can occur, but they do not guarantee it. Moreover, when one or more of these condi-tions is not met, the transformation may be rather limited or not even occur at all. We see some important limitations to the power of ecolabels alone in catalyzing market transformations. For instance, without demand for the attributes that ecolabels certify, we should hardly expect the needle to move on greening whatever activity or industry the ecola-bel covers. Likewise, the fundamentals of information problems are such that the market might stagnate and remain in its conventional, "brown" form without effective solutions to those information problems. Yet ecolabels hold promise when demand for greener markets is strong and information problems pose a significant barrier.

There may be multiple ways to accomplish the market transformation, and voluntary ecolabels are just one of them. We should be aware of other tools in the policy toolkit, and how these tools interact with each other. Mandatory disclosures, such as rules about labeling tobacco products, can compel major changes – but we ought to not expect complete and total market transformations. (Cigarette sales continue, and new smokers join the market every day.) Regulations that mandate certain technologies can radically transform how a market functions by brute force, such as how mandates over low-flow toilets or leaded gasoline essentially forced shifts away from certain types of production. Other conventional policy tools such as subsidies can work to transform markets. We see that story play out in other sectors like solar panels in the United States (Nemet 2019). These other policy approaches rely on voluntary action to varying degrees. Technology mandates lack the voluntary component, while tax and subsidy approaches steer the voluntary choices via financial incentives. Yet a core part of the Green Building Movement has been its reliance on the essentially voluntary nature of using market-driven forces through ecolabels to lead the market transformation. Finding ways for markets to voluntarily transform may be rare, but they have a compelling future when the conditions are right.

Despite the advantages of the voluntary approaches to greening the economy, these approaches will not always work to transform markets. They work best in certain circumstances. We have identified many of these conditions for this approach to flourish. These conditions may not be necessary nor sufficient conditions to guarantee success, but they all tend to play very important roles in setting the stage for the transformation. Further theoretical and empirical work is needed to refine and robustly establish specific conditions needed for Green Market Transformation. But, based on the research reviewed thus far, we expect that a final list will largely overlap with these supporting conditions. To review, the key conditions that make the context ripe for greener market transformation through voluntary mechanisms are:

1. **Substantial demand for greener attributes.**
   It is crucial that consumers demand greener attributes and that they are willing to pay a market premium for greener products. It is inevitable that greener products will cost more – at least at first until there is substantial market penetration. Ideally, these

attributes – goods, services, processes – affect multiple types of actors in the industry, from wholesalers to suppliers to retailers to consumers to investors. This allows pressures for sustainability to flow upstream along supply chains. Whether it is consumer-level demand for green that pushes upstream suppliers to go green, or industry suppliers adopt greener practices and technologies that permeate out to the consumer markets, demand for sustainability among a diversity of actors in the market can promote market change.

2. **Strong marketing signal value.**

   To facilitate the price premiums necessary to support greener products, it is essential to have a label or market signal that is recognized by the marketplace. This label makes it easy for consumers to recognize the attributes of products and for producers to receive a premium for the provision of greener products. While perhaps not necessary, it helps that the products in the market are publicly visible, symbols, or icons that can be marketed. Even if the attributes being certified are largely invisible, or the concept of sustainability itself is abstract and messy, the labeled product itself should be easily marketed so that the publicity can be claimed by those seeking the label. This advantage of marketability can also spill over to associated or attached products themselves, such as material inputs to the building, expertise by designers and architects, or financiers or clients of firms with green labels. Having high-profile, publicly visible "things" can be crucial to an effective ecolabel for that thing – and also to indirectly support greener activities and products associated with that "thing," but that might otherwise be less visible. Certain types of management practices, for instance, might be too invisible for an ecolabel to certify quality in such a way that fully transforms the marketplace for management practices. But an ecolabel that certifies a highly visible and complementary good – the firm's flagship headquarters – can provide more motivation for changing management practices in ways that are essentially bundled under the green building label. As we argue in the discussion of pilot and demonstration projects in Chapters 6 and 7, having information and learning about others adopting is vital for reducing risk and increasing pressure or incentives for others to subsequently adopt. Visibility and strong marketing value are thus key for ecolabels to effectively change behavior more broadly across an industry and in related sectors.

3. **Substantial benefits to adopters of the new technology.**
   There needs to be substantial benefits – private, market, or strategic – available to adopters of the new technology. This condition
   overlaps with Conditions 1 and 2 but represents an important
   distinction. The adopters themselves need to realize the benefits
   from adoption. Demand for the greener attributes might exist
   among some but not all stakeholders. Just having demand for the
   greener attributes in a downstream market is not sufficient to spur
   adoption if the adopters upstream do not realize benefits from
   doing so. For a green building, there may be important benefits
   for tenants, or benefits in terms of lower employee turnover or
   better morale. But just because others in the green building story
   can realize gains does not automatically imply that upstream producers will build it green. Thus, builders and developers must
   actually gain some benefit from adoption. This benefit might take
   various forms, such as financial (e.g., cost savings that occur at the
   time of construction, a price premium upon eventual sale), risk-
   related (e.g., mitigating climate or regulatory risk via design
   choices), or more strategic (e.g., joining the "green club" and
   positioning the firm as a market leader).
4. **Support from legal and regulatory institutions and stakeholders.**
   Having some background or bedrock support from regulation, and
   possibly other legal constructs such as strong rule of law, contract
   law, property rates, etc., can also help support the market transformation through ecolabels. It is not that regulations such as
   building codes drive the market transformation, but rather that
   those building codes actually follow the market transformation. In
   the particular case of building code, there was an extensive network
   of stakeholders who were invested in greening the industry. By the
   time the building codes changed, most of the building practice had
   already moved ahead or fully anticipated those changes. Yet having
   a lagging regulatory approach, and baseline rule of law, is not
   irrelevant for our story. We argue that it presents an important
   signal to actors in the marketplace about those trends. In the
   broader context of corporate social responsibility, a movement by
   stakeholders to incorporate social, environmental, and ethical goals
   into decision-making can change norms in an industry that lay the
   groundwork for regulations that then codify this behavior. In a
   sense, changing norms and then codifying these changes reaffirms
   the risk-taking and greener behavior by those early adopters. This

endorsement has some value. Perhaps most importantly, it signals the continuing ratcheting up of regulatory standards signals to the economic actors about the risk of future regulation. The presence of the risk of future regulation can motivate voluntary adoption of improved environmental performance (Lyon and Maxwell 2004). Ecolabels that work in conjunction with other traditional regulatory and policy approaches may be most effective (Costello and Kotchen 2020; Yokessa and Marette 2019).

While perhaps not as strong as the four conditions that enable Green Market Transformation, we observe a number of other factors that are present in the built environment that have been enabling factors. For example, the durability of capital is another useful condition for market transformation, whether this durable capital is productive capital like manufacturing equipment, human capital like expertise in green building design, network capital like valuable partnerships and trust in the industry, or some other form. The durability of buildings as capital stock, for instance, surely affects the calculus of decision-makers throughout the process of adoption of greener technologies. In addition, the idea of future (regulatory, climate) risk in Condition 7 plays a more prominent role when capital decisions being made today are long-lived and exposed to greater future uncertainty. For durable goods, like buildings that may last 30-plus years, there are additional future regulatory and price risks that are relevant that may induce additional preemptive voluntary action as a mechanism to hedge against risk. Those experts and firms working in the sector also have more incentive to invest in learning the innovative practices and technologies when they have decades ahead to recoup those investments.

The presence of an innovation ecosystem can help transform markets. In the particular case of the built environment, this innovation ecosystem is comprised of many invested stakeholders across industry, NGOs, and government. These stakeholders helped facilitate an institution of iterative demonstration projects that disseminated lessons across an industry, helped move policy targets, and leveraged public procurement to build supply chains and facilitate market development. In the case of the built environment, the interaction between demonstration projects, the ecolabel, and buy-in from the public and private sectors helped facilitate successful green market transformation. This brings us to the catalytic forces that can drive the transformation.

The Catalysts: Key Causal Mechanisms in Transforming Markets

A number of causal processes help explain the phenomenon of Green Market Transformation. This section reviews the various ways in which mechanisms like ecolabels, demonstration projects, and peer learning about green innovations can drive change to green markets for the built environment. Table 10.1 lists some major causal mechanisms and groups them by their impacts on market size and strength, their impacts on informational aspects like learning and risk, and their iterative or dynamic mechanisms. We reserve other chapters to focus on detailing how these catalysts bring about the Green Market Transformation, while this section reviews them and how they fit into this broader framework for understanding the transformation.

Impacts on Market Strength

In Chapters 3–5 we discuss the role that ecolabels can play in catalyzing transformation in the green building sector. In Chapter 3, we discuss how the design of ecolabels and, in particular, the pairing of

Table 10.1. *Causal mechanisms in green market transformation for green buildings*

Impacts on market strength	Ecolabels or demonstration projects build supply chains and reduce costs
	Ecolabels increase demand for greener technologies
Impacts on information	Ecolabels and demonstration projects increase knowledge about innovative technologies
	Ecolabels and demonstration projects decrease information costs
	Ecolabels and demonstration projects reduce uncertainty about performance
Dynamic mechanisms	Race to the top pressures participants to learn and improve (green) performance

public and private benefits associated with certification can induce participation in an ecolabel. In a review of past theory regarding the design of ecolabels, we observe that effective ecolabels induce the provision of public goods with a mixture of private benefits related to improved energy and environmental performance and the signaling of improved performance and the provision of public goods to the marketplace. We note that this design trait of ecolabels is key to inducing participation by private actors. We also identified design elements for green building certifications that can promote green market transformation. These key design variables include content, governance, and context. The *content* of a label includes what the label covers. Sustainability is a highly multi-dimensional concept, and content of the label can reflect a wide range of potential product and process attributes. We hypothesize that an appropriate balance between public and private benefits of ecolabels needs to exist in order for the label to be effective. We also suggest that an ecolabel design that allows sufficient flexibility and provides an appropriate mix of incentives to create both deep levels of commitment as well as broad participation is most likely to be highly effective.

Improved *governance* of an ecolabel is thought to increase its impact. We discuss governance characteristics that have received attention in the literature such as sponsorship, noting an array of potentially conflicting incentives that are likely to impact the stringency and impact of an ecolabel. Third party verification auditing has also received research attention and demonstrating, unsurprisingly, that ecolabels with third party verification are perceived as more stringent than those without it. We also discuss a range of additional governance characteristics of ecolabels that have received less attention in the academic literature: Stakeholder involvement and the process in which ecolabels are designed, revised, and implemented are promising areas for future research.

Finally, we discuss the *context* of ecolabels. The context refers to the broader political–economic space in which labels operate. It has been noted that the ecolabel space is quite crowded, with many competing certifications existing in individual industries. There are likely powerful intermediating relationships between product type, industry structure, and ecolabel design and impact that are worthy of investigation. Our "A Closer Look: Agricultural Ecolabels" subsection in Chapter 3 describes the application of these key theoretical constructs of ecolabels and how they help characterize a set of 51 agricultural eco-labels. We suggest that studies that traverse multiple ecolabels are still few, and there are likely significant opportunities to understand the impacts of variation across the plethora of ecolabels.

These concepts are applied to the world of ecolabels in the built environment in Chapter 4, describing and characterizing differences across 14 different built environment ecolabels, focusing in particular on the design and evolution of the LEED ecolabel, the most popular ecolabel in the built environment. For the practitioner, this chapter helps elucidate a world with dozens of labels and helps characterize the differences across the world of ecolabels in the built environment. To the scholar, this chapter helps demonstrate the utility of some of the theoretical constructs developed in the earlier chapters to characterize variation in ecolabels around the world. We employ the constructs of content, governance, and context in a limited fashion to help describe the LEED label in more depth. We encourage future research to sys-tematically characterize a wide range of ecolabels for the built environ-ment, and find relationships between the design of these labels and their impacts, and note that some recent research (e.g., DeLeon and Rivera 2009; Grabs 2020; Van der Heijden 2017) has attempted to make sense of these sorts of issues. More empirical research on busi-ness models and the "market for ecolabels" is needed, especially one that recognizes the complexity that arises from multiple pressures (mandatory and voluntary) and multiple ways firms can respond (Aragón-Correa et al. 2020).

In Chapter 5, we leverage information about the public and private benefits of a prominent ecolabel, LEED, and the types of investments that are made to pursue certification. These characteristics allow us to develop an improved understanding of the types of participants in ecolabel programs. We hypothesize that marketing benefits of achiev-ing LEED drive additional investment in environmental and energy technologies. Further, we suggest that there might be important inter-actions between public and private investments and the marketing benefits that induce organizations to invest greater resources in the technologies that lead to achieving the LEED ecolabel. These traits, *marketing* and *publicness* of investments, bring us to develop a typ-ology of four categories of LEED participants. *Pragmatists* pay little attention to marketing signals and invest in technologies that provide private returns. *Altruists* also pay little attention to marketing signals but invest in technologies that provide public returns. *Greenwashers* pay careful attention to marketing benefits and invest in technologies that provide private returns. And we define *members* of the ecolabel club as those who invest more heavily in technologies with public benefits but do so in a manner that maximizes marketing benefits.

This chapter is one of the first looks under the hood of ecolabel participants, into the types of strategies employed to certify green. Ecolabel participation, and the strategies that firms, governments, and other organizations use to comply with green labeling requirements, have rarely been transparent. We find evidence of variation in ecolabeling strategies across building ownership. Government organizations are more likely to build green in a way that delivers public benefits and with less emphasis on marketing benefits. For profit organizations and NGOs are more likely to emphasize the marketing benefits. And we observe that at higher tiers of certification, for-profit firms are more likely to invest in efficiency technologies that may not have been otherwise profitable.

Our second set of causal mechanisms associated with our theory of Green Market Transformation suggest ways that ecolabels and demonstration projects can change the demand and supply of innovative technologies, helping drive market transformation. For demonstration projects to be effective, we assume that there are important information problems with available remedies. Likewise, for ecolabels to catalyze transformations, there needs to be information problems for them to resolve and feasible means to address those problems. Credible third-party measurement and reporting of the greener attributers must be an available option. The information problems need not be "solved," but at least meaningfully reduced. Partial solutions might be the case in some situations for, say, credence goods or even some experience goods. Current technology or other (legal, political, economic) circumstances might make credible (third-party) monitoring infeasible. Ecolabels are not miracles that can overcome all challenges to difficult information problems.

Impacts on Information

While Chapters 2 and 5 allow us to understand the motivations and strategies that lead to investment in energy and environmental technologies, in Chapters 6 and 7, we turn our attention to the mechanisms that enable the diffusion of these technologies by lowering information costs. For green market transformation to occur, the adoption of advanced energy and environmental technologies needs to be widespread. We view ecolabeled demonstration projects as an important tool that can help catalyze green market transformation by addressing information barriers. In Chapter 6, we take a close look at the Kendeda Building for Innovative Sustainable Design. This building purports to be the most environmentally advanced building in the Southeastern United States and was designed with a goal to transform the market. A careful look at this building and discussions with the contractors who helped design and build it reveals an improved understanding of the barriers that inhibit the adoption of advanced environmental and energy technologies, and the process in which demonstration projects can help overcome these barriers.

Chapter 7 tests the hypothesis that demonstration projects can catalyze green market transformation. We find causal evidence that the presence of demonstration projects drives the uptake of a greater number of LEED labeled buildings, controlling for a vast array of factors that might also impact the adoption of LEED buildings. This finding, while limited to one particular ecolabeling program, suggests a mechanism that demonstration projects undertaken in the public or private sectors might be valuable by facilitating positive information spillovers and the uptake of advanced energy and environmental technologies.

To this point, our theory has presented a static view of mechanisms that lead to investment in advanced energy and environmental technologies, facilitating Green Market Transformation. But transformation is an inherently dynamic concept. We imagine an iterative process of transformation, and one where these dynamic processes drive changes that diffuse across industry. To conceptualize this process, we adapt a theory of jurisdictional competition to imagine a race to the top, facilitated by ecolabels and market premia.

Dynamic Mechanisms

Catalyzing a transformation to a greener market relies on triggering and sustaining a race to the top while preventing a race to the bottom. As discussed in Chapter 8, the conditions for inducing a race to the top from ecolabels include: participants getting greener, increasingly rigorous criteria for certification, and increasingly substantive participation in certification.

Competitive forces provide the pressure needed to motivate adoption of greener technologies. Competition for financing, for buyers, for tenants, and for other stakeholder support gives incentives for that race to the top (Rysman et al. 2020). It gives others in the supply chain incentives to compete to serve that greener demand (Yokessa and Marette 2019). These competitive forces need not apply only to commercial, for-profit firms. Nonprofits and even government agencies should still face competitive pressures, as they compete strategically to improve their position, garner more support from constituents and stakeholders, etc. Moreover, some competition – or at least the threat of competition – can be important to keeping the certifiers honest and innovating themselves. Complacency will stall out the transformation.

In Chapter 8, we consider the dynamic, iterative nature of green market transformation and hypothesize a set of conditions that can help facilitate a virtuous cycle and race to the top, spurred by a voluntary ecolabel. Ecolabels induced the adoption of advanced technologies by providing a marketing benefit, and the presence of early adoptions helped facilitate increasing numbers of adoptions. But this process occurs over a long period of time. And LEED participants, for example, interact and compete in a market. Borrowing from the literature on regulatory competition, in Chapter 8 we spell out conditions that can enable a race to the top or race to the bottom in the ecolabel context. For a race to the top to occur, participants need to be getting greener, the criteria for earning an ecolabel needs to be increasingly rigorous over time, and the participation in the ecolabel needs to be increasingly substantive. In the LEED ecolabeling program, we find evidence for all three of these conditions.

Limitations to Transformative Powers

We must recognize some important limitations to this theory of Green Market Transformation, in terms of the extent and desirability of the transformation as well as the applicability of the theory. As an ongoing process, the transformation may not be sufficiently comprehensive or complete, failing to transform important aspects of the built environment and its markets. Moreover, some of these changes may be unintended or hold adverse consequences for sustainability goals. Just because transformation is happening does not imply that some perfect market will emerge. And, of course, while our case for Green Market Transformation has been built primarily within the building sector, and its ecolabeling mechanisms rely heavily on the LEED label experience, the generalizability of this theory to the far reaches of the built environment and beyond – to markets for other goods – remains an open question. Each of these limitations warrant further discussion.

Limited Extent of Transformation

The evidence underpinning our Green Market Transformation story is growing, but it remains limited. To observe outcomes related to Green Market Transformation, we consider a number of key indicators. For example, we observe the number of green technology adoptions throughout the book as an indicator of market uptake. We review evidence of improvements in energy efficiency, environmental justice, and other environmental impacts in Chapters 2 and 8. And, in Chapter 6, we observe indicators related to the improved knowledge and understanding of innovative environmental and energy technologies. These outcomes are not exhaustive. Others have examined market premia (e.g., De Paola et al. 2020; Eichholtz et al. 2013; Li et al. 2021; Shewmake and Viscusi 2015; Zhang and Liu 2013), risk of mortgage default (An and Pivo 2020), and energy consumption associated with green ecolabeling or colocation of ecolabeled buildings (Rysman et al. 2020) as evidence of other trends that are consistent with Green Market Transformation. These important changes reflect the transformation in the building sector, and our theory predicts still more changes to result. Other potential outcomes, such as the spread of specific green-building knowledge and practice or the growth of green building practices without ecolabels, would also support our theory. Table 10.2 lists a few of these outcomes of interest, though others remain. As more data become available, we encourage others to advance research along these lines.

Other outcomes might arise, even if unintended or adverse consequences of this kind of transformation. Concerns about costs and accessibility to greener technologies and environments warrant top priority. We use Chapter 9 to help explore potential pitfalls of green market transformation, with a particular focus on equity and justice implications of using ecolabels to promote green market transformation.

Table 10.2. *Key outcome variables indicating green market transformation*

Increased frequency of green technology adoptions
Improvements in energy efficiency or other environmental impacts
Improved knowledge and understanding of innovative technologies
Alignment of building codes with ecolabel requirements
Adoption of business practices and processes aligned with using greener
    technology (e.g., favoring green procurement, relocating operations)

But, even among the key outcome variables we list in Table 10.2, the evidence is sometimes lacking. To be sure, transformation is happening. As we detail in previous chapters, the Green Building Movement is a global phenomenon that is gaining steam in nearly every market. The adoption of green building approaches spread rapidly even as the standards continue to rise and innovations associated with green buildings continue to be introduced. The expansion – wider and deeper – of green buildings is remarkable given that the movement ostensibly began only a few decades ago and the industry – buildings – is so vast and decentralized. The share of the largest commercial real-estate markets in the United States with green building certifications jumped from less than 5 percent to nearly 40 percent from 2005 to 2014 (Holtermans and Kok 2019). Green buildings dominate the markets in cities like San Francisco (71 percent) and Chicago (65 percent).

Yet for all its accomplishments, the market transformation is hardly complete or comprehensive (Fuerst et al. 2014). The race is not yet over. The US markets may be leading the pack, but take-up is lagging in other regions of the world – notably much of Asia and South America. Even with a late start, those regions with their major population centers have shown progress in recent years (Costa et al. 2018). There remains an open question as to whether green building practices can continue to gain in their prominence in all of these regions. Continued diffusion of green building approaches into other construction markets – notably those for smaller buildings such as smaller retail shops and residences – represents one of the more notable frontiers for green buildings to expand into. Larger buildings (corporate, commercial, office space, and high-profile buildings) and government buildings (easier to regulate) in larger metros have experienced faster transitions to green building approaches. The diffusion into smaller, private buildings that might not receive so much public (and investor) attention and pressure remains mostly "untapped potential" for the Green Building Movement. And, finally, given the durability of the capital stock when it comes to buildings, the vast majority of buildings – and their environmental and social footprints – includes older buildings that predate the Green Building Movement. Add in all of the recently built, nongreen buildings, and we can see that only a small fraction of the existing building stock today is meaningfully "green." Retrofitting and renovating these nongreen buildings represents a crucial challenge and frontier for the Green Building Movement. Unless these older buildings get retired much more quickly than they have been historically, even universal adoption of green building practices for new construction will have limited environmental impact. Transforming the building sector to become greener thus entails aggressive, widespread greener retrofits. Early indications suggest that this practice is taking root as the Green Building Movement's accomplishments and practices spill over into the existing building sector. But (technical, contractual, etc.) challenges for green retrofits remain.

This leads us be concerned about the distribution of access to green buildings, and the attendant equity implications. Research reviewed in Chapter 9 finds that, while affordability and access to green buildings might remain a concern, lower income and minority communities have more access to green schools. While this is a promising result, we note a number of caveats that temper our enthusiasm. While we observe more access to new green schools for lower income and minority areas, this result is conditional on schools being built. We do not observe the probability of schools being built. Further, our results are also correlated with local education levels, demonstrating an important role for education in driving green school adoption. All of this reinforces that our Green Market Transformation theory has little to say, a priori, about the distributional and equity consequences of such a transformation.

Limited Generalizability

Given the various conditions that help set the stage for market transformation, it is worth emphasizing where the "stage" itself begins and ends. There are boundaries to where the story likely applies. We expect that our story of market transformation through voluntary mechanisms does not capture situations where there is concentrated market power, where there is no market economy or strong rule of law, where the green attributes are not valued and do not provide benefits substantially to adopters, and also where information problems are not solvable through third-party verification. Perhaps most importantly, we suspect there are important characteristics of the attributes and products in question that may make some industries more ripe for transformation than others. The green building sector no doubt benefits from high visibility of the buildings themselves. The large size of the market helps create economies of scale that can support fringe innovations, at least those that are initially fringe when the market is at the beginning of the adoption S curve. Likely, the durable nature of the capital or product being invested in helps those in the Green Building Movement to capitalize on the marketing value. Being able to involve a diversity of actors from different sectors of a complex industrial organization, as well as from diverse climate and geographic regions, likely also increases the chance for the green demand condition (condition #1 above) to hold. When we are looking at an industry that is, say, perfectly vertically integrated, only has a few relevant components, or only operates in a very narrow geography, then we might not expect to see enough heterogeneity in demand to encounter sufficient numbers of unconventional, new, green demanders for the innovative product. In addition, the efficacy of ecolabels can be undermined by their complexity and the proliferation of multiple, competing, or substitute labels (Yokessa and Marette 2019).[1]

Areas for More Research

Additional research is necessary to examine what kinds of conditions might be needed in those circumstances that lie beyond the boundaries

---

[1] There is a balancing act here. With more labels as options, there are diminishing returns to additional labels (Waldrop et al. 2017; Yokessa and Marette 2019) and increasing complexity for buyers and stakeholders to sort through the alternative information tools. Conversely, some competition among certifying entities can help promote more credible signals, higher standards, and less greenwashing or fraud. More label competition might not help with environmental quality (Fischer and Lyon 2014).

of the market transformation stories that we tell here. It may be that markets dominated by one or a few single players can achieve (green) market transformations with rather different circumstances or conditions holding. Likewise, largely vertically integrated industries may require a different approach.

In this book, we have documented a number of processes and indicators that point toward Green Market Transformation in the built environment. Nevertheless, given the urgency of the need for decarbonization, it is essential to study the potential generalizability of this case to other markets and in other contexts where ecolabels and demonstration projects may play a key role in facilitating green market transformation.

A research agenda in support of a theory of Green Market Transformation through voluntary mechanisms would also build on some of the central themes raised throughout this book. This includes:

- *Learning processes and spillover mechanisms.* Though recent research (e.g., Blackburn et al. 2020; York et al. 2018) provides even stronger evidence of learning and spillovers among private actors in building markets, we should better understand how these learning processes operate and connect to environmental initiatives. Ecolabels like LEED are associated with spillovers from learning, procurement, competitive pressure, and signals of quality well beyond the individual building itself (e.g., to management, to the neighborhood, to tenants). Better understanding of these learning processes and spillover mechanisms can help improve future initiatives and ecolabel designs.
- *Interdependence of voluntary and mandatory standards.* Though this is a story of primarily voluntary mechanisms for market transformation, support from and engagement with government policymakers and regulations plays a role as well. The voluntary and mandatory standards of green buildings do not operate independently, and builders regularly consider both – especially expectations of future regulatory mandates (which themselves are often explicitly based on voluntary standards like LEED). Much research considers only a narrow set of policy tools in order to isolate the effects of a single initiative like an ecolabel or a building code change. Future research should embrace the interdependence of voluntary and mandatory standards, and of public and private pressures on builders'

decisions. Appreciating ecolabel efficacy often hinges on its broader context.

- *Timing for different instruments.* As we consider the interplay of voluntary mechanisms like ecolabels and other policy tools like regulation or pollution fees, more research into the optimal timing or sequencing of these instruments is needed. As these instruments can affect costs and information (risks, learning) for different actors (e.g., investors, producers, installers, retailers, consumers) differently, and spillovers among these actors may flow in particular directions, we might expect that the timing of implementation may affect instruments' effectiveness. We have more to learn about when and where to target these initiatives for optimal impact.

- *Necessary and sufficient conditions.* More work is needed to identify which conditions described in this book (see earlier in this chapter) are necessary or sufficient for green market transformation through voluntary mechanisms. It should be asking too much to strictly identify the conditions needed to support transformations across the myriad empirical settings we might hope to affect. But assembling additional evidence on which conditions most commonly foster green market transformation would help support and refine the theory advanced here.

- *Other (voluntary) causal mechanisms.* Similarly, we have highlighted several important causal pathways through which voluntary actions have engendered a Green Market Transformation for the built environment. The list in the previous section, however, may be incomplete. Future research should explore other catalysts for market transformations through voluntary mechanisms. As we argue in the next chapter, the stakes are so high and the alternatives so limited that casting a wide net for additional catalysts is warranted.

- *Other measures market transformation.* Future research should explore additional indicators, whether those are intended or unintended outcome measures. Table 10.2 lists a few prominent indicators, but surely more exist.

- *Recipes for effective and sustainable ecolabels.* As detailed in Chapter 3, the landscape of ecolabels is complex and diverse. The framework we provide in that chapter can help map that landscape and frame how we analyze the attributes of ecolabels that contribute to effective and sustainable ecolabels. As we seek sustainable ecolabels – not just those that promote sustainable practices but are themselves ecolabel programs that can support lasting change – questions remain about which business models to employ and how to best trade off among priorities (e.g., increasing label take-up versus increasing stringency, emphasizing public benefits versus private benefits). More research is needed to identify how recipes for effective ecolabels differ by their context. Designing ecolabels that support substantive environmental improvements depends on studying not just effective ecolabels like LEED but also ineffective or failed ecolabels.

Conclusion

As summarized in this chapter, this book lays out a blueprint for Green Market Transformation in the built environment. Certain preconditions support this kind of transformation, and key catalysts help make the changes a reality. Previous chapters detail the ways that these conditions and catalysts apply in our case study of LEED and green buildings. In theory, these voluntary, market-based transformations hold great promise for more sustainability. But just because an ecolabel like LEED has helped catalyze a remarkable transformation of the building sector does not mean that just any ecolabel can do likewise for any other market. The conditions outlined in this chapter help make the built environment ripe for transformation, and the LEED system has successfully catalyzed change through key mechanisms to strengthen the market, facilitate solutions to information problems, and induce a race to the top. Yet even this success story has its limitations. For example, we observe in Chapter 9 that there are several promising performance indicators associated with LEED buildings, though there are at times gaps between actual performance and expected performance. At the individual building level, the LEED label may not have as large of an impact as we might hope. Making green buildings greener is just one way the transformation can deepen. Opportunities remain for expanding this transformation along two margins, including more of the new construction (extensive margin) and including more retrofits of existing building stock (intensive margin). In the final chapter of the book, we turn our attention to how to overcome these challenges and where voluntary market transformations can take us next.

References

An, Xudong and Gary Pivo. 2020. "Green Buildings in Commercial Mortgage-Backed Securities: The Effects of LEED and Energy Star Certification on Default Risk and Loan Terms." *Real Estate Economics* 48, no. 1: 7–42.

Aragón-Correa, J. A., A. A. Marcus, and D. Vogel. 2020. "The Effects of Mandatory and Voluntary Regulatory Pressures on Firms' Environmental Strategies: A Review and Recommendations for Future Research." *Academy of Management Annals* 14, no. 1: 339–365.

Blackburn, Christopher, Mallory Flowers, Daniel Matisoff, and Juan Moreno-Cruz. 2020. "Do Pilot and Demonstration Projects Work? Evidence from a Green Building Program." *Journal of Policy Analysis and Management* 39: 1100–1132.

Costa, O., F. Fuerst, S. J. Robinson, and W. Mendes-Da-Silva. 2018. "Green Label Signals in an Emerging Real Estate Market. A Case Study of Sao Paulo, Brazil." *Journal of Cleaner Production* 184: 660–670.

Costello, C. and M. Kotchen, 2020. "Policy Instrument Choice with Coasean Provision of Public Goods."*NBER Working Paper*, w28130.

De Paola, Pierfrancesco, Vincenzo Del Giudice, Domenico Enrico Massimo, Francesco Paolo Del Giudice, Mariangela Musolino, and Alessandro Malerba. 2020. "Green Building Market Premium: Detection through Spatial Analysis of Real Estate Values. A Case Study." In *New Metropolitan Perspectives*, Carmelina Bevilacqua, Francesco Calabrò, and Lucia Della Spina (eds.), pp. 1413–1422. Cham, Switzerland: Springer.

DeLeon, Peter and Jorge Rivera (eds.). 2009. *Voluntary Environmental Programs: A Policy Perspective*. New York: Lexington Books.

Eichholtz, Piet, Nils Kok, and John M. Quigley. 2013. "The Economics of Green Building." *Review of Economics and Statistics* 95, no. 1: 50–63.

Fischer, Carolyn and Thomas P. Lyon. 2014. "Competing Environmental Labels." *Journal of Economics & Management Strategy* 23, no. 3: 692–716.

Fuerst, F., C. Kontokosta and P. McAllister. 2014. "Determinants of Green Building Adoption." *Environment and Planning B: Planning and Design* 41, no. 3: 551–570.

Grabs, Janina. 2020. *Selling Sustainability Short? The Private Governance of Labor and the Environment in the Coffee Sector*. Cambridge: Cambridge University Press.

Holtermans, R. and N. Kok. 2019. "On the Value of Environmental Certification in the Commercial Real Estate Market."*Real Estate Economics* 47, no. 3: 685–722.

Li, Weilin, Guanyu Fang, and Liu Yang. 2021. "The Effect of LEED Certification on Office Rental Values in China." *Sustainable Energy Technologies and Assessments* 45: 101182.

Lyon, T. P. and J. W. Maxwell. 2004. *Corporate Environmentalism and Public Policy.* Cambridge: Cambridge University Press.

Nemet, G. F. 2019. *How Solar Energy Became Cheap: A Model for Low-Carbon Innovation.* New York: Routledge.

Rysman, Marc, Timothy Simcoe, and Yanfei Wang. 2020. "Differentiation Strategies in the Adoption of Environmental Standards: LEED from 2000 to 2014." *Management Science* 66, no. 9: 4173–4192.

Shewmake, Sharon and W. Kip Viscusi. 2015. "Producer and Consumer Responses to Green Housing Labels." *Economic Inquiry* 53, no. 1: 681–699.

Van der Heijden, Jeroen. 2017. *Innovations in Urban Climate Governance: Voluntary Programs for Low Carbon Buildings and Cities.* New York: Cambridge University Press.

Waldrop, M. E., J. J. McCluskey and R. C. Mittelhammer. 2017. "Products with Multiple Certifications: Insights from the US Wine Market." *European Review of Agricultural Economics* 44, no. 4: 658–682.

Yokessa, M. and S. Marette. 2019. "A Review of Eco-Labels and Their Economic Impact." *International Review of Environmental and Resource Economics* 13, no. 1–2: 119–163.

York, J. G., S. Vedula, and M. J. Lenox. 2018. "It's Not Easy Building Green: The Impact of Public Policy, Private Actors, and Regional Logics on Voluntary Standards Adoption." *Academy of Management Journal* 61, no. 4: 1492–1523.

Zhang, Li and Hong-yu Liu. 2013. "Do Green Building Labeled Dwellings Fetch a Market Premium in China." *Journal of Engineering Management* 27, no. 6: 107–111.

11 | Conclusions
What Are We Building To?

We have put forth our theory of Green Market Transformation for the built environment via voluntary mechanisms. In so doing, we have advanced our understanding of how an ecolabel like LEED can work to disrupt and change a building sector in ways that go far beyond individual, certified buildings. The whole of this Green Building Movement is greater than the sum of its LEED-certified parts. This story contributes to the specific literature on the operations and impacts of LEED and green building labels. Our theory makes the connection to ecolabels more generally, contributing a case study to that broader literature and suggesting which factors key to LEED's success may also be key to other ecolabels achieving similar transformative impacts.

We must emphasize, however, that the LEED case is not merely an example of an ecolabel signaling green quality for some goods. Rather, it is a story of an ecolabel spurring spillovers, learning, and enabling stronger markets for greener products beyond the confines of particular certified projects (and their symbolic label). Thus, we are contributing to a broader literature on innovation and market transformation by showing how one mechanism – an ecolabel system like LEED – attracted participants and normalized greener practices. In some ways, the key market failures here are less about information asymmetries or pollution and more about informational public goods. Thus, we contribute to the growing literature on the primacy of informational problems in addressing social challenges like climate change (e.g., Gerarden et al. 2017; Giraudet 2020) by illustrating how voluntary mechanisms like ecolabels can help. Sure, LEED-certified buildings receive price premiums and other market recognition. But what makes LEED work in catalyzing major changes in the building sector is its promotion of positive spillovers from learning about new technologies and feasible greener practices.

278

Showing promise for voluntary mechanisms like ecolabels in addressing climate challenges can be particularly important for policy-makers if conventional policy tools struggle to remedy informational problems or simply if another arrow in the policy quiver is needed. Regardless, the lessons and insights we draw from this case are many. This concluding chapter elaborates on the implications of this case for management, planning, and policy in the face of climate change and other environmental challenges. First, we put the use of voluntary mechanisms into broader context for policy-makers and management. This section recognizes both the potential and the limitations of this approach. Next, we discuss how to guide and accelerate this kind of Green Market Transformation. The lessons of the building ecolabel story can inform how ecolabels can address frictions in the innovation lifecycle by helping to mainstream nascent technologies. Then, based on assembled evidence in the LEED case, we highlight some critical areas that can support more Green Market Transformations. Our recommendations offer both management and policy with promising areas to build better foundations to advance sustainability goals.

How Green Can We Go? Marshalling a Volunteer Army

How far can voluntary mechanisms take us? On one hand, we have demonstrated the potential of well-run ecolabel programs and voluntary initiatives in the building sector to develop and market higher quality buildings. This model has promise, but alas there are limitations.

Buildings and other consumer-facing goods are highly differentiable in the marketplace. And there is opportunity for users to experience something different. Many of the improvements made through green building programs work by pairing public and private benefits creating eco-friendly products that are also higher quality. A LEED Platinum building is a high-performance, high-quality building in a similar way that a Tesla is a highly desirable high-performance vehicle. Because these products are highly desirable – they sell at a premium – and buyers are willing to pay for the higher price.

The limitations of voluntary mechanisms may occur when those voluntary mechanisms collide with private interest. It will be very difficult to ask firms to leave oil in the ground or to voluntarily forego profits that can be earned through the burning of fossil fuels. Similarly, while some companies, property owners, and households adopt greener practices and make costly investments in sustainability, we might be skeptical that these exceptions will become universal practices. (It is a big ask to eliminate all or even most defectors in the prisoner's dilemma game discussed in Chapter 8!) Even if norms shift so everyone voluntarily "goes green," we may doubt that these efforts will go far enough. Success through voluntary mechanisms depends on breadth *and* depth of change.

Capitalism and markets, then, may be seen as the villain in this story. We sympathize with this view. Indeed, the ability to produce energy cheaply and discharge pollutants into the water and atmosphere is what got us here. It might be tempting, then, to assume we can correct the failings of these decentralized, market systems – which relied on free, voluntary choices for so long – by adopting top-down interventions to solve our environmental problems. In some respects, this approach forms the core principles behind an economic approach to remedy environmental harms: If the market is broken when it comes to the environment, then policy should intervene to fix the markets. When prices – the information signals and incentives in markets – send the wrong message, then economists tell us we need to "get the prices right." When polluting is free, we will do too much of it. When innovating greener solutions is too costly, we will shy away from taking those risks. So often, we assume that if externalities were priced appropriately, then efficient markets would result. From the 1997 Kyoto Protocol until the 2016 Paris Climate Accords, the assumption was that a top-down international treaty would create carbon markets that would solve carbon pollution.

While we sympathize with – and have even taught our students for decades – this canonical approach to undertaking optimal policy, we need to pause to take stock of this simple framing of the problem. Our solutions come from how we frame the problem. In this case, there is a natural tendency to see or create a dichotomy between markets and government interventions. Certainly, the public discourse is filled with this binary simplification. It is easy to cast the situation as either/or. We can either have markets or socialism. We can either have "free" markets or "command-and-control" regulation. If the markets fail, then we need policy-makers to fix it. When decentralized, voluntary approaches let us down, then enlightened experts should implement top-down interventions to correct behavior. And so on.

There is a strong tendency to reduce complex situations into simple stories with heroes and villains. Even as environmental awareness has spread and grown markedly over the generations, the history of public debate surrounding the environmental movement is replete with villainizing. The adversarial approach often taught us more about political gamesmanship and self-interest than it did about how society's systems actually produce the results we see every day. It is refreshing and rare (and risky) to hear an appreciation for environmental problems that transcend the polarizing, binary perspectives. In late 2004, major controversy erupted when Michael Shellenberger and Ted Nordhaus circulated their "The Death of Environmentalism" essay (Shellenberger and Nordhaus 2004). As they despaired the insufficient efforts to address climate change, they saw the progressive environmental movement more as an obstacle than the hero. Environmentalism as a special interest, casting sustainability as an "environmental problem" (for greens and environmentalists to tackle) rather than a societal or business problem, and fetishizing technical policy fixes without regard to political efficacy were recipes for failure in this century. They called for a new approach, a broader and more inclusive vision, one which eschewed political turf wars in favor of embracing the interests of workers, industry, and communities in charting a greener path forward. In their "strange bedfellows" politics, they see the necessary intertwining of prosperity and environmental sustainability. Shellenberger and Nordhaus take the bold and surprisingly uncommon stance that our best path forward marries markets and policy. No wonder that controversy and criticism ensued. Almost 20 years ago, they saw vital opportunity in (public) investment in greener R&D and other approaches that mobilized entrepreneurship and market innovations to improve our environment. In that sense at least, they represented a breakthrough seeking more breakthroughs. Miscasting our problems as a markets versus regulation debate misses opportunities to leverage their inherent duality for greener goals.

What is key to understand, perhaps, is how institutions – characterized by the incentives and information they create – got us here, and how we can reform these institutions to produce solutions. Markets and regulations are not enemies, but instead key components in a larger system. Most "free" markets rely on property rights, rule of law, courts, and often substantial state capacity (roads? police? education?) to function well. Reasonable people can disagree about the right amount of government intervention into those markets, but the debate is really a matter of degree rather than an either/or decision. As contemporary markets flourish under some government rule, prudent regulation can often enhance their efficiency.

Yet, if regulation and government intervention can be good, surely we can experience too much of this good thing. To solve environmental problems, especially at scale, we need the power of markets. Engineers often think that we can "solve" environmental problems by implementing specific technologies and optimizing processes. In this utopian world, all-knowing bureaucrats, somehow insulated from the fickle winds of politics, can devise the perfect set of regulations that will incentivize optimal efficiency and optimal outcomes. But carbon emissions are diffuse. No one lever pulled is going to solve climate change. It is inconceivable that thousands of government administrators could pull just hard enough on all the right levers, in all the right places. Woe unto those who appreciate the limitations and self-interest of private decision-makers in markets while discounting that our also-human policy-makers work in institutions with their own incentives and imperfections. For some, idealized policy-makers in an effective government provide shelter from the certain disappointment of real-world capitalism and markets. Yet the track records of top-down government interventions and regulation for producing environmental gains are also mixed. Pollyanna Principle aside, even perfect policy-makers may struggle to make sufficient progress. There are limits to the extent of what top-down policy can regulate, especially when we are talking about regulating on a micro scale (e.g., how we construct and use buildings) and at a global scope. At some point, the limits of top-down regulation must give way to the realities of countless, diffuse decisions by firms and individuals scattered across all sorts of contexts.

Rather than frame the problem of markets versus regulation, we recognize the limits of both and seek to harmonize them. When the ecological crises facing us require massive solutions, then we might look to *harness* the power of market forces rather than sideline one of our most effective institutions. We need to devise policies and institutions to provide the right set of incentives so that markets can help develop solutions that do not rely on technological mandates set by administrators. We can think of it as a course-correction for previously unfettered markets which arguably scaled-up our environmental woes. Instead of casting markets aside or shackling them, we see a vital role for policy to guide and foster markets to find and implement *solutions*. The scale of the problems facing us demands a grassroots, bottom-up approach that enlists the efforts of households, workers, and firms around the planet. The challenge for policy-makers is in facilitating that, in devising and supporting mechanisms so that voluntary action also serves the greater public benefit.

Sustainability in this large and complex world will rely more on polycentricity (Ostrom 2010) than on exclusive top-down or unregulated markets. Nobel Laureate Elinor Ostrom helped introduce this notion of polycentricity – many different, overlapping-yet-independent centers for decision-making – as a way of thinking about a much more complicated world as it actually exists. Recognizing that markets are really good institutions for providing private goods and that governments are best for (nonprivate) public goods, Ostrom saw the emerging dichotomous worldviews as missing the complex, diverse, and oft-chaotic sets of institutional arrangements that actually exist. Just as one-size-fits-all prescriptions tend to fail, the simplified extremes of markets versus government also fall short. Ostrom embraces the messy, often hybridized, locally or regionally adapted institutions as not just reality. These local or regional institutions survived because they were generally superior to the either/or sorts of stylized extreme markets *or* regulation. Polycentric institutions, developed from the bottom-up (while perhaps guided and facilitated by higher authorities), allow local solutions to match local conditions aligning with local preferences. The diversity of polycentric arrangements can also foster more experimentation – allowing other communities and markets to learn from successes and failures *in governance* elsewhere. Innovation is not just about better water filtration technology or building design, it also includes innovating institutional design.

Effective approaches must also be dynamic. Just as diversity in our approaches involves some hybridization or harmonization between markets and regulation, how we strike balances will evolve over time. Like an adaptive-management approach (Norton 2005), continual adjustment can help balance the competing interests among private actors like firms and households, the public interest in healthy environments, and other important constituencies. The pendulum may swing back and forth, favoring at times a longer or a shorter leash for market actors. Here, voluntary mechanisms play an interesting role in the middle of this dynamic back-and-forth. These mechanisms can help signal and smooth transitions between more or less stringency from regulators. As regulators ramp up their attention, for instance, they might start by fostering more voluntary action and, if that proves inefficient, more coercive measures follow their initial signal. Conversely, as market actors push toward more sustainability, regulators can roll back or freeze mandates while supporting more voluntary approaches to push the sustainability frontier.

Voluntary private action certainly cannot do it all. However, ultimately, voluntary action will constitute the great bulk of what we do. We will need to lean on it heavily. For all those promising, world-changing ideas and practices that can advance sustainability goals, voluntary actors will play the most important role in finding those opportunities and demonstrating their successes. The challenge is to design institutions that can encourage those innovations and the diffusion of best practices. We do not expect one-size-fits-all prescriptions to work in solving the institutional design problem. But we do expect that voluntary mechanisms will play a key role in most or all of them. A solely top-down approach is doomed to fail to adequately address our environmental problems simply because its inherently political nature leaves it very limited in practice. A purely market-based approach might be better at causing the environmental problems than it is at solving them, but its power may be a vital component in addressing these problems at scale. Voluntary mechanisms discussed in this book are key to harnessing market forces to these ends.

What the Green Building Context Can Tell Us

What Has Been Accomplished by the Green Building Movement?

We are at an inflection point. The first "wave" of the Green Building Movement has ended – resulting in newfound attention to the sustainability characteristics of buildings. We are at the beginning of a new wave, with increased attention to performance and increased focus on making buildings an instrument to help restore and improve the environment. Technological innovations such as rooftop solar, heat pumps, improved windows, and LED lighting are becoming commonplace and included into building codes. Practices such as testing the thermal envelope and monitoring energy consumption are becoming more widespread. Mass timber may serve as a way to sequester carbon long term in the structure of buildings. Building automation can help smooth load curves and store thermal energy, helping to enable a transition to renewable energy. Increasingly, building managers are taking advantage of building analytics and are monitoring the performance of buildings in real time. We expect these technological developments to become more widespread and enable a transition to an improved built environment.

The first wave of green building acknowledged that energy efficiency and other best practices in building were under-invested, and the Green Building Movement sought to encourage builders and developers to adhere to best practices. They were encouraged to benchmark their energy models for the building to seek improvements in the energy-efficiency performance through upgrades to the HVAC system and the building envelope. They sought to encourage building developers to think carefully about the employee and consumer experience from everything to siting the building near public transportation and including bike infrastructure into the building design to thinking about natural lighting and air quality inside the building. The movement sought to encourage building developers to think about the building within the broader context of the location within the urban environment – and bring focus to the role of the building in managing stormwater, producing electricity, or simply being a purchaser of renewable energy. These upgrades to buildings made improvements to the environmental footprint of buildings and demonstrated a market for a greener approach to building. They improved the user experience and launched a movement that focuses on the intersection of human health and the built environment.

Not Unlimited Gains

While this first wave of green building conceptualized the role of buildings in reducing harm, it perhaps did not go so far as to reimagine the role of buildings as a vital component of a sustainable socio-techno-ecological system that could begin to reverse harms and contribute to more sustainable infrastructure. The early versions of LEED, like many ecolabel programs and other corporate sustainability programs, focus on reducing harm, as opposed to reimagining the way that industrial activity engages with the natural environment. Questions exist about the overall environmental footprint of the built environment and how this footprint can be fundamentally rethought. This criticism is not unique to buildings per se but has been a mantra across industrial activity for the past several decades, where researchers argued the need to refocus on pollution prevention and rethink how production occurs, as opposed to implementing end-of-pipe solutions. The goal of the Living Building Project is to create buildings that are restorative to the environment: They go beyond simply reducing harm, but are intended to *improve* air, water, and waste processes.

Further, despite some successful efforts to push advanced building quality into schools and use the Green Building Movement to provide for equitable outcomes, little effort has been oriented toward the residential building sector thus far. There are well known inequities in household building stock that contribute to the energy burden, where low-income residents pay an average of 8.6 percent of their income in energy bills.[1] While there are over 80 competing green certification systems for homes in the United States,[2] this area is not well understood, and market penetration remains quite low. As we describe in Chapters 3 and 4, the presence of many competing labels has the potential to create confusion in the marketplace. Without broad market recognition of what a label is and what it means, certified homes are less likely to gain a market premium or serve the purpose of verifying the performance of the buildings. This conundrum leads to the need for increased focus on building codes to establish minimum standards in the residential sector in the absence of effective ecolabels, and on retrofitting programs to address existing building stock.

A shifting minimum standard for building quality or greenness can help to bring up the laggards, but it might have some unintended consequences. Insofar as these approaches increase building costs, they can reduce affordability, a major concern if we are seriously concerned about the equity implications of greening the built environment. Further, raising the costs for new buildings can induce decision-makers to postpone new construction or prolong their stays in older, less

---

[1] www.energy.gov/eere/slsc/low-income-community-energy-solutions
[2] hwww.newhomesource.com/learn/green-home-program-right-for-you/

environmentally friendly buildings. Smarter contracting, reducing transaction costs, and better incentives are all needed to address the big (brown) elephant in the room: the vast existing capital stock of not-very-green buildings already covering the planet. Like brownfield redevelopment can redirect greenfield development, retrofitting to avoid new construction holds considerable promise along another new frontier. According to an estimate from a US Department of Energy calculator, adopting best retrofitting practices in the United States over the next 30 years can reduce building-related CO_2 emissions by 35–60 percent, reducing the emissions footprint associated with existing buildings by 7.7 to 12 gigatons of CO_2, and saving 246 quads of energy use.[3] In addition, applying current best practices in new construction will reduce emissions by up to 4.2 gigaton of the total expected 7.7 gigaton footprint. Yet the policies and institutions that can enable this massive potential are not well understood. We have much to do to better harmonize the regulations and markets to induce voluntary retrofits around the developed and developing world. As Figure 1.1 shows, take-up rates of ecolabels are dominated by just a few markets, with little activity in the developing world.[4] A real challenge remains for standards (and ecolabel initiatives like LEED) to effectively map the frontier of best practices available, set the bar there (custom-tailored for different markets), and keep raising the bar. Ecolabels cannot rest on their successes of today. The race to the top requires ratcheting up standards. Efforts are needed to care for those individuals and sectors that might be "left behind" in the transitions.

Guiding and Accelerating Market Transformation

New policies and financing approaches are needed to help solve some of these problems. As we have identified throughout the book,

---

[3] Our analysis using scout.energy.gov building energy models.
[4] Although our theory of Green Market Transformation may not apply well to many emerging market country contexts, as conditions like those outlined in Chapter 10 may not be present, many of the lessons discussed here still apply. Advances made in innovating greener buildings may become available sooner and cheaper to emerging economies as they learn from gains made elsewhere in the Green Building Movement. But concerns about appropriate mix of policy tools, affordability of greener buildings (and wide-and-shallow versus narrow-and-deep), and how best to spur green innovation in those contexts remains paramount.

information barriers have led to a market for lemons in buildings – where builders and developers build and sell low-quality buildings and not much else. When developers do not typically hold on to their properties for long periods of time, there is little incentive to invest in building quality that pays off over time. Because building quality is difficult to observe, the majority of buildings sold are low quality, even when higher levels of quality might be preferred by the purchaser. How does one align incentives between the original developer and the potential owner and operator of a building? In the residential sector – how does a builder profit from creating a higher-quality product? While ecolabels are one way to signal quality and allow a premium product, we believe that there are other innovative ways to promote improved building practices and improve the performance of ecolabels.

First, there likely needs to be increased standardization in the green building area and more coordination across labels and national contexts. Label sponsors and coordinating associations are already working on this, but free entry to ecolabel markets can undermine coordination and create congestion. With a deluge of labels on the market, there is less understanding of what each label signifies and less recognition for each individual label. This is particularly true in the US residential housing market. In the international commercial buildings market, however, investors need to be able to compare the characteristics and performance of buildings across the world. A lack of harmonized practices and performance metrics impedes the ability of building managers to leverage data analytics and the information economy to improve the performance of buildings. Large investors (developers, real estate investment trusts, pension funds) want to direct investment into high-performing buildings and optimize the performance of those buildings. They want to have comparable information across the globe and want to be able to compare performance metrics. To do this requires harmonized practices and data collection. At the same time, there needs to be recognition for local control for local priorities and complexity. Alternative transportation means something different in India than it does in Sweden.

Second, we need to figure out ways of allowing organizations to benefit from longer-term investments. This problem is ubiquitous across the building sector. Developers typically turn buildings over after two years. Homeowners occupy their homes for an average of

13 years.[5] While the federal government may occupy buildings for the entire building lifespan – greater than 30 years – federal budgeting rules often limit the accounting of costs and benefits to just 10 years, limiting the opportunity to take advantage of investments that pay off over a longer period of time.[6] There are several approaches that can allow smarter decisions to be made that will increase building quality.

Improved building codes. For a complex range of reasons, building codes are balkanized and out of date in a bizarrely political process, where local developer interests often have significant sway over building-code adoptions. As a result, states and localities often outsource their code development to the international building code standards, though they often lag many years behind the most recent version of the standards. LEED Silver has taken the place of certifying best standard practices, and many localities (Washington, DC; Chicago; etc.) require LEED Silver or equivalent. Nonetheless, for the most challenging sectors of the built environment – the residential single-family and multifamily sectors – codes often remain out of date with what seem to be cost-effective practices. Improved building codes (and their enforcement) would reduce emissions significantly going forward. Small, incremental costs up front are likely to reduce energy consumption significantly and to mitigate the problem of having to deal with equipment and construction that is new but inefficient. After all – at the moment that a building is built – it is no longer a new construction issue, but rather a retrofitting issue. Yet new construction is expected to last more than 30 years. Inflexible and outdated codes put building owners in the position of needing to retire equipment early in order to retrofit it.

On-bill financing programs. We can adopt financing approaches that allow investments in energy performance to be financed with monthly payments on energy bills. These investments can be amortized over the expected performance period and yield savings to the building operator. Because utilities have the best information about the energy performance of a particular building, they are in a position to be able to optimize energy investments in those

[5] www.nar.realtor/blogs/economists-outlook/how-long-do-homeowners-stay-in-their-homes
[6] www.ase.org/blog/primer-espcs-uescs-and-cbo-scoring-problem

buildings. Further, utilities often have access to low-cost capital that can enable them to make these longer-term investments. Utilities can roll these energy-performance upgrades into their rate base and profit off of energy savings. Similar approaches have been used by the federal government in Energy Savings Performance Contracting. In the private sector, on-bill financing allows building owners to take on a longer-term perspective on the cost-effectiveness of energy investments. Nevertheless, there are potential pitfalls with this approach. Knowing that future building owners or tenants may have to pay for these investments, building owners may overinvest in energy upgrades. Or utilities, who are incentivized to increase their rate base, may recommend that owners over-invest in energy performance upgrades. Further, cultural barriers to these sorts of programs need to be overcome. Utilities have not always been keen on shifting their approach from electricity generation and distribution to a new role that entails energy-efficiency audits, retrofitting, and capital investment financing. This model is a far more complex business model than utilities are accustomed to.

Public financing programs. Similar programs can leverage public funding to enhance energy efficiency investments. These include Qualified Energy Conservation Bonds, Property Assessed Clean Energy financing (PACE), and a variety of other publicly funded energy financing approaches. In this case, state energy offices or local municipalities bear the risk for the financing of energy investments. While these programs are promising and already exist in most states, there has been little attention to their performance, impact, and what the barriers are to scaling up these programs. Some studies that have looked at the performance of individual PACE and related programs have demonstrated significant promise (Kirkpatrick and Bennear 2014; Rose and Wei 2020). Other models, such as using crowdfunding models such as Citizenergy or Startengine, to finance renewable energy investment and retrofitting in schools and other facilities represent innovative approaches to facilitating clean-energy investment. This is a fruitful area for research, further funding, and policy development.

Data analytics. As in so many sectors of society today, data analytics represent a growth area that is potentially transformative. Buildings have been managed in a low-tech way that has remained relatively unchanged for over a hundred years. Building

Automation, Smart Thermostats, and Data Analytics can be used to leverage the nearly unlimited data that has been created by the multitude of sensors. GBCI's Arc platform has the potential to transform the management of the built environment by integrating a platform to collect finely grained data that will enable harmonization and coordination of performance-based metrics. Creating *smart* buildings that are integrated with sensors and real-time data is essential in order to utilize other emergent technologies. Some of these emergent technologies include using the built environment for thermal storage, a key component in a smart energy grid that helps generate and manage the supply and demand for electricity.

Transforming through Voluntary Mechanisms

The lessons from green building – and in particular the ways that voluntary mechanisms intersect with policies and markets – help us think about a broader framework that can enable us to build better institutions that align incentives and leverage policies and markets to create market transformation. To summarize our theory of market transformation detailed in this book, these early entrants are rewarded with a price premium for providing a new, superior, green product to the market. A highly recognizable and marketable label like LEED Platinum or being Living Building Challenge Certified enables this premium. As more companies enter this market, three things happen. First, to differentiate the next building, a builder or owner needs to out-do the previous building in a race to the top. The market premiums available to early entrants at these higher performance tiers enable the race to the top. Second, by entering the market, supply chains are developed, injecting competition for the supply of high-performance green buildings. Learning and competition by these suppliers helps drive down prices and enable a more widespread adoption of these technologies. Third, information, provided by the early entrants, reduces costs and uncertainties associated with constructing high-performance green buildings, increasing the demand for these products. The professional networks that govern the green building certifications play a key role in helping to disseminate this information and stimulating the demand for higher quality green buildings. This virtuous cycle creates market transformation when what were previously market-leading practices become the market standard. This creates an opportunity for new market-leading practices that continue to push the bar and improve the performance of the built environment.

While we have dealt mostly with the built environment and the Green Building Movement in this book, it makes sense to consider how generalizable our story is for other areas. How useful are ecolabels in other sectors of the economy? How generalizable is our theory of market transformation – with or without the inclusion of ecolabels?

The built environment has some characteristics that are common to many other – though not all – industries. For example, the built environment is highly consumer facing – in the sense that buildings are occupied by people and it is easy for employees, customers, and investors to observe ecolabels and derive benefit and utility from an ecolabeled building. In Chapter 4 we also explored the use of ecolabels in agriculture. Certainly, for some consumer facing products like coffee, seafood, and organics produce and commodities, ecolabels have been commonly employed. It seems less likely, however, that products that are primarily business-to-business and are commodity items such as oil and gas will be successful as green products that procure a price premium. This is perhaps for two reasons: First, these products are uniform in nature when it comes to private consumption. The difference in these products is their production process. As discussed in Chapters 4 and 5, one of the key design features of successful ecolabels is that they pair attributes that have private benefit with those that have public benefit. It is simply not possible to distinguish between fossil fuels or kilowatt hours of electricity at the point of consumption. We suggest that the success for credence goods is likely more limited, as it relies solely on the willingness of pay of consumers for public benefits of improved production processes. There are some cases where labeling of electricity sourcing, commodity foods, and other goods that are primarily sold business-to-business seem to gain traction in the ecolabels movement. Nevertheless, it is hard to imagine going to the pump and relying on an option to purchase "green" gasoline (say, gasoline produced through direct air capture of CO_2 or with emissions offset through carbon sequestration) as a way to meaningfully move toward a net zero economy. Similarly, while airlines have offered voluntary carbon offsets for passengers for years, it is hard to imagine that relying on individuals to pay extra to offset emissions will transform the airline industry. In these cases, the green product is strictly costlier than the eco-product, and transformation is fully dependent on individual voluntary financial donations. Altruism alone will not transform the markets as needed to achieve our sustainability goals.

In the entirety of the innovation lifecycle, ecolabels are effective at driving market uptake of nascent technologies and practices in order to make them more mainstream. However, there are other frictions in the innovation process that require remedies – the kinds of policy tools that have received less attention than direct economic incentives, mandates, or other more common approaches. When considering the innovation lifecycle, products or processes are invented through R&D. These products then often struggle to become a commercial product at all. These barriers have to do with high startup costs associated with achieving economies of scale; the difficulties of getting traction with distributors, suppliers, and contractors; and a slew of other barriers in the market. Subsidized loans via public–private partnerships, and early-stage investing by risk-tolerant innovation funds may be one way of seeding the commercialization of nascent technologies. These loan subsidies and guarantees for large, risky, projects – while politically contentious and dotted with high-profile failures – have helped achieve notable successes in the US solar industry and in the electric-car industry. Tesla received several large government-backed loans on its way to becoming the largest automaker by market capitalization.[7,8] There may be several opportunities to accelerate nascent technologies through these sorts of partnerships in carbon capture, hydrogen infrastructure, or other emergent green technologies. Incentive policies complement voluntary ecolabels like LEED well and can promote green building adoption (York et al. 2018).

Guiding and Accelerating Market Transformation

Once advanced energy and environmental products exist in the marketplace, there are multiple ways to accelerate their adoption. Neoclassical economics points to carbon prices, subsidies, and taxes as both the most efficient and primary ways of transitioning to greener technologies. For the past generation, economists and policy analysts have advocated market-based instruments as the most effective way to

---

[7] www.washingtonpost.com/news/innovations/wp/2017/03/16/this-government-loan-program-helped-tesla-at-a-critical-time-trump-wants-to-cut-it/

[8] www.bloomberg.com/news/articles/2020-06-09/tesla-got-a-major-boost-from-2009-u-s-stimulus

move markets. These policy instruments, however, have had little political success in the United States. Even in places where limited carbon prices or cap-and-trade programs have been implemented (RGGI, California, Europe, and many other parts of the world), the prices in these systems remain well below the globally efficient social-cost-of-carbon. Consider that current prices for carbon in most systems range from $5 to $15 per ton, in comparison to recent global social-cost-of-carbon estimates that put the median costs in the range of $177 to $805 per ton (Ricke et al. 2018). Even at lower estimates of roughly $50 a ton, as estimated by the US Interagency Working Group in 2016, prices of existing carbon pricing systems do not come near to approximating these damage estimates, and have proven to be politically malleable, as evidenced by the Trump administration's use of values as low as $1 per ton in many regulatory decisions.

The inability for politicians to implement efficient pricing for carbon stems from an inability of politicians to withstand political opposition to price changes that are disruptive to existing interests. Further, the complexity of global coordination in carbon markets makes individual countries, states, and regions hesitant to act unilaterally. As recent research and government reports have suggested politically feasible prices of carbon in pricing schemes seems unlikely to decarbonize the economy rapidly (Metcalf 2019). Even prices as high as $50 per ton will likely only reduce emissions by 30 percent by 2050 (Barron et al. 2018). It is not a technical or practical failure of our policymaking apparatus. Political institutions lack a track record in successfully addressing climate change. A variety of researchers have suggested that the difficulty of carbon prices to gain policy traction invites exploration into additional policy tools that address additional market barriers and failures for energy transitions.

Nascent technologies do not gain market traction because they are expensive, but also because they are undeveloped and unknown. And because they are unknown, they do not reach economies of scale – and thus they stay expensive. This paradox is known as the Valley of Death, where promising technologies fail to gain a foothold in the market. There are several ways to break this paradox. Using a very simplified approach of breaking the innovation cycle into several stages, we consider challenges of developing new technology, gaining a foothold in the market, and, ultimately, gaining widespread traction for these technologies.

Building Better Foundations

Research and Development

It is well known that research and development is subject to market failures. Firms tend to underinvest in research and development because they are unlikely to be the only ones that benefit from this spending. When firms invest in R&D, much of the benefit of that R&D may accrue to market competitors. These public-good and positive-externality traits of R&D mean that too little of it is provided to the market. While the federal government produces R&D directly through national labs and outsources R&D through grants to universities and firms, society needs even more R&D to help develop improved technologies to meet the challenges required by decarbonization.

Pilot and Demonstration Projects

Pilot and demonstration projects, as discussed in Chapter 7, might be appropriate ways of achieving these economies of scale and spillover effects. These smaller-scale investments – particularly when iterated – can help refine nascent products and provide a signal to the marketplace that these new technologies are ready for broad-scale deployment. Pilot and demonstration projects, and public investment in these projects, may be justified through the provision of positive *information* externalities. Intriguingly, with pilot and demonstration projects, these are not limited to public-sector spending. Universities, nonprofits, and individual firms can play a big role in helping push the boundary of new technologies. That is, when doing a pilot or demonstration project, the builder of that project provides information to the market about the performance of nascent technologies that accrues outside of the owner of that project and, perhaps, to the market at large. While some economic theorists (e.g., Kotchen and Costello 2018) have considered the value of experimentation and learning *within* a particular organization, too little attention has been paid to the value of experimentation and learning as a public good or as a positive externality that accrues outside of an individual organization. We believe this to be key to our quest for a greener economy. Private actors play a big role in boosting green building adoption all around them (York et al. 2018). When governments and other organizations provide information to the market as a way to transform markets to a low-carbon economy, we can reap this knowledge's significant value. This approach highlights opportunities for public–private partnerships to foster the co-creation and distribution of valuable information (Huguenin and Jeannerat 2017). Going forward, more attention should be paid to the role that public and private actors can play to stimulate market uptake through the supply of pilot and demonstration projects. This includes more attention to how to effectively utilize ecolabels to foster market reputation and provide value and recognition for the early movers willing to absorb the increased expense and risk that accompanies these investments.

Government Purchasing

Increasing the use of government purchasing can be a key way to drive the market for nascent technologies. Government entities may have higher willingness to pay for several reasons. First, they are likely to operate assets longer than the private sector. Private developers often hold a building for a year or two, while governments (as well as universities, hospitals, and other organizations) own and operate buildings for decades. This long-term time horizon should make governments more willing to pay for improvements that pay off over long time periods. Because governments are beholden to stakeholders to provide public goods, it is reasonable to consider the use of government spending to promote the deployment of green technologies that provide positive externalities such as reduced carbon pollution. While it is challenging to align incentives appropriately for private firms to provide public goods (though, as we describe throughout this book, ecolabels are certainly one way to do it!), it is often easier to require public entities to provide public goods. As discussed in Chapter 2, a range of cities and states have required public buildings and schools to adhere to LEED standards. The federal government has at times required federal buildings to be built to LEED standards, but the instances where private buildings are required to do similarly have been much more limited. Still, as we discuss throughout the book, public spending can spill over to the private sector. This may be due to the size of government achieving economies of scale in a product or market, allowing a new product to reduce its price as production quantities increase, or it may be due to building supply chains in a way that creates knowledge diffusion throughout an industry. Using

NGO-led labels like LEED paired with government purchasing may be an easier way for government entities to produce public goods and reduce the costs associated with governments formulating their own labels that are less likely to be trusted.

Market-based Instruments

We began with the use of market-based instruments as a perhaps simplistic approach to thinking about the use of policy tools to overcome the challenges of market transformation. It is also likely that the use of market-based instruments like purchase subsidies or carbon prices can help push emergent products into the mainstream. Consider the success of Tesla, which has relied on the US federal automobile fuel-economy standards to acquire fuel-economy credits that have helped make Teslas more affordable and the firm profitable. While a $25 per ton carbon tax will only affect the price of electricity by a couple of cents or a gallon of gasoline by about 25 cents, these incentives can help move customer options at the margin and reduce the costs associated with opting for improved technological options. Impacts of these conventional market-based instruments may be small, but at least they point in the right direction. In contrast to the traditional environmental economics literature that considers market-based instruments as the primary mechanism to efficiently transition markets and consider total social costs and benefits of improved technologies, we see market-based instruments as one tool that can help move customer behavior at the margin once a variety of choices are market ready. Market-based instruments can provide the final price nudges that lock in superior environmentally friendly products once those products are broadly available in the market.

What Is Next for Voluntary Environmental Mechanisms?

What then is the role of voluntary environmental mechanisms beyond helping establish a foothold for nascent technologies, and where can these approaches be leveraged in the future? In an era where gridlock in government has been unable to produce substantive and consistent policy signals, voluntary mechanisms suggest alternative ways for individuals and firms to engage in collective action and help shift culture and politics to an equilibrium that values sustainability as an outcome.

The promise of voluntary environmental mechanisms brings a politics of innovation and opportunity, as opposed to a culture and politics of fear. Gas and carbon taxes spur fears of increased costs of living and of big government pressing its thumb on the scale of individual choice and "leaving behind" workers in disfavored industries. Mandates evoke even stronger fears about a potential lack of consumer choice, reduced profitability for firms, and a lower quality of life.

In contrast, in a world where investors are repositioning assets to align with ambitious carbon reduction targets, the promise of innovation and opportunity dominates the politics of fear. These greener, cleaner, innovative, and higher value-added products provide promise. The recent developments with the Business Roundtable formally acknowledging a wide range of stakeholder interests and a social license to operate reinforces a perspective where sustainability is not confined to the public-relations division of the corporation, but starts to permeate decision-making throughout the corporation.[9] Employees of major corporations want to know that their firm is doing something to move the ball forward, rather than to stymie progress, and these goals are beginning to align with the core strategies of firms. The commitment by large investors to target net-zero emissions, and the commitment by many large firms to sign up for the Science Based Targets Initiative and set targets aligned with the Paris Climate Accords also provides some hope.[10]

Of course, a challenge of even a green-product-driven economy is the culture of consumerism and the difficulty of reducing emissions even while buying more "stuff" and growing production. One perspective that provides optimism observes that, over the past decade, wealthier economies – even the United States – have increasingly valued "experiences" over stuff. We see greater shares of wealth spent on goods and services that are less emissions intensive. Further, even when wealth is spent on stuff, a greener product with a smaller environmental footprint might provide greater value to the consumer than a brown product with a larger environmental footprint. This change in values – to valuing the handmade over the mass produced, to valuing the sustainable over the disposable, and to valuing products and services that tread lightly on the planet – may be a powerful way to

---

[9] www.nytimes.com/2019/08/19/business/business-roundtable-ceos-corporations
.html
[10] https://sciencebasedtargets.org/

leverage markets using voluntary mechanisms. If purchasing brown products has a yuck factor, and purchasing green products comes with a side of halo, then indeed, green production and green marketing can help drive market transformation. If consumers are willing to pay more for products that have a smaller footprint because they feel better about those purchases, perhaps voluntary action can have more impact. This process, catalyzed in part by ecolabels, can be iterative, as NGOs, governments, and markets continue to raise the bar on the expected quality of goods.

We believe that these factors are working so far, at least in the green building sector. We are optimistic that large shifts in the way that people think about consumption and sustainability have helped shift the conversation and make solving climate change – or at least avoiding the worst impacts of cataclysmic climate change – a feasible goal. The job is not yet done. There are no guarantees that this trajectory is going to hold. There are likely to be hiccups along the way. In particular, while technology exists to get us much of the way to net-zero emissions, there are some areas that are going to be quite challenging. Green hydrogen and hydrogen-powered airplanes and freight, for example, remain more of a hope than reality.

To overcome these obstacles, we look to markets, innovation, and increased research and development as a pathway forward. In many cases, there are existing technologies that need to gain widespread adoption. In other cases, we need research and development to bring these products to market to meet carbon reduction targets. Still, if one looks at the state of technology in the early 1990s compared to today, it is apparent that polycentric solutions can align voluntary mechanisms, regulations, and markets in such a way as to bring new technologies to market, bring down their costs, and promote widespread adoption by 2050, helping meet carbon reduction targets. To achieve these targets, however, it is essential to leverage all of the tools in the toolbox to get there. Regulations alone will not succeed. Voluntary mechanisms alone are unlikely to have the universal impact necessary to drive markets. And decentralized markets alone are unlikely to provide the appropriate incentives to tackle the problem. But if voluntary mechanisms work in concert with regulation and other policy tools such as government purchasing, R&D, and market incentives, we can leverage markets in a transformative way to meet the sustainability challenges of tomorrow.

References

Barron, Alexander R., Allen A. Fawcett, Marc A. C. Hafstead, James McFarland, and Adele C. Morris. 2018. "Policy Insights from the EMF 32 Study on U.S. Carbon Tax Scenarios." *Climate Change Economics* 9, no. 1: 1–47.

Gerarden, Todd D., Richard G. Newell, and Robert N. Stavins. 2017. "Assessing the Energy-Efficiency Gap." *Journal of Economic Literature* 55, no. 4: 1486–1525.

Giraudet, Louis-Gaëtan. 2020. "Energy Efficiency as a Credence Good: A Review of Informational Barriers to Energy Savings in the Building Sector." *Energy Economics* 87: 104698.

Huguenin, Ariane and Hugues Jeannerat. 2017. "Creating Change through Pilot and Demonstration Projects: Towards a Valuation Policy Approach." *Research Policy* 46, no. 3: 624–635.

Kirkpatrick, A. Justin and Lori S. Bennear. 2014. "Promoting Clean Energy Investment: An Empirical Analysis of Property Assessed Clean Energy." *Journal of Environmental Economics and Management* 68, no. 2: 357–375.

Kotchen, Matthew J. and Christopher Costello. 2018. "Maximizing the Impact of Climate Finance: Funding Projects or Pilot Projects?" *Journal of Environmental Economics and Management* 92: 270–281.

Metcalf, Gilbert E. 2019. "On the Economics of a Carbon Tax for the United States." Brookings Papers on Economic Activity, Spring: 405–484.

Norton, B. G. 2005. *Sustainability: A Philosophy of Adaptive Ecosystem Management*. Chicago, IL: University of Chicago Press.

Ostrom, E. 2010. "Beyond Markets and States: Polycentric Governance of Complex Economic Systems." *American Economic Review* 100, no. 3: 641–672.

Ricke, Katharine, Laurent Drouet, Ken Caldeira, and Massimo Tavoni. 2018. "Country-level Social Cost of Carbon." *Nature Climate Change* 8, no. 10: 895–900.

Rose, Adam and Dan Wei. 2020. "Impacts of the Property Assessed Clean Energy (PACE) Program on the Economy of California." *Energy Policy* 137: 111087.

Shellenberger, M. and T. Nordhaus. 2004. *The Death of Environmentalism: Global Warming in a Post-Environmental World*. Available from: https://s3.us-east-2.amazonaws.com/uploads.thebreakthrough.org/legacy/images/Death_of_Environmentalism.pdf

York, J. G., S. Vedula and M. J. Lenox. 2018. "It's Not Easy Building Green: The Impact of Public Policy, Private Actors, and Regional Logics on Voluntary Standards Adoption." *Academy of Management Journal* 61, no. 4: 1492–1523.

Index

Printed in the United States
by Baker & Taylor Publisher Services